The Internet For Mac
For Dummies, 2nd Edition

W9-BIA-320

Cheat Sheet

Your Internet Mini-Phonebook

Enter the numbers here so you won't lose them.

Service	Local Connect Number	Help Line Number
1.		
2.		
3.		
4.		
5.		

Note: Write your password for each service in the index of your favorite cookbook.

Five Fun Sites on the Web

Face it, 80 percent of Web cruising is probably just for goofing off.

Site	Description
Mr. Showbiz web3.starwave.com/showbiz	Just what the name implies, lots of show business information.
Amazon Books www.amazon.com	A reader's paradise, with more than a million titles.
Cool Sites cool.infi.net	Changes-every-day list of interesting Web sites.
Hotwired www.hotwired.com	The hottest online magazine.
Hollywood www.hollywood.com	Everything about movies.
Rockweb www.rockweb.com/wri	Everything about popular music (more than just rock).
Suck! www.suck.com	A viciously funny, energetic trouncing of dumb stuff on the Web.

Searching the Web

There are tree-directory style searchers and keyword searchers for finding what you want on the World Wide Web.

Service	Type of Service	Description
Yahoo www.yahoo.com	directory	Yahoo is probably the easiest place to start.
Galaxy www.einet.net	directory	Galaxy is also easy to navigate, like Yahoo.
Lycos www.lycos.com	keyword	Lycos claims to index the largest number of URLs.
CUSI web.nexor.co.uk	keyword	This site links to many others.
WebCrawler www.webcrawler.com	keyword	The fastest keyword search service.
Infoseek www2.infoseek.com	keyword	A wide-ranging, multi-service searcher.
CUI cuiwww.unige.ch	keyword	This university-maintained site in Switzerland has lots of unique material.

COMPUTER
BOOK SERIES
FROM IDG

The Internet For Macs® For Dummies® 2nd Edition

Cheat Sheet

Sample Addresses via Online Services

To Send To	With This Address	Use This Address
AOL	Bob Wilson	bobwilson@aol.com
CompuServe	70340,701	70340.701@compuserve.com
Delphi	bwilson	bwilson@delphi.com
eWorld	Bob Wilson	bobwilson@eworld.com
GEnie	WILSON318	WILSON318@genie.geis.com
Prodigy	HBNM07A	HBNM07A.prodigy.com

Internet by Mail

This is the lowest-order type of Internet usage, but you can still use it if you only have an e-mail address. This isn't as cool as surfing the Web with Netscape, but it works with severely limited hardware.

Archie

Send an e-mail message just like this:

```
To: INTERNET:archie@archie.sura.net
Subject:
prog <file you want>
```

You get the results by e-mail. You may need to use an alternate (less busy) Archie server.

FTP

To get coolfile.txt from the ftp.helpful.com site, send the following e-mail message:

```
TO:INTERNET:ftp.helpful.com
Subject:coolfile.txt

reply <your own Internet address>
connect ftp.helpful.com
chunksize 24000
get coolfile.txt
quit
```

For chunksize, use a number that is 1000 less than the maximum mail message size your service allows.

Five FTP Mac Software Sites

Four rules for you:

1. Don't hit these sites during their working hours.
2. Get games and so forth from an online service instead.
3. Try to get in and out quickly.
4. Just type the FTP address in your Web browser as a URL.

Location	Number	Directory
ftp.dartmouth.edu	129.170.16.54	/pub/mac (Dartmouth)
boombox.micro.umn.edu	128.101.95.95	/pub (gopher, more)
ftp.rrzn.uni-hannover.de	130.75.2.2	/ftp1/mac [sumex]
ftp.ucs.ubc.ca	137.82.27.62	/pub/mac/info-mac
shark.mel.dit.csiro.au	144.110.16.11	/info-mac [sumex]

IDG BOOKS WORLDWIDE™

. . . For Dummies: #1 Computer Book Series for Beginners

THE INTERNET FOR MACS® FOR DUMMIES®

2ND EDITION

THE INTERNET FOR MACS® FOR DUMMIES®

2ND EDITION

by Charles Seiter

Foreword by David Pogue

Macworld Contributing Editor and author of *Macs For Dummies*

IDG Books Worldwide, Inc.
An International Data Group Company

Foster City, CA ♦ Chicago, IL ♦ Indianapolis, IN ♦ Braintree, MA ♦ Dallas, TX

The Internet For Macs® For Dummies®

Published by
IDG Books Worldwide, Inc.
An International Data Group Company
919 E. Hillsdale Blvd.
Suite 400
Foster City, CA 94404

Library of Congress Catalog Card No.: 95-81440

ISBN: 1-56884-371-2

Printed in the United States of America

10 9 8 7 6 5 4 3 2 1

2A/TQ/RR/ZV

Distributed in the United States by IDG Books Worldwide, Inc.

Distributed by Macmillan Canada for Canada; by Computer and Technical Books for the Caribbean Basin; by Contemporanea de Ediciones for Venezuela; by Distribuidora Cuspide for Argentina; by CITEC for Brazil; by Ediciones ZETA S.C.R. Ltda. for Peru; by Editorial Limusa SA for Mexico; by Transworld Publishers Limited in the United Kingdom and Europe; by Al-Maiman Publishers & Distributors for Saudi Arabia; by Simron Pty. Ltd. for South Africa; by IDG Communications (HK) Ltd. for Hong Kong; by Toppan Company Ltd. for Japan; by Addison Wesley Publishing Company for Korea; by Longman Singapore Publishers Ltd. for Singapore, Malaysia, Thailand, and Indonesia; by Unalis Corporation for Taiwan; by WS Computer Publishing Company, Inc. for the Philippines; by WoodsLane Pty. Ltd. for Australia; by WoodsLane Enterprises Ltd. for New Zealand.

For general information on IDG Books Worldwide's books in the U.S., please call our Consumer Customer Service department at 800-762-2974. For reseller information, including discounts and premium sales, please call our Reseller Customer Service department at 800-434-3422.

For information on where to purchase IDG Books Worldwide's books outside the U.S., contact IDG Books Worldwide at 415-655-3021 or fax 415-655-3295.

For information on translations, contact Marc Jeffrey Mikulich, Director, Foreign & Subsidiary Rights, at IDG Books Worldwide, 415-655-3018 or fax 415-655-3295.

For sales inquiries and special prices for bulk quantities, write to the address above or call IDG Books Worldwide at 415-655-3200.

For information on using IDG Books Worldwide's books in the classroom, or ordering examination copies, contact Jim Kelly at 800-434-2086.

For authorization to photocopy items for corporate, personal, or educational use, please contact Copyright Clearance Center, 222 Rosewood Drive, Danvers, MA 01923, or fax 508-750-4470.

is a trademark under exclusive license to IDG Books Worldwide, Inc., from International Data Group, Inc.

About the Author

Charles Seiter wrote his first computer programs on ancient IBM iron in the 1960s and, at one point, had a college summer job writing FORTRAN code for Atlas missile guidance simulation. That's right, he *is* a rocket scientist.

Well, not really. He got a Ph.D. in chemistry from Caltech and then worked as a chemistry professor for years. His academic career was derailed by winning a pile of money on a television game show, at which point he freed himself from the job of flunking a certain percentage of pre-med students in freshman chemistry every year and moved away to a redwood forest in northern California.

He began consulting on the design of DNA sequencing equipment and other biochemistry hardware for firms in the Bay Area and, by chance, just happened to be hanging around when *Macworld* was founded. Over the course of ten years, he has probably reviewed more Mac technical software than anyone in history. *The Internet For Macs For Dummies, 2nd Edition,* is his twelfth computer book. He is also author of IDG Books' *Everyday Math For Dummies* and *The Internet For Macs For Dummies Quick Reference.*

Welcome to the world of IDG Books Worldwide.

IDG Books Worldwide, Inc., is a subsidiary of International Data Group, the world's largest publisher of computer-related information and the leading global provider of information services on information technology. IDG was founded more than 25 years ago and now employs more than 7,700 people worldwide. IDG publishes more than 250 computer publications in 67 countries (see listing below). More than 70 million people read one or more IDG publications each month.

Launched in 1990, IDG Books Worldwide is today the #1 publisher of best-selling computer books in the United States. We are proud to have received 8 awards from the Computer Press Association in recognition of editorial excellence and three from Computer Currents' First Annual Readers' Choice Awards, and our best-selling ...*For Dummies*® series has more than 19 million copies in print with translations in 28 languages. IDG Books Worldwide, through a joint venture with IDG's Hi-Tech Beijing, became the first U.S. publisher to publish a computer book in the People's Republic of China. In record time, IDG Books Worldwide has become the first choice for millions of readers around the world who want to learn how to better manage their businesses.

Our mission is simple: Every one of our books is designed to bring extra value and skill-building instruction to the reader. Our books are written by experts who understand and care about our readers. The knowledge base of our editorial staff comes from years of experience in publishing, education, and journalism — experience which we use to produce books for the '90s. In short, we care about books, so we attract the best people. We devote special attention to details such as audience, interior design, use of icons, and illustrations. And because we use an efficient process of authoring, editing, and desktop publishing our books electronically, we can spend more time ensuring superior content and spend less time on the technicalities of making books.

You can count on our commitment to deliver high-quality books at competitive prices on topics you want to read about. At IDG Books Worldwide, we continue in the IDG tradition of delivering quality for more than 25 years. You'll find no better book on a subject than one from IDG Books Worldwide.

John J. Kilcullen

John Kilcullen
President and CEO
IDG Books Worldwide, Inc.

Acknowledgments

The author would like to thank Diane Steel and Milissa Koloski at IDG Books for seeing this book to a second edition, and Jim Heid and Maryellen Kelly for talking me into the first one. Thanks also to Nancy Dunn, for getting me into this racket in the first place. The staff at *Macworld,* particularly Carol Person and Galen Gruman, have shown great forbearance about my frequent and unseemly disappearances into cyberspace.

I would also like to thank Tim Gallan, my project editor at IDG's Indianapolis office, for not flying to California and strangling me with his bare hands. That's true professionalism. Thanks also to Suzanne Stefanac for last-minute help with the project, to K. Calderwood for discussions on TCP/IP, Web marketing, and other matters, and to David Pogue for the hilarious foreword.

Loretta Toth, rather than see an acknowledgement about "my wife putting up with long hours blah blah blah" realized at once that she should just do her own book project at the same time. Look for a book by "Julia Chapman" at a store near you. I hope this sparks a domestic tranquillity revolution in publishing in which contracts are issued in pairs.

Finally, I would like to thank the pioneers of the Internet, some famous and some unsung, who put together this remarkable system. Bit by bit they made an entity with its own living intelligence and its own strange dreams.

(The Publisher would like to give special thanks to Patrick J. McGovern, without whom this book would not have been possible.)

Credits

**Senior Vice President
and Publisher**
Milissa L. Koloski

Associate Publisher
Diane Graves Steele

Brand Manager
Judith A. Taylor

Editorial Managers
Kristin A. Cocks
Mary Corder

Product Development Manager
Mary Bednarek

Editorial Executive Assistant
Richard Graves

Acquisitions Assistant
Suki Gear

Production Director
Beth Jenkins

**Supervisor of
Project Coordination**
Cindy L. Phipps

Supervisor of Page Layout
Kathie S. Schnorr

Pre-Press Coordination
Steve Peake
Tony Augsburger
Patricia R. Reynolds
Theresa Sánchez-Baker

Media/Archive Coordination
Leslie Popplewell
Kerri Cornell
Michael Wilkey

Project Editor
A. Timothy Gallan

Editorial Assistants
Constance Carlisle
Chris Collins
Stacey Holden Prince
Kevin Spencer

Technical Reviewer
Brian Combs

Graphic Coordination
Shelley Lea
Gina Scott
Carla Radzikinas

Production Page Layout
Brett Black
Anna Rohrer
Kate Snell
Shawn Aylsworth
Michael Sullivan

Proofreaders
Jon Weidlich
Gwenette Gaddis
Dwight Ramsey
Robert Springer

Indexer
Sharon Hilgenberg

Cover Design
Kavish + Kavish

Contents at a Glance

Cartoons at a Glance

By Rich Tennant

Table of Contents

Foreword

by David Pogue
Macworld Contributing Editor and author of *Macs For Dummies*

Some topics don't make good *Dummies* books. I doubt the phrase "flying off the bookstore shelves" would ever apply to *Escalators For Dummies, Flossing For Dummies,* or, for that matter, *Neurosurgery For Dummies.*

The Internet, however, begs — pleads — *screams* to be a *Dummies* book.

You must understand that the Internet is our solar system's largest information network, accessible only by computer modem. It's a tangled, seething mass of cobbled-together wiring and computers, designed by a bunch of tangled, seething scientists and government bureaucrats 30 years ago. When I *picture* the Internet, I usually envision something like a set design out of *Alien* or *Brazil.* Abandon hope, ye who enter.

Those Internet designers had in mind a secret network, a huge underground maze of circuitry, so cruelly cryptic that invading Russians would throw up their hands and march right back to their submarines in disgust. The Internet requires its own silly language, in which things like

```
sumex-aim.ncsa.uiuc.edu@ftp(*)
```

means "Yo." The Internet was designed to run on huge humming mainframe computers that dwarfed Manhattan warehouses and had 4K of memory. The Internet is so complex that even complete reclusive computer nerds with few social opportunities had to write utilities like SLIP and WAIS and WWW to manage the Internet's utilities.

And during every step of the tangled, seething construction of the Internet, there's one thing nobody ever stopped to consider.

You.

Nobody intended for the typical, well-meaning American of above-average intelligence and a decent education to be able to make any sense of the Internet. Until *Time* and *Newsweek* and *The New York Times* began hailing the Internet as the biggest news story since Baby Jessica, it was the sole domain of scientists and hackers (the Internet, not the baby).

You haven't a prayer for making your way through the snarled, tangled techno-mass of the Internet without Charles Seiter. He was born with some kind of double-recessive gene, a freak rarity, that lets him make technical topics as accessible as the fridge. Good grief, sometimes I even catch myself reading his *Macworld* articles on things like statistical analysis and quantum physics, just because they're funny and interesting.

In this book, Charles offers two ways for you to get onto the Internet without losing unduly large hair tufts. First — the Great *Internet For Macs For Dummies* Dirty Little Secret — you can avoid the crumbling, archaic dirt roads of the military/university computers entirely. Instead, you can drive on the new, smoothly paved freeways provided by friendly services like America Online.

Second — if clicking a few colorful icons is too sissified for you — Charles also shows you how to get onto the Internet the *regular* way (huge humming mainframes, and so on). And he tells you what few silly Internet-language codes you really need to negotiate the hostile electronic waters — but friendly fellow cybernauts — of the Internet.

Either way, you're likely to be blown away and probably consumed for hours a day by the awesomeness and depth of the information and people you'll find there. Billions of Mac programs. Trillions of facts. Hundreds of messages a day about *Seinfeld*.

And 60 million people.

Correction: 60 million and one.

Welcome to the Internet.

David Pogue
New York City

Introduction

· ·

*W*elcome to the second edition of *The Internet For Macs For Dummies!*
When I started taking my Macintosh onto the Internet, I found that there
was a lot to learn, mainly because the Internet was not built with the Mac in
mind. But I'm going to save you plenty of Internet time and trouble because

- ✔ I've already chewed my way through all the hassles.
- ✔ You were kind enough to buy this book.

The Internet is a gold mine of information, but the programs you could use in
1994 or so to access Internet services were based on early-1980s state-of-the-art
programming — in other words, stuff people admired before the Macintosh was
invented. The Internet is a large part of what experts call the information
superhighway; I must say, however, that the paving was chock full o' potholes.
Then the big Internet service providers and the national online services got
busy and made everything fairly easy. If you're just now getting on the Internet,
you saved yourself a lot of problems by waiting a bit!

I assume that because you're a Mac user, you don't want to learn a bunch of
mysterious three-letter commands from a different computer operating system
just to send an e-mail letter to someone. In the Mac world, of course, things are
supposed to be easier. Every chance I get, I'm going to show you ways to work
around the complicated, old style of Internet access.

This book is full of cutting-edge material — the eWorld Web browser, for
example, was two days old when the eWorld chapter was written. In fact, it may
be the first non-obsolete Internet book for the Macintosh because it was written
after the big interface revolution. Any service that really wants your Internet
business now has a nice, stable, easy-to-use, real, Mac interface. I've kept lots of
technical stuff about MacTCP and SLIP and PPP, since these more advanced
connection modes still offer higher access speeds than, say, America Online.
But the good news for 1996 is that you won't have to spend much time on
cryptic communications details, unless you absolutely insist.

About This Book

I wrote this book to get you onto the Internet and point out its many interesting features. All the material here has been tested on ordinary users. By *users,* I don't mean the people who hang around at user groups comparing shareware; I mean people who call me with questions about using the spell checker in MacWrite.

This book will be easier to follow than, say, a *Macworld* article. But be sure to skim most of this book before picking a way to sign on the Internet: I compare the costs and benefits of many different approaches.

Here are some key points explained in this book:

- ✔ What the Internet is (and isn't)
- ✔ How you get connected
- ✔ What you'll find
- ✔ How to get free software
- ✔ How to make friends on the Net
- ✔ How to access a whole universe of computers
- ✔ How to surf the World Wide Web

Using This Book

If you just want to get on and get out there, this is the right book for you. This is a reference book, but that doesn't mean that it's a computer-systems manual. It's a guide to launch you onto the Net, and it's a map to help you navigate the system after you get connected.

I prefer real Macintosh, point-and-click software. Nonetheless, some of the services described here still have a plain old text interface, which has the advantage of speed. When you have to type something (such as file name, directory name, Internet address, or newsgroup), I'll indicate it in a monospaced font like so:

```
upload goodies.txt
```

In general, it makes a difference whether you type a command in lowercase or in capital letters, so do it exactly as shown.

Not Just a Job, It's an Adventure

Learning about the Internet is not just another computer chore, such as learning Adobe PageMaker shortcuts. When you sign on to the Internet, you are participating in one of the most exciting intellectual adventures in history. Out there on the Net is a big chunk of all the information accumulated by the human race since the dawn of time, from satellite photos to Shakespeare. Many of the coolest people on the planet are out there, too. It's now also a great place to look for jobs and a great place to go shopping.

Nobody knows where all the Internet is headed, how big it's going to get, or how it will evolve next. For example, although businesses have flocked to the Internet, specifically to the part called the World Wide Web, at the moment it's an open question whether the Web will really pan out as a general purpose business tool. All I know is that hundreds of millions of intelligent people will be able to communicate and do business all over the planet (or *off* the planet, according to some Internet UFO discussion groups). Because you're reading this book, you're going to be able to help determine the future.

What's in This Book

This book is divided into five parts; each has a different function.

Part I: Internet and Web Basics

In this part, I explain the world of the Internet — what's in it, how it came to be, and who's there. You can read this part to learn some Internet background so that you can impress your friends and associates, or you can use the new knowledge to plan real adventures.

Part II: Online Services for Internet Access

The easiest Internet access is through the big online services. Not only do these people want your business, they are furiously upgrading their Internet capabilities on a monthly basis, just to make you feel welcome.

Part III: Big Business, High Speeds

If you want to play in the big leagues, I tell you what you need in this part. Sometimes it makes sense to be your own Internet site and sometimes it doesn't, so I cover the options.

Part IV: The Part of Tens

Some of these top-ten lists are serious, and some are just for fun.

Part V: Appendices

In the appendices, I reveal some extra hints and tips. I also offer you some useful lists that are too long to put in the middle of the book.

Icons Used in This Book

Hey, look here, everyone: Pictures in a computer book.

Technical Stuff

Believe me, the Internet has plenty of technical aspects. You can skip these sections if you like, but read them if you're curious.

Tip

A Tip is a recommended way to accomplish an Internet task with your Mac. Often, a Tip is a shortcut.

Remember

This icon flags background information that you should keep in mind. "Eat your dinner first and then eat the salad" would be a Remember icon for traveling in Italy.

Warning

"Drive on the left" would be a Warning for traveling in Britain.

Navigate

This icon alerts you that I'm going to tell you how to get to some cool places on the Internet. Hey, on the highway, do it my way.

Mac Psychology

Every time I can turn the Internet into a Mac-friendly environment, I signal so with this icon. Here you'll find some of the distinctively Mac stuff in the book.

What's Next?

It's time to take the plunge.

But first, I'd like to offer a few words of encouragement: Some parts of the Internet world are fairly confusing. If you find them confusing, it's not just you. Some aspects are hard — the way English-language spelling is hard — because the Internet evolved through a series of historic accidents.

I've been the contributing editor in charge of stuff-that's-too-hard-for-English-majors at *Macworld* for ten years. And I've found some fancier aspects of Internet use to be as hard as, say, advanced topics in Microsoft Excel. So if you are puzzled by the Internet from time to time, remember that it's not your fault.

IDG Books is paying me to make this easy for you. I think that this addition to the good ole . . . *For Dummies* series will make Internet access almost as easy as word processing — and considerably more fun.

Tell Us What You Think

Please send me your comments; you can reach me at

IDG Books Worldwide
7260 Shadeland Station
Suite 100
Indianapolis, IN 46256

I'd give you my Internet e-mail address, but it's already so jammed with stuff that I'm more likely to find your comments on paper! Here's a hint though — if you look at some of the screens in this book, you can figure out my name on various online services. I'm stuck belonging to all of them to produce works like this.

Part 1
Internet and
Web Basics

The 5th Wave   **By Rich Tennant**

"EXCUSE ME— IS ANYONE HERE <u>NOT</u> TALKING ABOUT
THE INTERNET?"

In this part...

The Internet is the wild and woolly frontier of electronic communication. A huge part of all the information ever accumulated is out there somewhere on the Internet. It's just a matter of finding a way to navigate this digital ocean with your Macintosh.

That's why I'm here. This is the first second-generation Internet book. It assumes that you want to use the Internet the same way you use a Macintosh, with icons, menus, and lots of the little details smoothed over.

In this part, you'll travel the Internet, seeing what it has to offer and how you get it for yourself. I hope you enjoy the journey!

Chapter 1

Welcome to the
Net — Internet Basics

. . . .

. . . .

What Is the Internet?

At one time, people thought that the Internet was the natural habitat of rocket scientists. But lately, every newsmagazine in America has told us that the Internet is happening for everyone — most newspapers now have weekly Internet columns. People talk about *surfing the Net* or *surfing the Web*, a peculiar sport played by people who rarely get wet. And commercials about the so-called information superhighway promise that you'll soon have data coming out of your ears and that a portable fax machine strapped to your wrist will be proper fashion for a beach vacation.

Whew.

Well, when you get into the Internet, you'll find out two things:

- ✔ It really is pretty amazing.
- ✔ You don't have to be a rocket scientist anymore to use it. And it won't follow you on vacation, unless you insist.

Caught in the Net

Most computers in offices or universities can talk to each other over *networks*, or sets of wiring and software that let computers communicate with each other.

The Internet is a way for these computer networks to connect to other computer networks. In fact, you can contact people all over the world from your computer through the Internet.

You see, the Internet lets you send files from one computer to another over a big, high-speed system of computer network connections, which the U.S. government paid for, installed, and then turned over to a private group of companies in 1995. Because all these computers all over the planet can transfer files or look at information anywhere, anyone (even you) can access any information that someone wants to place in the *public domain*, meaning that it's available to everyone with no restrictions.

That's right, people develop programs and other valuable stuff and give them away. They also develop a lot of amusing nonsense and give that away too. With the rise of the World Wide Web as a major Internet component, everyone from Apple to little Timmy Wilson of Fried Trout, Idaho can be an Internet citizen. The problem used to be mastering the technical details of file transfer; now it's coping with the explosion of both useful and non-useful stuff out there. And besides files and World Wide Web pages, there's now an e-mail address for just about everyone.

Macintosh, the easy network machine

Even if you're just sitting at your own Mac and aren't wired to anyone else, you have network capability anyway. The Mac's survival originally hinged on its success in the graphics/printing market, so Apple had to provide a way for several Macs to hook up to one (expensive) laser printer. (Three Macs and a printer is your basic example of a small network.) *AppleTalk,* a piece of software that lets Macs talk to each other and to a printer, became an essential part of the Macintosh system.

AppleTalk is too slow for larger networks, so vendors produced Mac-compatible hardware for *Ethernet,* a much faster networking connection. Fortunately, Ethernet is simple enough that lazy Mac users, like you and I, can use it without daily access to a network guru.

Combining all this information with electronic mail (or e-mail) means the following:

✔ You can send messages to anyone across the Internet, and they get the messages in a few minutes, usually.

✔ You can find thousands of useful files and free (!) programs.

✔ You can *chat* online with people anywhere (computer chatting is like talking via CB radio).

✔ You can get all sorts of instant, up-to-date news.

If you're having trouble visualizing the Internet as a network of networks, check out the schematic known as Figure 1-1. Still confused? Read on. (Sure, sure, I know that a picture is worth a thousand words. But, hey, give me a break: I get paid to write, not draw.)

That's you, at your own Macintosh, in the lower left of Figure 1-1. Using a modem, you dial into a central computer that many users can connect to. The central computer has a direct connection to the Internet, so it can dial up any other Internet-connected computer across the country. And that computer can look for files, at your request, on the big, federal computer located just outside Washington, D.C., or on any other computer that's been assigned a type of Internet address. To summarize: After you make an Internet connection, you can reach tons of files or information on any Internet computer. This process isn't *hacking*, or gaining illegal access to files; it's legitimately accessing files that people on other networks *want* you to see.

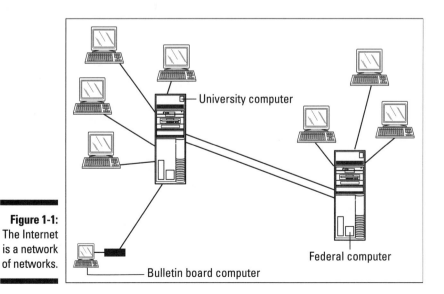

University computer

Federal computer

Bulletin board computer

Figure 1-1:
The Internet
is a network
of networks.

Mail: snail versus electronic

Snail mail is computerese for letters delivered by the U.S. Post Office. *E-mail* is computer messages (which can now include sound and pictures) that get sent over a network. When you send a piece of e-mail, it gets there almost immediately. (The only catch is that the person receiving the mail has to connect to the network to receive it.) As a result, the Internet is evolving into an international instant post office because it can pick up e-mail on one network and deliver it to another.

Internet Archaeology

How did all this Internet stuff happen? In the 1970s, the Defense Department decided that research efforts would speed up if investigators with funding from the Advanced Research Projects Agency (ARPA) could communicate from one network to another. Usually, these networks were at big national labs like Los Alamos or universities like MIT.

 ARPANET, as the new networking setup was called, originally linked about 30 sites, most of which used computers that are now ancient (Burroughs, Honeywell, and early DEC hardware). Some of the first ARPANET designers were hired for another project that would let ARPANET connect to radio- and satellite-based computer communications. This effort defined the communications hardware and software that make an Internet connection (that's why some of it is so weird, in modern computing practice).

In the 1980s, the old ARPA sites converted to the new Internet connections. Then the National Science Foundation (NSF) put together a high-speed network for Internet sites. Companies selling gateway hardware and software (a *gateway* is the actual connection from one network to another) for connecting to the NSFNET began to appear. Commercial Internet service networks were born. By 1995, the whole shooting match was so big that the Feds bowed out and turned maintenance of the Internet backbone over to a consortium of private companies.

Letting all existing networks connect to the single, big Internet produced the well-documented explosion of Internet connections; now almost every business card has both an @ address and a http:// address. At the heart of the system is the nationwide, high-speed NSFNET, which has been funded for the next five years as a sort of government experiment in communications infrastructure.

The number of people connected to the Internet has simply exploded in the last four years (see Figure 1-2). Some authorities are guessing that the system can handle almost a billion users eventually, with some rework of connection strategies. After that, the Internet may need to handle e-mail addresses differently — just as phone companies have had to adjust over the years to the increase in telephone use.

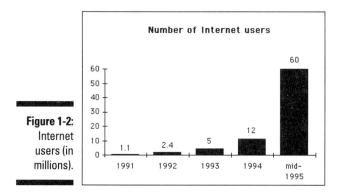

Figure 1-2: Internet users (in millions).

This amazing growth is one of the reasons that it took a while for Internet access to show a decent interface for Mac users. In January 1993, the typical Internet user had a research job and was used to dealing with a clunky interface (for example, see the archaic Internet commands listed in Figure 1-3). Very few people involved in designing the Internet, way back when, foresaw that you and I would be pounding on the gate(way)s by 1995, demanding a user-friendly Mac interface to Internet services. But several million Mac users beating down the doors at America Online, Prodigy, eWorld, and elsewhere have radically changed the game.

```
& help
cd [directory]              chdir to directory or home if none given
d [message list]            delete messages
e [message list]            edit messages
f [message list]            show from lines of messages
h                           print out active message headers
m [user list]               mail to specific users
n                           goto and type next message
p [message list]            print messages
pre [message list]          make messages go back to system
                            mailbox
q                           quit, saving unresolved messages in mbox
r [message list]            reply to sender (only) of messages
s [message list] file       append messages to file
t [message list]            type messages (same as print)
top [message list]          show top lines of messages
u [message list]            undelete messages
v [message list]            edit messages with display editor
x                           quit, do not change system mailbox
z [-]                       display next [previous] page of headers
!                           shell escape
```

Figure 1-3: Internet commands circa 1992.

E-Mail, the Internet, and @

If you glance at a business card for someone who works in a technology business or large company, it's likely that a line on the card will list an e-mail address (look for the @). (And to think, six years ago most cards didn't even list a fax number.) For example, an Apple employee named Kermit T. Frog could have the following e-mail address:

```
kermitf@apple.com
```

The @ is the tip-off that this code is actually an Internet-valid e-mail address; the notation .com (the Internet *zone designation*) means that the address is a business. When you read this address, you say "kermit-eff at apple dot com" (the @ is pronounced "at" and the . [period] is pronounced "dot").

Here's why addresses are important: If you have an @ address, you can communicate with anyone else on the planet with an @ address — that includes everyone who's anyone in the computer business and many of the powerful people at most organizations. To be taken seriously as a computer user or business person in the next few years, you're going to need your own @ address.

For example, today you can send a message to

```
vicepresident@whitehouse.gov
```

and help educate Al Gore on environmental issues. ("Sir, I'd like to volunteer several distant states as nuclear waste dumps.")

By the way, the zone designation .gov means that the e-mail address is at a government site. Professors at universities usually have addresses that end in .edu (for education). Sometimes, an address will be a location instead of a job category. For example, I have an address at well.sf.ca.us, which means that you can reach me at a bulletin board site called the WELL near San Francisco, California, in the good ol' United States. See Table 1-1 and/or Appendix A for more examples.

When you get your own @ address, I promise that you'll feel very official. I know I did.

Table 1-1	Ten Internet E-Mail Address Types
Address	*Interpretation*
@post.queensu.ca	Queen's University in Canada (.ca by itself means Canada, whereas .ca.us means California)

Address	Interpretation
@coombs.anu.edu.au	Australian National University
@netcom.com	A commercial Internet service provider
@aol.com	America Online, another commercial Internet service provider
@nic.ddn.mil	A military site
@whales.org	A (mythical) nonprofit organization
@nsf.net	The National Science Foundation network
@unicef.int	An international organization
@informatik.uni-hamburg.de	A computer science department in Germany (.de means Deutschland)
@leprechaun.ie	A fantastic address in Ireland

In 1995, the Internet saw an explosion in World Wide Web addresses (see Table 1-2) for businesses and organizations as well. A Web address, called a Uniform Resource Locator or URL, lets you connect, using a piece of software called a Web browser, to *Web pages* with graphics, sound, and occasional bits of video. Web pages are typically full of *hyperlinks*, underlined words that lead you to yet another page with its own URL address. In this way you can jump from one page to another for hours, in a determined research effort or in a random day's goof. You'll see lots more on the Web elsewhere in this book, and even more in IDG's *Yahoo! Unplugged* (by myself and some friends), a book on the Web Index site called Yahoo. These addresses follow the same conventions as e-mail addresses (.gov means government, .com means business, and so forth).

Table 1-2   Some World Wide Web Addresses

Address	Interpretation
http://www.yahoo.com/	The Yahoo index site, now a business (it used to be an .edu inside Stanford)
http://www.wustl.edu/	Washington University
http://www.netscape.com/	Netscape, developers of the most popular Web browser
http://www.amazon.com/	A store with a million books online!

Electronic Libraries on the Net

To recap: As an Internet user, you can exchange messages with other Internet users, from Brazil to Baltimore, and look at Web pages. By itself, that capability makes the Internet extremely useful. But, wonder of wonders, you also can use the Internet to access incredible files of information stored all over the world.

The Library of Congress, for example, contains copies of all the books (and nearly all the magazines and newspapers) published in the United States. (Of course, only 40,000 or so of the most useful books have been prepared for you to access through the Internet, but several library groups are working to get the whole collection ready for the Internet.) The U.S. Patent Office has files on all the patents it has ever issued. And university libraries across the country (Harvard, Yale, and Illinois are the largest) house all sorts of foreign research material not found in the Library of Congress. Heck, you can find comic books and campaign fliers and recipes and jokes and back issues of *TV Guide* on the Internet. There's going to be instant access to everything, including junk.

All this stuff is being merrily scanned into a text-file format that your Macintosh can read. All you must do is retrieve the file from the Internet.

Now, on-screen reading isn't great for novels — try scrolling through an 800-page paperback at the beach on your laptop. It's ideal, though, if you're looking for specific pieces of information because you can search the files for key words.

Greek to me

Just about everything ever written in Latin or ancient Greek is available online as part of a huge project involving Classics departments all over the world. You can, for example, consult the author Lucian, who provides these three rules for getting through the day:

1. When things aren't working, stop for a minute and smile.

2. Remember not to take it too seriously.

3. See whether you can make the situation better by trying harder, or see whether you should try something else.

This advice comes in handy when, every now and then, the software keeps crashing and you're getting busy signals from your modem and you get "connection refused" messages. The classical stuff is especially nice because you can read *finished* documents — I don't think that these authors will be writing new editions any time soon. These ain't betas.

Light reading?

Here's an example: The library in the small town where I live recently got its own Internet connection. (Your library will get a connection soon because Internet access is *the* hot topic at librarians' meetings in the '90s. Come to think of it, it's about time the poor old librarians had a hot topic.) Last week, from my house, I checked the local university library for holdings on a particular topic. I didn't find what I wanted, so I clicked into libraries at the University of California at Berkeley and at the University of Illinois, Champaign-Urbana. I could have tapped into libraries at Oxford, for that matter. Finally, I came back to my own library and made an interlibrary loan request for a book at Berkeley. Not bad for ten minutes work at my own Mac! In the next few years, with faster modems and more books online, even this interlibrary loan stuff will disappear, and a huge assortment of reference books will just be routinely downloaded.

In other words, even if you're sitting in front of your Macintosh, you can browse the stacks of most of the world's libraries. Although you may not always be able to get individual books transferred to a library near you, the information in these books is, as I write, steadily being converted to online files that you can download.

A connected world

The Internet isn't all serious. Sure, it has resources on programming languages and mathematical physics. But the Internet also is the planet's chief pipeline to news and plain, old, silly gossip.

For example, I regularly check comments made by fans of the TV program *Mystery Science Theater 3000*. This program has thousands of avid fans who chatter away online every day in a huge, open bulletin board, called a *newsgroup*. Because *MST3K* specializes in obscure, funny references, any given line from the show is capable of generating an endless stream of linked messages from fans explaining various perspectives on the wisecrack.

Inevitably, the Internet reflects what's on people's minds. Just as Egyptians filled their tombs with pornographic graffiti, and just as the first artsy pictures of naked ladies appeared within a year of the invention of photography, many private computer bulletin boards specialize in adult material. And many of those boards are connected to the Net. In fact, it's a matter of record that two of the newsgroups most frequently accessed are `alt.sex` and `rec.arts.erotica`. Most Web index sites will no longer carry references to naughty pictures, not because they have any basic objection but because if they let millions of people find the stuff fast, the connection simply blows out under the access load.

Actually, if you want online access to dating service communications, bulletin boards are hotter than the Internet.

Looking for love?

The Internet has a service called *Internet Relay Chat* (IRC), a sort of global conference call. But the chat lines on bulletin boards and big online services, such as GEnie, are actually better for this stuff than the Internet. There's no point clogging up the poor old Net if you can have more fun anyway with a specialized connection.

All Aboard!

Well, the Internet is not just for universities anymore. Millions of people — cyberpunks, grandmothers, business people — have a legitimate need for Internet access. And plenty of Internet users advocate the idea that nearly everyone should be connected.

On a drizzly, spring morning in San Francisco, I decided to find out what sorts of people were willing to take a beginning Internet class. The class was organized by the WELL (415-332-4335), a San Francisco-area computer bulletin board that's probably the finest service of its kind in the country. The East Coast equivalent is ECHO (212-255-3839). The crowd, amazingly enough, consisted of equal parts of

- ✔ Generation X-ers, complete with the occasional nose ring and I'm-an-artist-don't-bother-me-OK? fashion
- ✔ Retired high-school teachers
- ✔ Mysterious business guys in suits on a Sunday

This pattern has held through several rounds of classes (by the way, you can add entrepreneurs to the mix — to them, the Internet represents a new business opportunity). Of course, I don't quite know what this means. Lately, I've been asked to give Internet talks to every community group north of the Golden Gate Bridge, so my guess is that the sociological profile of Internet users is probably going to look just like the general population within a year or so. The latest explosion is interest in Web pages, since they allow you to post pictures. Bed-and-breakfast inns in the Wine Country with five rooms (!) now have Web pages providing tiny pictures of all five rooms. It's OK; the rooms are tiny too.

You and Your Mac

Mac users buy a Mac for straightforward, point-and-click access to serious computer power. Naturally, you and I both want Internet access that uses a traditional Mac interface. If you have free Internet access (for example, you're a university student or your employer has given you an account), you should check out the special considerations in Chapters 14 and 15. The aim of most of this book, however, is to explain Internet access to people who don't have large organizations with systems administrators supporting them.

In the first edition of this book, I said there was no way to get full Internet access easily in a single software or service package. That's all changed, in the space of eleven months. If you have a Mac, a modem, and a credit card number, it's no more trouble to get on the Internet than to run Microsoft Word.

A year ago, you might have an Internet connection that expected you to remember that

```
!sx -a myfile.txt
```

is the command for downloading a file. That's all over now. The available Internet services are still quite different. Delphi has real Internet, but it uses a text-based menu for navigation. America Online (AOL) and eWorld not only have a real Mac interface, but it looks the same in both cases because they bought it from the same company (InterCon).

Besides direct Internet access through a service provider, I'm going to discuss the pros and cons of Internet access with

- ✔ America Online
- ✔ CompuServe
- ✔ Prodigy
- ✔ eWorld
- ✔ and maybe a few more services

In Part II, I detail these services so that you can see what you'll get before you pay to join. I promise, I'm going to make this Internet stuff easy.

Think about it. If there's a research topic that you've always wanted to pursue, you can command the resources of most of the world's universities with your fingers. If you're an Australian frustrated by America's utter lack of interest in cricket (or in Australian-rules rugby, or really in anything but Foster's), you can get yesterday's scores by making a local call. If you just want to find a large group of people who share your obsessions, you no longer have to leave your home.

And, in most cases, as long as you observe a few basic rules of decorum, you'll find that you are welcomed into these new electronic communities. It's not just the future — it's already happened!

NAVIGATE

Check these topics

To motivate you and to give you some idea of what's out there, I list here some of the kinds of information on the Internet. You also can take it for granted that there are gigabytes of hard-core techie stuff, too.

✔ Urban legends: Folklorist Jan Harold Brunvand, author of *The Choking Doberman* and *The Mexican Pet*, maintains files on urban myths in a newsgroup called alt.folklore.urban. You can check here to convince yourself that all known poodle-in-a-microwave stories are fiction. I personally think the ghostly-hitchhiker stuff is true, however.

✔ QuarkXPress at Indiana University: Authors of books on Quark have downloaded files to this huge archive of tips and information on using QuarkXPress. Now you can look at this week's tips instead of last year's. By the way, sometime you should notice the huge concentration of computer publishers in Indiana.

✔ GUTENBERG: Project Gutenberg is the name of an initiative to put almost everything important that was ever printed into online form. Time for a bigger hard drive, huh?

✔ Hong Kong Polytechnic: The address @library.hpk.hk takes you into the li-

brary of this college in Hong Kong (the country code is hk, naturally). I mention this address because most of the other high-tech places on the planet (Korea, Hong Kong, Singapore, Holland, and so forth) that have computers are as connected as the United States. The curious exception is Japan; the Japanese government telecommunications office hasn't quite decided what to make of all this Internet stuff.

✔ Is funny, nyet?: There's an Internet service that reports jokes from the former Soviet Union. These days they need all the humor they can get.

✔ Agriculture: On a huge range of university-maintained databases, every bit of agricultural research ever assembled is indexed and available. If you're a farmer, there's no need any more to wait for the agent from the ag school to get around to your county.

✔ Sumo: The Yahoo index started out as a graduate student's after-hours Web-page project to provide some basic information on the Japanese sport of Sumo. Then he added more stuff, and then more stuff, and then dropped out of school to run Yahoo as a business that indexes more than 50,000 Web sites!

Chapter 2
The Whole World Online

- -

In This Chapter

▶ A network of networks

▶ Newsgroups, the first Internet fun

▶ And now, the Web!

▶ Is this educational?

▶ Greetings from the government

- -

The Internet Is a Collection of Nets

The basic story is that the U.S. Defense Department set up the prototypes of the Internet as a sort of nuclear-attack-proof communications system for the military. What got devised, and then became the Internet, was actually just a messaging system that allowed computers to forward messages over a network. Some part of the network could be missing, but the software would find a way to get a message from the originating computer to the destination computer. So what really came out of these efforts was a universal e-mail scheme.

But at the same time that the government agencies were working on a communications protocol for connecting research networks, computer use by ordinary people exploded. In the early 1980s, as the earlier military-based Advanced Research Projects Agency system gave way to the Internet, Apple II sales soared into the millions, and the IBM PC essentially became a new industry. Meanwhile, cheap, fast modems appeared, making computer bulletin boards and assorted online services practical for the first time.

Lots of Connections

When you start exploring the Internet, you'll find all sorts of information, opinion, and outright bafflement. Not only are there nearly 60 million Internet users, but there are comparable numbers of people connected to other nets that pass information to the Internet. Some of these other nets are just tiny,

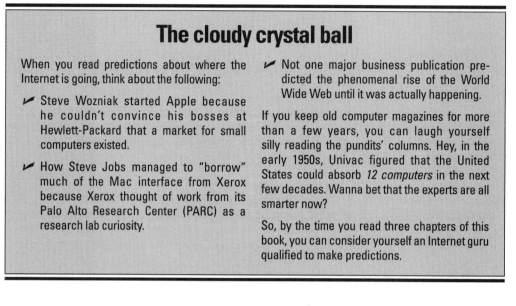

The cloudy crystal ball

When you read predictions about where the Internet is going, think about the following:

✔ Steve Wozniak started Apple because he couldn't convince his bosses at Hewlett-Packard that a market for small computers existed.

✔ How Steve Jobs managed to "borrow" much of the Mac interface from Xerox because Xerox thought of work from its Palo Alto Research Center (PARC) as a research lab curiosity.

✔ Not one major business publication predicted the phenomenal rise of the World Wide Web until it was actually happening.

If you keep old computer magazines for more than a few years, you can laugh yourself silly reading the pundits' columns. Hey, in the early 1950s, Univac figured that the United States could absorb *12 computers* in the next few decades. Wanna bet that the experts are all smarter now?

So, by the time you read three chapters of this book, you can consider yourself an Internet guru qualified to make predictions.

private bulletin boards that service five people per day. Some of them are government networks that span the whole globe and connect thousands of solid citizens in white shirts and ties.

Although thousands of nets can exchange messages and data with the Internet, only a few are really important. Four big sources (Usenet, university special-interest groups, government organizations, and the exploding World Wide Web) contribute most of the stuff that you find on the Net, so in this chapter, I'm going to give you a quick rundown on them.

What's This Newsgroup Stuff?

Although the Internet was designed as a sort of e-mail equivalent of the world-wide telephone system, it didn't take people long to find a way to use e-mail to set up interactive conferences on particular topics of interest. It was quite simple, really — all it takes is a program that will forward collections of e-mail messages from one computer to another so that everyone who is "signed up" with an interest group gets automatically updated on all the group's messages.

When people think of the Internet, they often think of cool characters swapping sophisticated information on every topic under the sun. Actually, lots of that action takes place on what's technically another network, called Usenet. But plenty of Internet sites also are Usenet sites, so the information tends to slosh across the two systems. On the Internet, you can talk to Usenet people, and they can talk to you. Usenet was really the first "fun" use of the Internet, and it is still sufficiently interesting that good World Wide Web software also gives you access to Usenet.

Usenet newsgroups are the source of the most entertaining text-based material on the Internet. For example, the newsgroup `rec.humor.funny` is the most-accessed topic on the Internet; `rec.humor.funny` includes jokes selected diligently from the material found in the larger selection `rec.humor`. That's right, someone screens out the unfunny jokes for you! Is this a great service or what?

Usenet also is the source of serious stuff. If you want to study mathematical chaos, for example, you can join a newsgroup called `sci.nonlinear`.

Getting network news

More than two million users participate in a scheme referred to collectively as network news; Usenet is the set of newsgroups at the core of the collection. Essentially it's just a set of conferences (organized discussion groups) that allow network discussions of different topics, together with an organized system for passing the discussions along to different nets.

An amazing amount of Usenet material is contributed by graduate students from various distinguished institutions of higher learning. (Considering the many afternoons I whiled away at dear old Caltech playing billiards when I should have been taking magnetic resonance spectra, I find that I envy today's students, whose every wisecrack is recorded for posterity. Now get back to work, folks.) At least they make for lively reading.

TIP

Short-sited?

After you make an Internet connection through an online service or bulletin board, you can ask the system operator to add your name to the subscription lists for different newsgroups. If your connections site does not carry a particular newsgroup, ask your system operators to add it; they almost always are willing to do so.

Conference calls

Table 2-1 lists a tiny sample of the conferences on Usenet that you can join from an Internet site. In the chapters where I tell you how to sign on, I tell you how to get a current list — many changes occur every few months.

Usenet sites, as a rule, use the operating system UNIX. One of my goals in writing this book is to insulate you from UNIX; I don't want you to have to learn a lot of UNIX commands just to get Internet access.

The reason UNIX appears all over the Internet is that UNIX is a real industrial-strength, bulletproof, network operating system. It's also very efficient with computer resources, and both computer memory and computer time used to be more expensive. It's nerd heaven, too. If you feel the urge to learn more, just check out IDG's *UNIX For Dummies* or the UNIX command sections in *The Internet For Dummies*.

Table 2-1	Welcome, Stranger!
Newsgroup	*Topic*
comp.ai	Artificial intelligence
soc.culture.thai	The latest from Bangkok and elsewhere
sci.med.aids	Current AIDS information
alt.hotrod	Souped-up vehicles, natch
alt.rush-limbaugh	Please note the hyphen
alt.sports.baseball.chicago-cubs	Seminar on congenital optimism
talk.abortion	Abortion controversies of all kinds
rec.arts.poems	Write a poem, put it here
misc.answers	About Usenet itself
comp.sys.mac.wanted	Macs for sale

Drinking from a fire hose

The relatively specialized newsgroup for magnetic resonance lists about a hundred messages a day. But face it, even though magnetic resonance has elbowed its way into hospitals, it remains a pretty obscure subject. My point:

Newsgroups for popular topics (in other words, where practically anyone may have an opinion) really run some high volume. Figure it out: If magnetic resonance is worth a hundred postings on a good day, how much traffic do you think showed up Summer 1995 in `alt.fan.hugh-grant`?

If you join lots of newsgroups indiscriminately, I promise that you won't be able to find the time to read most of the stuff.

The World Wide Web Takes Over

There's loads of fun to be had with Usenet newsgroups, but they consist mostly of text messages and typing. (OK, all the dirty pictures are in newsgroups too, but they're encoded as text files.) So it was inevitable that in a TV culture people would want pictures, and they finally got them when the World Wide Web moved to center stage on the Internet by early 1995. The Web spent a few years waiting in the wings, but when it arrived it was certainly ready for prime time. If you look at the typical newsgroup screen in Figure 2-1 and then at the typical Web screen in Figure 2-2, you will see at once why a nation of channel-surfers voted with their modems as soon as access became available.

Web history is worth a brief mention. Around 1989, a fellow named Dr. Tim Berners-Lee wrote a modest computer program for his own use in research. It was basically a sort of notepad program, with the interesting wrinkle that individual pages of notes were linked by keywords. You could call up a page about a scientific conference, for example, and click on the title of a particular lecture, and the program would then call up an abstract of the lecture. The abstract itself might contain other links to articles or reference tables. His supervisors at CERN in Geneva (a big physics lab) thought it would be interesting to develop this idea to become a general-purpose way of exchanging information among the other far-flung big-time physics labs around the globe. If you could dial up a central computer, and if you had one starting-point page with an index, it would be possible to access all the latest and greatest in physics research from anywhere, assuming that someone had set up the information and established the links. A group at CERN did just that, and in 1991, the first World Wide Web site was set up at CERN as a service to the world's physicists.

Dr. Berners-Lee made a formatting language that would support hypertext links as well as plain text formatting (bold, italic, size, fonts, and so forth) and called it *Hypertext Markup Language,* the now famous HTML. HTML, with a few extensions over its original version, is still the basis of the World Wide Web.

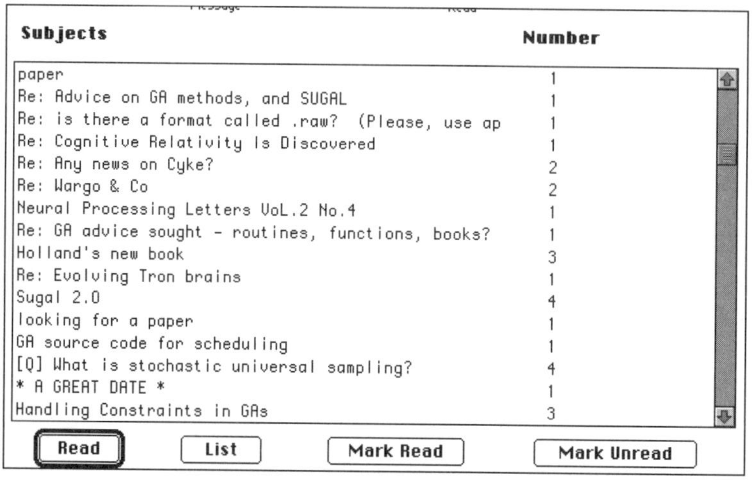

Subjects	Number
paper	1
Re: Advice on GA methods, and SUGAL	1
Re: is there a format called .raw? (Please, use ap	1
Re: Cognitive Relativity Is Discovered	1
Re: Any news on Cyke?	2
Re: Wargo & Co	2
Neural Processing Letters Vol.2 No.4	1
Re: GA advice sought - routines, functions, books?	1
Holland's new book	3
Re: Evolving Tron brains	1
Sugal 2.0	4
looking for a paper	1
GA source code for scheduling	1
[Q] What is stochastic universal sampling?	4
* A GREAT DATE *	1
Handling Constraints in GAs	3

[Read]   [List]   [Mark Read]   [Mark Unread]

Figure 2-1:
A look at a
newsgroup.

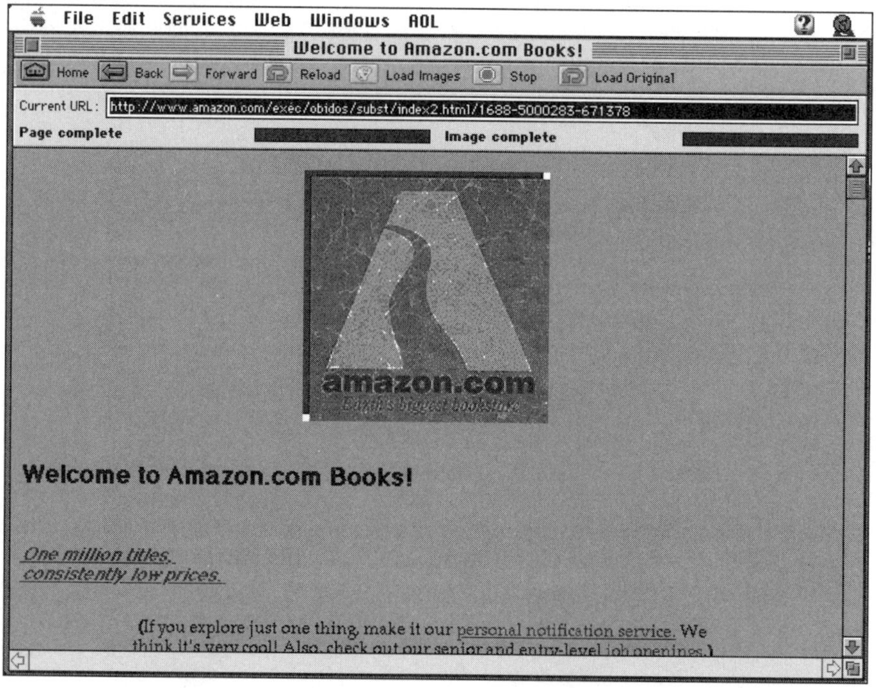

File Edit Services Web Windows AOL

Welcome to Amazon.com Books!

Home Back Forward Reload Load Images Stop Load Original

Current URL: http://www.amazon.com/exec/obidos/subst/index2.html/1688-5000283-671378

Page complete   **Image complete**

amazon.com

Welcome to Amazon.com Books!

One million titles,
consistently low prices.

(If you explore just one thing, make it our personal notification service. We
think it's very cool! Also, check out our senior and entry-level job openings.)

Figure 2-2:
A look at a
Web page.

The first version of the Web was essentially text-only, with hypertext links scattered throughout long passages of scientific literature. But at the National Center for Supercomputing Applications in Illinois, a graduate student named Marc Andreessen decided to do something amazing. The amazing thing he did was produce the text-plus-graphics NCSA Mosaic, the first really cool Web browser software, and then *give it away*!

This development put the Web at the center of Internet computing. Mosaic has an interface that's fun to use, and it encourages the use of pictures and sound clips. The offspring of Mosaic (AIR Mosaic, Spry Mosaic, Spyglass Mosaic, and Andreessen's own Netscape) have focused on speeding up graphical Web browser work over the punky, old 14.4K-bps modems that most home users have, but they are still recognizably the same software. Mr. Andreessen is now one of the principals of Netscape, which was the biggest stock-market news in 1995 when the company went public. Now he's rich, from giving a program away. There is some justice in this world — it's just rare.

Anyway, you'll see more on the Web in the next few chapters since it's where the action is on the Internet these days. When the first edition of this book went to press, there were 120 commercial Web sites. As this current book was written, there were 90,000, and the number is doubling every four months or so. The Gold Rush was a lazy Sunday afternoon by comparison.

Too Cool for School?

There are hundreds of regional Internet service providers offering full Internet access to one and all. The big national online services have finally set up almost-complete Internet access with really simple software, too.

You can find all sorts of shareware to download. You can find special-interest groups with an unlimited (and, I dare say, unhealthy) interest in the details of old Partridge Family shows. You can track the entire universe of day-to-day data (stock quotes, sports scores, weather). One really unique feature of the Internet, aside from its unmatchable vast connectivity, is the contribution made by university networks: If you want to look up biographical details on Marilyn Monroe, you can do so in a library. If you want to keep up with developments in molecular biology, you need the Internet. Internet access means access to most of the important areas of modern scholarship.

In fact, special initiatives now exist on the Internet for a sort of virtual reality international conference for biologists, in which scientists compare data and analysis — including journal figures and photos — online. In a more pedestrian Internet mode, Internet files are increasingly the standard repository for fast-moving information.

The Internet may someday help level the research-competitive playing fields between richer and poorer institutions. Already, Internet access — and particularly the World Wide Web — have enabled people in some fields, most notably mathematics, to enjoy a level of contact that's a vast improvement on the traditional once-a-year-let's-all-meet-in-D.C. style of interaction.

Classes at Electronic U

Universities are using the Internet not just to exchange research results but to offer courses. Think for a moment about the quality of student/teacher interaction in a freshman physics course: It's not uncommon at large universities to stuff 400 students in a lecture hall (and those sitting at the back have to watch the lecture on TV monitors). Doesn't a private online tutor sound more desirable? The window in Figure 2-3 is an example of an early version of Internet courseware.

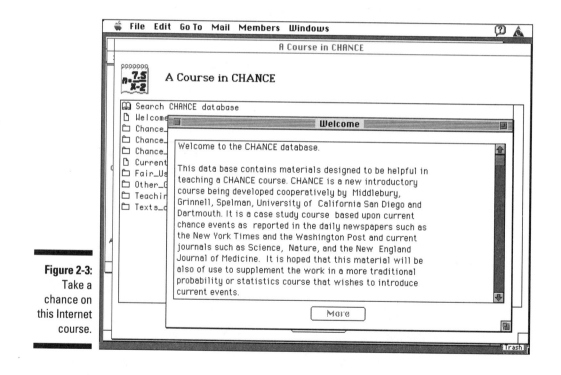

Figure 2-3:
Take a chance on this Internet course.

One big argument in favor of online courses is the appallingly short shelf life of course material. For example, there's not much you could have learned in a digital-design course in electrical engineering ten years ago that would look very compelling in your personnel file today. In most engineering professions, it's taken for granted that the whole stock of information needs to be over-hauled every five years. The need for fluid information flow keeps many schools interested in online education despite the hassles involved in designing a new instructional format.

Personally, I really hope that Web-based classes develop into a major part of the degree process and adult education market. I'm old enough to remember *television* being touted as a fabulous new educational medium, so I'm not 100% convinced this will work out, but it would solve a tremendous number of financial problems in education.

If it's new, it's here

Lots of the academic journals on the shelves of a university library now have a *one-year* lead time. That time lapse may be OK for medieval historians — the last time I looked, Charlemagne was still dead — but it's not fast enough for biotechnology or AIDS research or dozens of other hot topics. On the Internet, you can encounter not just newsgroups discussing current research but also databases that are updated almost daily by diligent university types.

Caution: People at work

Right now, there is open access to huge areas on university-maintained net-works that maintain Internet connections. Stanford University and the University of Minnesota, just to name two, do heroic public interest work. Stanford, in particular, has enough Macintosh stuff to keep you happy for years.

Of course, if millions of people start logging onto these university networks in the middle of the day, users will complain. And when it becomes clear that the university network is jammed with users downloading Snoopy screen-savers, the powers that be are going to change the open-access rules. Fortunately for now, most of the big sites have added capacity rather than restrict access.

Your Tax Dollars at Work

Universities around the world contribute a great deal to the information base of the Internet, but the U.S. government started it all and maintains a big presence. It used to pay for the Internet hardware backbone, too, until April 1995 when it turned maintenance of the Net over to a group of private companies.

It's pretty clear that almost no one in the government had any idea (what else is new?) what was being created when the funding for the high-speed NSFNET and another net called NASA Science Internet was approved. Actually, I'm talking about a trivial amount of money by Defense Department standards — remember, we live in a world where new fighter-plane designs cost tens of billions of dollars. It would have taken Nostradamus to realize that the world could be stood on its ear by a few hundred million doled out over a few decades to scientists.

Good guys and bad guys?

Although many Internet old-timers are convinced that the U.S. government in total is too dumb to impose any sort of regulation on the Net, lots of advanced thinkers working for the government have become quite agitated about the prospect of a high-speed, nearly anonymous, nonwiretappable international communications network.

As a result, topics of Net access and security are controversial. Most traditional Internet people favor unrestricted use, but a minority favor some way of guaranteeing law-enforcement access to suspicious activities. It's probably naïve to disregard the possibility that some Internet users will find a way to use the Net to foster criminal activities (send opinions to psuarez@medellin.cartel.com?), but it's also naïve to suppose that there's an unobtrusive way to check a significant fraction of messages. Expect plenty of debate in these areas in the years to come.

If you have access to one of the national services that carries an online version of *Time* magazine, you can watch government concern express itself by doing a search on the keyword "Internet". Almost every title you find is a horror story, from credit scams to what-if-the-North-Koreans-are-watching to the notorious, entirely-fabricated cover story on child access to porn. *Time* is a pretty accurate reflection of the concerns of the Washington establishment, and it's clear that unlimited access to all types of information gives the establishment a case of the whim-whams.

Dear Congressman (from a concerned citizen who can afford a computer)

You can find lots of old-time government data on the Internet (I tell you where in the access chapters). Some of it is the kind of info the government's printing office still ships from Boulder, Colorado, with a hundred fun recipes for powdered milk, or pamphlets on *The Soybean, Our Versatile Friend*, or travel tips on avoiding exotic diseases.

Another way to use the Internet is to make yourself heard in the corridors of power. Because newspapers have many staffers in the forefront of the online revolution, you're likely to find Internet e-mail addresses for everyone with the slightest pretensions to authority, including state legislators, congressional representatives, governors, senators, and cabinet members. Usually these @ addresses are listed on the editorial page of the paper (sometimes printed as a shameless way to fill space).

The handful of people I know who have worked this contact channel (some old hands at PeaceNet and EcoNet, for example, pioneering public-interest network groups) claim to have obtained better results electronically than with traditional paper and pen. You can throw letters right in the trash, but you have to clear e-mail or it clogs up your electronic in-box.

Despite the millions of Net residents now online, the whole scheme is probably new enough to politicians that an Internet message still has a certain mystique. And if you send an Internet message to a politician, you're more likely to be taken seriously. The U.S. Senate, by the way, now has an anonymous FTP site with files of current Senate information.

How Did All This Stuff Get Here?

Before most day-to-day Mac users heard of the Internet, people were pumping out information and discussions from Usenet, university special-interest groups, and government labs and organizations. They were doing it in the United States, and they were doing it everywhere else, too. In the last year, every business that could afford a computer has been flooding the Net with Web pages.

Finland, for example, jumped on the Internet early. Finland is snowed-in five months of the year (they're the world champs at icebreaker-ship technology), so online communication makes plenty of sense compared to frozen snail mail. A big Internet presence keeps Finnish researchers in contact with the rest of the planet.

As you head out into cyberspace, I have good news and bad news. The bad news: The landscape is even more crowded. You're visiting the big, international, 60-million-user Internet, not the old, chummy 2-million-user Internet. That makes it harder to navigate. The good news: Since the landscape is more crowded, it's richer.

To get your hardware set up to cruise this strange new world, turn to the next chapter.

The 5th Wave

Larry's newsgroup friends pay an in-person visit.

Chapter 3

Modem, Your Wire to the World

You Gotta Have a Modem to Get on the Net

All the wonderful information on the Internet is out there on other computers. Your Macintosh is sitting on your desk. If you want to join the Internet, a cable has to connect your Mac to the rest of the world.

That cable plugs into the little port with a picture of a telephone on the back of your Mac. The other end of the cable goes to a modem, which plugs into your phone line. That's all there is to it. Unless, of course, you decide to get really fancy and go for a high-speed ISDN connection (more on that later). But for most people in most places, a good modem is the answer to all connection questions.

Now, this assumes that you're an individual Mac user. If someone has handed you a network-connected Mac at a university or business, you're a separate case. You can skip this chapter, unless you also want to get online at home.

A modem is one of the more mysterious computer accessories. In the Mac world, for example, a printer is fairly self-explanatory. That's because the Macintosh was *designed* to be the first computer that worked easily with printers.

A modem, in contrast, is distinctly *not* self-explanatory. The bulk of the modem business is still in the hands of electrical engineers who don't have much interface-design expertise. Nearly all modems respond to a command code developed in the 1970s, and Apple itself is powerless to save you from the confusion this situation produces. I am going to try to get you through modem installation as painlessly as possible. Consult the "Warning signs for modem users" sidebar in case I succeed too well — and you become a modem junkie.

What You Should Buy?

Modem-buying calls for a little background. For historical reasons, modem speeds are based on funny multiples of 300 bits per second, and several different data compression formats are current. Manuals for modems tend to feature cable-connect pinouts, timing diagrams, arcane CCITT standards jargon, and tables of the time-honored Hayes AT commands. The Hayes company declared bankruptcy in 1995, but the AT commands will apparently live on to eternity.

In the Mac world, external modems are much more common than internal modems. An external modem comes in its own case. An internal modem is a card that you stick into a slot inside the Mac. They don't differ much operationally, except that internal modems tend to be a bit cheaper. External modems have the advantage that you can see the little flashing lights, so at least you can tell if they're working. PowerBooks are a special case, as the "Power to the people" sidebar explains.

Warning signs for modem users

You can get into this modem stuff too deeply. Review these warning signs to make sure that you aren't turning into a wirehead.

- ✔ You hum dial tones in the shower.

- ✔ You can make modem sign-on noises with your nose.

- ✔ You remember which colors mean what on the phone jack's teensy wires.

- ✔ You absentmindedly reset the clock on a friend's VCR.

- ✔ The blinking lights on the front of your modem send secretly coded messages that only you can understand.

If any of these things happen, go to some live concerts to restore your equilibrium.

Power to the people

PowerBook owners should note that everything I say in this chapter applies to PowerBooks as well, with the provision that the same specs cost $100 more for PowerBook internal modems than for desktop Macs, a sort of surcharge for miniaturization engineering. Very small portable external modems (pocket modems) are also available, with the advantage that you can unplug them and use them with your desktop Mac. Little pocket modems typically run off their own 9-volt batteries. This feature helps when you're on the road, since PowerBook internal modems tend to run down the PowerBook's own battery at a frightening rate.

Understanding Modems

Despite all the hardware jargon, a modem's job is really fairly simple: it takes output from your files or your keyboard and converts the pattern of zeroes and ones into an equivalent pattern of tones. The telephone line can handle the tones reliably, so the message gets sent.

The other common communications accessory is the fax machine, so these days, modem makers tend to build fax capability into the modem. A fax/modem's job isn't much harder — it converts the document into a set of lines containing dark bits and white spaces (blocks of zeroes and ones) and performs the same tone conversion on this data. One of the major Mac communications mysteries is why fax software is often so troublesome. Things are, however, getting better.

The circuit boards inside these products reflect this simplicity. They usually contain just a few chips (and there are only a few popular chip vendors for data communications circuits) and other components. In portable modems, the holder for the nine-volt battery is often the biggest physical component. Because there's really not much in them, prices for modems fall steadily every year as the chips get cheaper. Yesterday's $600 modem is today's $99 bargain, and yesterday's mainstream modem is sitting on a closet shelf.

Can I use an older modem on the Internet?

The short answer to this question is No.

Millions of 1200-bps (bits per second) modems are floating around, and if you plan to contact an online service only occasionally and then only use it for e-mail, you can get along with one of them. Frankly, you shouldn't *buy* one — try to cajole someone into giving you one instead. The typical Mac users group includes dozens of people who have upgraded their communications and may be willing to donate their old ones to you. You won't be happy downloading Internet files at 1200 bps.

What does "good enough" mean?

You can still buy a 2400-bps modem without a fax as a basic communications system. Sometimes you find them bundled with introductory offers for national online services. As the next sidebar explains, they sometimes come bundled with your Mac.

The reality is that you are probably going to want to plunge into the fabulous new universe of the World Wide Web. Most modems made before 1994 didn't anticipate this situation. You can limp along on the Web at 9600 bps, you can be reasonably happy at 14.4K, and you will find things pretty satisfactory at 28.8K. Anything slower just won't work on the Web. "Good enough" was 2400 bps five years ago, and now good enough means 14.4K.

By 1995, most bulletin boards and network connections upgraded to 14.4K access nationally, with 28.8K access in big cities. They have also dropped surcharges for faster service, adjusting to the reality that World Wide Web access calls for access at ten times the speeds that were common a few years ago. When you download lots of pictures, you simply need an order of magnitude faster access than you did with plain text.

What should I buy?

To be happy with a modem connecting to the Internet, you should plan on buying at least a 14.4K-bps modem — or 28.8K if you can afford it. The reason is simple. Once you get used to file transfers at 28.8K, even 9600 feels like you're wading though bean dip.

Honest, they gave me this thing!

Apple sold at least a million Performa models with built-in modems and communications software. The catch in this arrangement is that the modems are 2400-bps units, for which Apple paid about $20. The built-in modem is fine for getting oriented to Internet services, but once you start doing anything serious, it's going to be out with the old and in with the new, modem-wise. If you plan to access the World Wide Web, the old built-in modem is an obstacle, not a help.

With a built-in fax, 28.8K bps costs a bit more than $100 in January 1996. You would think that 14.4K modems should be proportionally cheaper, but that's not the case. In a store, a 14.4K modem isn't particularly a bargain — the cheap way to get one is to have a Nethead friend who can't stand to use it any more.

If you are the kind of person who wants a $3,000 trail bike and who bought a Power Mac the first day they appeared, you should know that faster options are also available (see Table 3-1).

Table 3-1	Modem Standards
The Standard	*What It Means*
V.22*bis*	2400 bps
V.32	9600 bps
V.32*bis*	14,400 bps
V.Fast	28,000 bps
ISDN	56,000 bps

(ISDN requires a modem-like card and a special arrangement with the phone company.)

Telephone systems themselves are being upgraded to carry more data — at 28,000 bps, the noise in ordinary voice lines becomes a big problem. That's why many national online services took their time about providing faster access. In the first edition of this book, I predicted that it could take a few years to get faster access. But phenomenal demand for Web services forced everybody to upgrade in a matter of months! Most national online services are planning special hardware/software ISDN packages for their members by early 1996.

The Software Connection

The modem, of course, does nothing but sit there until a piece of software tells it what to do. (Also, make sure that it's turned on — believe it or not, I've been called out on consulting calls where pressing the On button was the issue.)

Three kinds of software are important for your Internet journey. First is the software provided directly by online services. If you're going to connect to America Online for Internet service, AOL sends you its own software disks. (Actually, you can walk into any grocery store in the U.S. and find AOL disks bagged into computer magazines.) The second kind of software is represented by the special communications programs you have to use with direct Internet connection (I tell you about these programs in the next two chapters). Finally, basic communications software lets you connect to bulletin boards and online services that have a plain vanilla, no-icon, text-style interface.

Here's a bit of distinction between these programs. For basic Internet connection, the national online services have all come around to offering most of what you need. But as these companies have big legal staffs, a lot of material is censored. For really wild material, or material that appeals to special interest groups (Chippendale furniture collectors), or local interest stuff, you need software to access bulletin boards. The programs in this section are just that: basic software to connect to bulletin boards. Get yourself a copy of *Online Access* or *Boardwatch* for a quick look at "what's out there."

ZTerm, the last word

David Alverson wrote a terminal program called ZTerm that shows up (in earlier versions) on bulletin boards and in the software libraries of online services. If you have a PowerBook with an internal modem, the vendor probably gave you ZTerm (see Figure 3-1) as part of the package. The editors of *Macworld* always pick ZTerm as the best communications software. Computers, you see, are still a funny kind of business. One good programmer — for example Mr. Alverson, working by himself in Mason, Ohio — can do better work than a whole three-story building full of mediocrities on the West Coast. The manual for this product, however, is not the greatest.

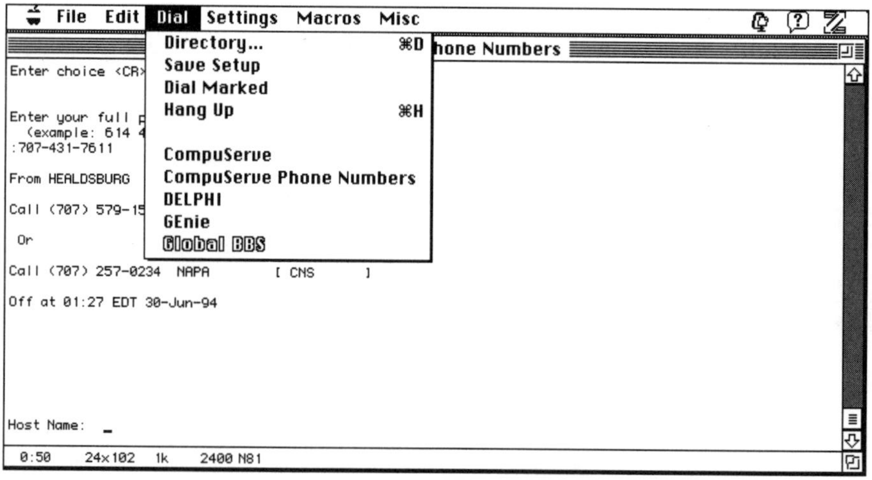

Figure 3-1:
ZTerm is fast, clean, efficient, and usually free.

Microphone LT (for lovable terminalware)

A majority of new Mac modems ship with Microphone LT from Software Ventures Corporation (510-644-3232). It lacks the automation features and some of the high-end capabilities built into the full-scale version of Microphone, but it's certainly good enough for using your Mac as a text-based terminal. For signing onto a free Internet connection at a library or for any other dial-up Internet service that works on text commands, it has everything you need.

If you know your modem's speed and the phone number for your connection, you can pretty much leave Microphone LT's default settings in place (see Figure 3-2). Microphone LT also lets you specify VT-102 as the terminal type in a simple terminal settings window (see Figure 3-3). Lots of people on the Internet, especially inside universities, still use real hardware VT-102 terminals, so you're in good company.

One of this program's great virtues is that it keeps a record of your online session, and it's just about impossible to lose this record by accident. Instead of downloading files, often it's more convenient to read them on-screen and then later open the Microphone LT record of the session by using your favorite word processor.

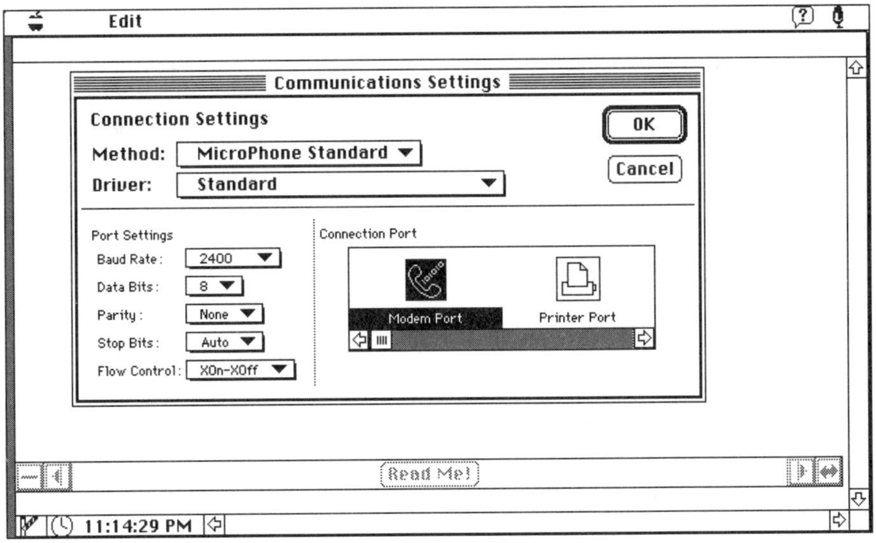

Figure 3-2: Microphone LT asks you to make only a couple of setup decisions.

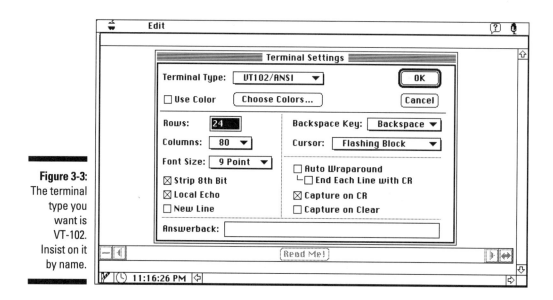

Figure 3-3:
The terminal
type you
want is
VT-102.
Insist on it
by name.

ClarisWorks — I've seen better; I've seen worse

ClarisWorks 4.0, which is bundled with an amazing number of Macs sold through consumer channels, includes a communications module. It's neither as capable as Microphone nor as easy to use (see the dialog box in Figure 3-4); however, if you already own it, you can learn to live with it. It doesn't have as many friendly, built-in reminders as the best communications software and was clearly something of an afterthought to Claris, but if you use ClarisWorks all the time, it gets information into the other modules (word processing and database) conveniently.

Microsoft Works: a glimpse of the past

You're a back-to-basics sort, right? No frills? Chip your own stone tools on weekends? (Remember, flint can be *sharp!*) Microsoft Works has a communications module just for you.

Somewhere far to the west, a brooding Bill Gates, richest man on earth, lies in bed and stares up at a vaulted ceiling in his giant mansion. What's keeping him up nights? The nagging thought that somehow, somewhere, someone got something for free from Microsoft. The word processor in Works is designed,

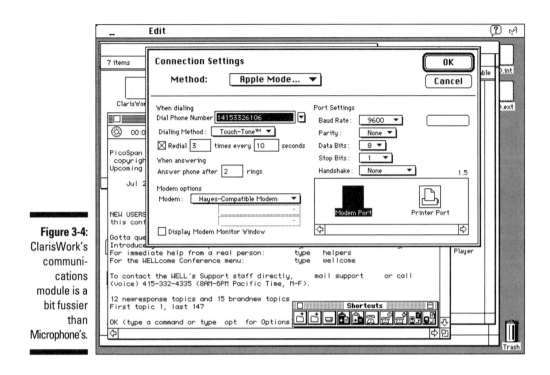

Figure 3-4:
ClarisWork's
communi-
cations
module is a
bit fussier
than
Microphone's.

for example, to force you to buy Microsoft Word from sheer frustration some-day. Microsoft acquired the communications module from a third party in a no-cash-exchanged transaction essentially as a marketing consideration.

If you have Works, one of the first things you should do on the Internet is use it to download a better terminal program by using the screen shown in Figure 3-5. I tell you how in Chapter 5.

Fancy stuff

Figure 3-6, the sign-on screen from America Online, shows you what Mac communication software is supposed to look like. I don't show you the configu-ration and settings screens because usually you need to enter only modem speed and phone number, which often have been preset.

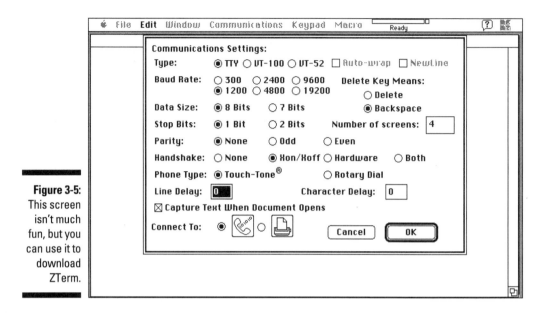

Figure 3-5:
This screen isn't much fun, but you can use it to download ZTerm.

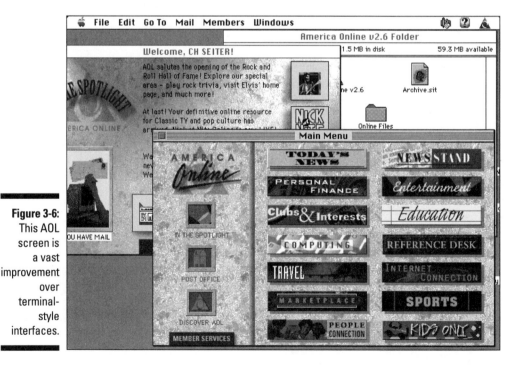

Figure 3-6:
This AOL screen is a vast improvement over terminal-style interfaces.

More Info for the Hyper-Curious

In this book, I only want to tell you enough modem stuff so that you don't buy something that's disastrously wrong. As you can see, the Internet itself is a big enough subject to occupy your attention. The definitive work on modems is Tina Rathbone's *Modems For Dummies, 2nd Edition,* another fine IDG product (there's also *More Modems for Dummies*, too). With these preliminaries out of the way, I show you how to communicate with everyone on earth in the following chapters.

Chapter 4

E-Mail — The World on the Wire

• •

• •

What's the Story on E-Mail?

You can send e-mail to any one of the Internet's 60 million users if

✔ You own a Macintosh and a modem.

✔ Your Mac is on a network, and the network has a modem.

✔ Your Mac is directly connected to a network that is an Internet *host* — a computer system with its own Internet numerical address. You don't even need a modem in this case.

The first e-mail services open to the public (businesses have had in-house e-mail since the 1960s) were national organizations like MCI Mail and CompuServe. In the beginning, if you had an MCI account, you could send mail to anyone else with an MCI account, but you couldn't send mail out of the system. Actually, you could have had an MCI message delivered on paper to a regular street address for a discouragingly high fee.

By the early 1990s, however, everyone involved in the e-mail business had figured out that universal connection was the future of e-mail. If CompuServe, MCI Mail, and Prodigy became Internet hosts, then users could easily send messages from one service to another. It was obviously a good idea. Surprisingly, they actually followed through. Every commercial service that can afford to advertise in a magazine is now connected to the Internet and has universal e-mail capability.

Hosts, mailboxes, and you

Suppose that you sign up with a major Internet service provider, such as Netcom (408-554-8649). Netcom gives you a local dial-up phone number. You use the name "Joe Cool," and you choose "joec" as your Net name. Your Internet address, then, is joec@netcom.com. Netcom is the *host,* meaning a computer system with its own Internet numerical address. You, in turn, are a user attached to that host, but you are not a host yourself.

As a service for outgoing e-mail, Netcom becomes the equivalent of the corner mailbox. You send a message to your pal Michael Nifty, miken@world.com. Netcom routes the message to the receiving Internet host, world.com. The receiving host acts like one of those big office mailbox systems with hundreds of pigeonholes. It finds miken, stores the message, and notifies your pal that he has new mail. Usually, he sees this notice the next time he logs into the world.com system.

Oh, there really is a world.com, provided by The World. It's another big-time commercial Internet service (based in Boston, it was one of the first), and you can reach it at 617-739-0202. One shift in Internet access that took place in 1995 is that more familiar names, such as America Online or Prodigy, came to be much more common as Internet addresses than those of Net pioneers like World or Netcom.

These connections work, in part, because the messages are primitive. The e-mail messages I'm talking about are plain text; these messages can be created on any type of computer and read on any other. And because they're just text, they're compact — a one-page color picture file is 500 times bigger than a file containing a page of text. That makes a difference when you use a relatively slow modem (9600 bps) for Internet connection. Someday soon, you will be able to send systemwide sound-plus-picture messages across the Internet. Even now, it's possible to send sound and picture *files* with a few tricks (more on this subject later), but sounds and graphics are not generally available in Internet e-mail yet because services haven't uniformly implemented multimedia mail standards.

Dear Mr. President

Using only the simplest version of a mailing system, I'm going to give a little e-mail tour now. The way I show you is not the best way to do e-mail, but this simple way is common. Some national online services have convenient and intuitive mail systems, and you can use a Mac-specific mail program called Eudora if you are a host (or have a direct link to a host). But the typical Internet service-provider setup uses a plain vanilla UNIX mail program like the one in this chapter.

First step

You get an account and log into your system. All you need is your name, your password, and a phone number. Most likely, you'll use one of the communications programs described in Chapter 3 (most chapters in this book explain the details of signing on one way or another, so for now, just come along for the ride). After you log in, you get a prompt (no menus here, folks); a common prompt is the %. That's right, the computer sends you this symbol — % — to assist you in figuring what to do next. Thanks for all the help.

This situation explains why nearly 3 million people have signed up for America Online, with far easier e-mail, in the last year alone. I'm tracking this process in the old style so that you can see some of the machinery underlying the Net — you may be using a friendlier mail program, but that program is issuing most of the commands you will see here.

If you read the manual, you know that at the prompt you can type

```
mail president@whitehouse.gov
```

to start the mail program. By the way, if you find yourself stuck using this kind of interface, at the % prompt you can also type

```
man
```

and the main system (the host system — it's the host, you're the user) fills your screen with pieces of the operating system's manual.

Helpful advice

After you type **mail** and an address at the prompt, you're rewarded with something a bit more informative. Now you see the following:

```
mail president@whitehouse.gov
Subject:
```

You may as well compose a good general-purpose Internet presidential letter — one with a long shelf life. After you give a subject name and press Return, type this message:

```
mail president@whitehouse.gov
Subject: Such a Deal
The deficit in the Federal Budget is running close to a bil-
        lion dollars a day. I have developed a spread-
        sheet in ClarisWorks that can reschedule interest
        payments on the national debt by half-day incre-
        ments to save $10 billion a year, and I only want
        payments of $1 million a day (it's a licensing
        arrangement) for it. Look at it this way: I may
        even be right, and $1 million a day is well
        within the range of accounting error in your
        system. As far as you can tell, it wouldn't cost
        you anything even if I were wrong!
Yours sincerely,
Joseph M. Cool
```

Now what? Well, if you read the manual, you know to press Ctrl-D (hold down Ctrl and D at the same time). The system sends you

```
EOT
```

for end of transmission.

Out into the Net

That's the end for you, but the computer system has just started working. It attaches an ID to your message and finds a path through the Internet to the target computer — in this case, a computer at the White House.

Sometimes this process is very straightforward, but the message path may go through a whole set of computers with their own weird Internet addresses.

At the receiving end, the president sees your message with a header that contains all sorts of system information. Actually, I'm just kidding about the president — it's a lead-pipe cinch that he won't see anything you send personally (there is a staff that sends out automated thank-yous). But the header is there (see Figure 4-1).

If you make a mistake in the address, the message won't get through. Some

```
Path:search01.news.aol.com!newstf01.cr1.aol.com!uunet!MathWorks.Com!europa.eng.gt
efsd.com!library.ucla.edu!csulb.edu!csus.edu!netcom.com!zzz
From: zzz@netcom.com (Louis Zzizz)
Subject: Re: Mac Ftp Mirrors
Message-ID: <zzzCqFHpC.AoC@netcom.com>
References: <2s1fq9$f8c@news.CCIT.Arizona.EDU> <fujii-260594031300@ts7-
38.upenn.edu>
Date: Sun, 29 May 1994 21:15:11 GMT

Subject: Re: Mac Ftp Mirrors
From: zzz@netcom.com (Louis Zzizz)
Date: Sun, 29 May 1994 21:15:11 GMT
Message-ID: <zzzCqFHpC.AoC@netcom.com>

>> Where else can I ftp to get the Umich and/or Info-Mac files?

Here are two sites that are updated every day:

ftp.univie.ac.at      131.130.1.4     mac/info-mac           1/1
ftp.ucs.ubc.ca        137.82.27.62    pub/mac/info-mac        1/1

Louis Zziz         zzz@netcom.com      San Jose, CA
```

Figure 4-1: A typical Internet e-mail message, preceded by a header with more than you want to see.

systems tell you after a brief delay that the address isn't working. Typically, however, the message goes out on the Internet and gets bounced back to you hours later — you'll find it returned the next time you connect to your host system. In other words, it's critical to get Internet addresses exactly right. Unlike the Post Office, the Internet has no way to work around your typos. I once got a letter addressed to C. Smelter in Hellburg, CA — there is nothing corresponding to this kind of creative interpretation online.

UNIX Stuff (Groan)

The Internet For Dummies includes a description of a somewhat-improved UNIX-based mailing system called *elm*. This program has a nice repertoire of commands and a full-screen editor. By UNIX standards, it's a big improvement. There are half a dozen other mailing programs, too.

But the fact is, they're all absolutely pitiful even compared to a simple Macintosh shareware mailing program. Nonetheless, only shareware programs are available for many kinds of basic Internet connections.

Here's why: Back when the Mac could run only MacPaint and MacWrite, UNIX was a highly evolved, nearly uncrashable operating system that could handle big networks. The best way to make a low-cost, multiuser system in the mid-1980s was to get a single, powerful UNIX computer and a bunch of cheap terminals that offered only character-oriented display. Hundreds of universities, government organizations, and businesses — the same ones that make up a big part of the Internet today — set up UNIX systems. Even now, there are more

Sun workstations running UNIX as Internet servers than any other kind of hardware box.

In the mid-1990s, therefore, Internet services often want you to take your lovely, graphics-oriented Macintosh, capable of QuickTime movies and stereo sound, and operate it as a character-oriented terminal. The machine at the other end of the wire thinks that you actually have a character-oriented terminal. I wish that some wise guy would write a program that mimics a terminal with a black screen and green dot-matrix characters to remind me of the time I spent as a child at a real VT-100 terminal. Oh, well. All this is rapidly being swept away as national online services get their multimedia act together.

Ten Internet e-mail tips

1. The best way to find someone's address is simply to ask for it over the phone. Sometimes you can even state your message. Ain't technology neat?

2. If tip 1 fails, try looking up the address in *The Internet White Pages*. There is an online version of this resource available on most services.

3. Make your Internet name recognizable instead of using `squiggy@netcom.com` or something like that.

4. DON'T USE ALL CAPITALS. THEY MAKE IT SEEM LIKE YOU'RE SHOUTING.

5. Remember the Golden Rule because everyone else can do unto you automatically. Over and over. Over and over. Over and over.

6. E-mail jokes don't always work. In plain text, it's harder to tell when you're kidding, you lamentable buffoon (just kidding).

7. Try to keep it short. U dnt hv 2 wrt lk ths, but *Moby Dick* doesn't fit down a wire.

8. Make sure that the person receiving the message can tell who you are (put name and phone number in the text of the message).

9. Unsolicited messages should put a ? first in the subject line, as in `?are you the joanm who went to high school in greenwood, wi.`

10. Pay attention to discussion of electronic security in newspapers. Watch Big Brother instead of letting him watch you.

BBS Is Bttr

Check out the mail system in Figure 4-2. It's a text-based but menu-driven system — you don't necessarily have to memorize the commands or keep a cheat sheet in your lap while you're typing because help is available at all times.

The difference between this mail system and classic UNIX mailing systems, like so many things, has to do with money. In the stock UNIX situation, you had access to a computer system by using UNIX, and you took what you got. Don't like the mailing system? Then write people notes in purple crayon on paper towels.

A typical bulletin board system (BBS) or conferencing system wants you to sign up, wants you to be happy, and wants to charge you a fee. If the mailing system is intolerable, two problems arise: You don't want to write messages, so you won't stay connected (and the service usually charges an hourly fee). And eventually you quit, an even worse situation. Even if the BBS is free, the BBS operator pays for the software, so any way you slice it, there's more incentive to offer a decent mailing system.

Figure 4-2:
This mail
system isn't
Mac
software
yet, but it
makes a few
concessions
to the user.

```
            COMMAND OPTIONS FOR USING EMAIL

mail userid  ...Send email to another WELL user.  You will be prompted for
             a "Subject". Type a short subject header and hit Return.
             Then, enter the text of your message, hitting Return at
             the end of each line (about 70 chars wide).  To abandon
             the message without sending it, hit control-c twice.

             To send the letter, go to a new line, type a dot (.),
             and hit Return.

mail         ...Read your mail.  You will see a list of your mail items
             and a prompt which looks like this:  &   ...To read each
             consecutive mail item, hit Return at this "&" prompt.

             Type: r     ...to respond to the current message.

             Type: dt    ...to delete the current message.

             Type: q     ...to quit email.
```

Mac Access

Two years ago, I would have felt compelled to offer a few pages full of UNIX mailing commands in a cheat sheet. Now, I can duck the whole, ugly mess. Even UNIX hotshots themselves are converting their systems wholesale to an interface called X Windows, which looks for all the world like a small-print version of a Macintosh screen.

You can get Internet e-mail access in lots of ways. You can use the plain, guess-your-next-command style that's standard with UNIX, or you can get a really friendly mail interface from America Online or eWorld. Ironically, Internet e-mail access probably costs between $10 and $20 a month, whichever type of access you pick. Allow me to underline this distinction by presenting two mail-access screens (see Figures 4-3 and 4-4) back-to-back. Look, you had enough sense to pick a Mac in the first place — make your own decision.

```
Sun Mar 13 23:50:20 PST 1994
crl1% mail
Mail version SMI 4.0 Fri Jul  2 11:55:02 PDT 1993  Type ? for help.
"/usr/spool/mail/chseiter": 1 message 1 new
>N  1 wilson          Sat Mar 12 26 05:59   36/1103  Macworld note

& mail chseiter@aol.com
Subject: comm1
Hi. If you can read this, you're not having fun.
.
EOT

New mail has arrived.
crl2% mail
Mail version SMI 4.0 Fri Jul  2 11:55:02 PDT 1993  Type ? for help.
"/usr/spool/mail/chseiter": 1 message 1 new
>N  1 MAILER-DAEMON    Sun Mar 13 23:53   24/719
Returned mail: User unknown
& d 1
& quit
|
```

Figure 4-3:
The traditional Internet mail interface.

 File Edit Go To Mail Members Windows   ⑦ ◢

To: `anyone@zyx.com`   cc:

Address Book

Subj: `Macintosh software`

Attach File   File: `               `   ☐ **Return Receipt**

This is what a real Macintosh interface looks like on communications software

Send Later

	Mail you have sent	
🖫 6/3/94	IDG BOOKS	for L. Smith/Mac INet Ch. 6 rev
6/2/94	Mactivity	the show
🖫 6/2/94	IDG BOOKS	for LaurieSmith/MacInetCh3/c.se
🖫 6/1/94	IDG BOOKS	for Laurie Smith
6/1/94	digger@mai…	Re: user directory searches
5/31/94	IDG BOOKS	to: L. Smith
5/28/94	erjablow@c…	Re: Mystery Science Theater 300
5/24/94	marca@netc…	Mosaic plans
5/24/94	marian@mic…	Re: Solid State NMR
5/19/94	apalmer@ro…	Matlab notes

Send Now

Help

[**Read**]   [**Status**]

[**Delete**]   [**Unsend**]

Figure 4-4:
Internet mail meets the Macintosh.

Names and Numbers

Once you're on the Internet and people know that you're a master of e-mail, you may find yourself called on to chitchat about esoteric topics. That is, I propose to get you up and running with minimal fuss, but if I don't fill you in on a few gory details, you won't be able to impress your friends. Net old-timers complain constantly that *anyone* can get on the Internet. In one plaintive newsgroup message I read recently, a hard-core Nethead complains that he just received a message from his grandmother!

A class system

Internet hosts have machine addresses composed of four numbers separated by dots. Thus the WELL in San Francisco is called

```
well.sf.ca.us
```

but other Internet machines know it as

```
198.93.4.10
```

The numbers between the dots range from 1 to 254. In other words, there are 254 x 254 x 254 x 254 possible addresses — about 4 billion.

The same conventions apply to the World Wide Web, in the sense that Web addresses are fitted into the same scheme as overall Internet addresses. When you try to connect to

```
http://www.yahoo.com
```

instead of an @-address, the system has a so-called "nameserver" that looks up the number for Yahoo company and routes you to the WWW server on Yahoo's network (actually located at Netscape).

A, B, and C

Because there are different ways to do the network address assignment, the people who assigned them made up three classes: A, B, and C. Class A networks can support about 16 million hosts (that's a big network!); class C networks can handle 254 hosts. Because a host computer on a network can handle several incoming lines, there's a lot of room out there.

Inside a big network, a method called *subnetting* simplifies addressing from one network to the next, and another method called *supernetting* lets organizations effectively address several smaller networks as though they were one big network. I wouldn't bother you with a word of this, except that it will come back to haunt you when I tell you how to make your Mac a host. Figure 4-5, for example, shows the setup screen from MacTCP. You have to know how to fill in the blanks, or you can't get connected with a high-speed SLIP or PPP connection.

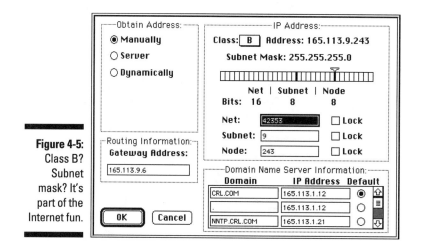

Figure 4-5:
Class B?
Subnet
mask? It's
part of the
Internet fun.

The 5th Wave   By Rich Tennant

Chapter 5
Beyond E-Mail — The InfoSphere

Piles o' Files

E-mail contains everything that someone thought up an hour ago and wanted to communicate. The rest of the Internet is everything that someone thought up *ever* and wanted to communicate.

The Internet currently has something like 200 gigabytes of text files that you can access with no special security clearance. (This book is about half a megabyte of text, so I'm talking about roughly 200,000 books this size.) Programs and pictures are available, too. In addition, gigabytes of information slosh back and forth between BITNET and USENET sites and thousands of bulletin boards.

The original Internet scheme can be thought of as a way of extending universal e-mail to a form of universal file transfer. Therefore, most of the first generation of Internet facilities concern themselves with files and file transfer. In the more graphics-oriented system of the World Wide Web (that's the topic of the next chapter), things are a little different, mostly because the Web represents a more advanced way to organize and index Internet information. Meanwhile, for historical reasons that date as far back as 1994, this chapter looks at the grand old Internet tradition of file-handling.

Finding What You Want

The first problem you face, in Internet file operations, is finding what you want. Thousands of big computers are on the Internet — so where's the good stuff? The next problem is hauling the good stuff back to your own computer (you actually have to transfer a file to your own hard drive to use it). Both problems have a standard Internet solution and a Macintosh solution.

The most common Internet tools for finding files are probably Archie, Gopher, and WWW (World Wide Web) indexes (see Chapter 6). I provide some basic exercises in these programs so you can see what a search is like. A program called FTP (*file transfer protocol*) is the standard tool for retrieving files — all national online services have implemented a version of Internet file transfer protocol (besides their own internal file services).

The stand-alone Macintosh programs for searching and transfer are, as you may expect, even better than the originals. TurboGopher and Anarchie are just fantastic pieces of software, and Mosaic is pretty cool, too (see Figure 5-1). The Mac program Fetch, from Dartmouth University, is a file retrieval program that makes users of other computers drool enviously. The catch, and it's not a small one, is that you need a direct Internet connection to use these particular tools. That means that either 1) you're a Mac user on a network host, 2) you're paying for an expensive full-time direct connection, or 3) you have bought a SLIP or PPP account (see the following sidebar). Fortunately, although this chapter features examples of these stand-alone programs, the big national services have implemented their own work-alikes for these, making it possible to do the same things without a SLIP or PPP connection.

Key to the Highway

At first, the assortment of Internet navigation tools can be somewhat bewildering. How are you supposed to figure out what tool to use when?

I'll tell you how. It's all very simple. It came to me in a blinding flash after this book was 95 percent finished. I looked back over several chapters and realized that in 15 different sections I was talking about the same thing. Here it is.

There is only *one* trick on the Internet. The trick is the ability to jump from one computer to the next. Everything else is just a file-management utility.

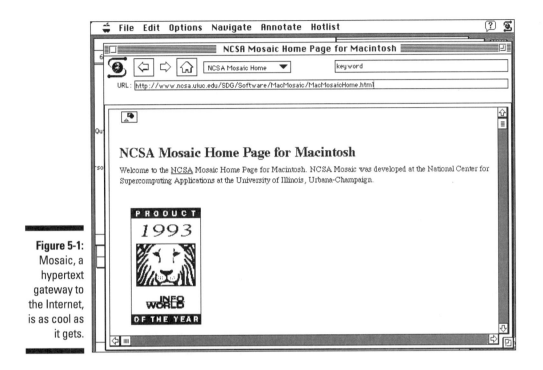

Figure 5-1:
Mosaic, a
hypertext
gateway to
the Internet,
is as cool as
it gets.

Two steps out

Here's the scenario. You get an Internet account and a password at a service provider. You sign onto your host service. There you are on your host computer, which probably has all sorts of interesting files itself. But let's face it. You want more. You want *power*. So you type the command

```
telnet fedix.fie.com
```

At this command, your own host computer then calls up a big computer network that's another Internet host (see the sidebar "Remote possibilities"). This one is full of government databases. You see the dazzling display of character-based graphics in Figure 5-2. Don't worry about this bland readout for now — you'll see lots of dolled-up World Wide Web connections shortly.

You will be asked to log in, but fortunately this particular system tells you how:

```
Enter your FEDIX/MOLIS USERID, or NEW if you are a new user,
or PRIOR if you have forgotten your USERID > new Logged in
as new
```

```
Hello, Welcome to FEDIX on fedix...


Last login: Mon Jun  6 18:53:20 from uclink2.Berkeley
Up - Sat May 28 12:08:04 EDT 1994
SunOS Release 4.1.2 (FEDIX2) #1: Tue May 25 11:51:11 EDT 1993
          FFFFFFFFF EEEEEEEEE DDDDDDD   IIIII XXX   XXX
          FFF       EEE       DDD  DDDD   III    XXX XXX
          FFF       EEE       DDD   DDD   III     XXXXX
          FFFFFF    EEEEEEEE  DDD   DDD   III      XXX
          FFF       EEE       DDD   DDD   III     XXXXX
          FFF       EEE       DDD  DDDD   III    XXX XXX
          FFF       EEEEEEEEE DDDDDDD   IIIII XXX   XXX


***************************************************************
***************************************************************

logged in on - /dev/ttyp5
Internet
```

Figure 5-2:
Yikes! It's
the Feds
(sort of). But
they're
smiling!

SLIPpery business

SLIP (Serial Line Interface Protocol), as implemented in the programs MacSLIP and InterSLIP, lets you connect directly to the Internet over an ordinary phone line. Get a fast modem (at least 14,400 bps) and a SLIP account from an Internet service provider, and you can have your own Internet address number. You can even get assigned an address to be a host.

SLIP service by phone involves a few minor difficulties. It's great for transferring files, but mail to your new address only works when you're online. If you hang up the phone line, as far as the rest of the Internet is concerned, you're a "Host not responding" site. That's why most SLIP account users have another way to get mail 24 hours a day: through a national online service like CompuServe or through a *shell* account

(standard dial-up access) at the SLIP provider.

Another minor difficulty is that getting SLIP up and running can be frustrating. It's also likely that the customer support people at the service provider won't be Mac authorities. Sometimes these guys are a bit strange anyway. Here's an authentic hot-off-the-Internet joke:

Q: How do you recognize an extroverted network engineer?

A: He stares at *your* shoes when he talks to you.

Since 1995, PPP (Point-to-Point Protocol) has started to edge out SLIP as a direct-connect style. The gruesome details of direct connection (as opposed to lazily letting eWorld or another service do your electrical engineering) are covered in Chapter 13.

Remote possibilities

Telnet is the standard command in UNIX for connecting you to another computer network (you're on one now; it connects you to another one). Another command called rlogin, for remote login, is similar. If you type **!man telnet**, most systems give you a little manual about telnet to read. What's remarkable about this is that *connected means connected*; when you telnet to a computer at the National Center for Supercomputing Applications, you're just as connected as users in Urbana, IL (except they have a megabit-per-second line, and you have a punky little modem).

If you don't have advance information, you usually won't know what to do at the login prompt

that you see. If you have to guess, use "guest" or "public" as your name and your Internet address as a password. A better approach is to get the information from your own host. Usually, if you read about an interesting telnet site in a magazine or newspaper, the login information will be provided.

Some networks you reach with telnet have prepared a lovely menu system to help you navigate. Some haven't. If you get into a network that just gives you a % prompt, try typing **ls** or **dir**. You should get a directory of files. If the directory doesn't make any sense to you, type **bye** or **quit** and read the rest of this chapter, like a good Net citizen.

After this point, all you have to do is follow the menus. That's good, because there's a ton of material there — just look at the menus in Figure 5-3. You keep answering questions; the system keeps giving you choices. When you get to the World Wide Web chapter, you'll see how *hyperlinks* have simplified navigating the information seas.

```
FEDERAL  INFORMATION  EXCHANGE
*************************************************************

Item  Description
----  ---------------------------------------------
  1   Federal Opportunities (FEDIX)
  2   Minority College & University Capability Information (MOLIS)
  3   Higher Education Opportunities for Minorities & Women (HERO)
  8   New System Interface (Lynx http://web.fie.com/) *** PLEASE USE ***
      (From Mosaic, Cello or Lynx; URL=http://web.fie.com/)
  9   Download FEDIX/MOLIS Files
  0   Exit

What is your choice  - > 9
         Currently files are available from:

      FEDIX System
      1 -- Air Force Office of Scientific Research (AFOSR)
      2 -- Department of Energy (DOE)
      3 -- Department of Agriculture (USDA)
      4 -- Federal Aviation Administration (FAA)
      5 -- Federal Minority Opportunities
      6 -- National Aeronautics and Space Administration (NASA)
      7 -- Office of Naval Research (ONR)
      8  MOLIS System

Which agency do you want a file from?
```

Figure 5-3: The Feds answer your every question.

One step back

You, the astute reader (hey, I figure you're all astute because you had enough sense to get this book) may raise some questions at this point. How did I know *where* to telnet? Actually, I got the information from a list provided by my own Internet host as I experimented. Unless you have the worst service provider on earth, customer support at your own service can send you a list of telnet sites to try (send an e-mail message to customer support). If you want to try the telnet trick from a big national service such as CompuServe, you will find that the service has posted a list of hot telnet sites besides providing telnet capability.

There's a Macintosh HyperCard stack called HytelNet that has a big directory of resources you can search off-line. You can also try sites from Table 5-1, my list of Ten Telnet Treasures.

Table 5-1	Ten Telnet Treasures	
Telnet to:	*Login as:*	*It holds*
fdabbs.fda.gov	bbs	The latest FDA warnings!
michel.ai.mit.edu	guest	A strange virtual reality world
sparc-1.law.columbia.edu	lawnet	Legal databases
coast.ucsd.edu	gopher	Everything about the oceans
nisc.jvnc.net	nicol	Directory of Internet resources
bbs.oit.unc.edu	bbs	General-purpose Internet facilities
hnsource.cc.ukans.edu	history	The login says it all
mb.com	mb	A simple shopping service
fedworld.doc.gov	bbs	Piles of government documents
nebbs.nersc.gov	new	K-12 education

As you might expect, you can find stuff in a more organized way than logging into one computer after another in search of gems. That's why the rest of this chapter is about searching.

Another "astute" question: How do I get those files from the big computer over there to my little Macintosh over here? That's the function of FTP (*f*ile *t*ransfer *p*rotocol), which is a sort of telnet-with-download-built-in that's the standard file transporter for networks on the Internet. I give you an FTP tour, too.

In fact, FTP is not just a good idea: It's the law (more or less). It does a high-speed file transfer from the remote computer to your Internet host. That lets other high-speed traffic pass you on the information superhighway. You can then get the file from your host to your Mac in your own quiet modem-based slow lane on the side. Most sites insist that you do your file transfers with FTP, rather than with any of the several UNIX utilities for file copying.

First You Search, and Then You FTP

A kindly bunch of people at McGill University in Canada have set up a computer that maintains lists of the files on a huge assortment of Internet networks. Instead of going around to computers one at a time by telnet and poking through the files, you just go to the computer at McGill. The computer is called an *Archie server*, because it maintains archives and lots of people can use it at the same time.

Archie in action

Other places, mostly universities, soon installed their own Archie servers, and there's a sort of built-in Archie in the nationals (AOL, eWorld, Prodigy, CompuServe, and others). Figure 5-4 shows a sample search. As a demonstration, I looked for files with the name "MacTCP" in them. As a good citizen, I did the search on an Archie server in Finland at 4 a.m. Finnish time. There are only 4 million people in Finland, and even Finns have to sleep sometimes (you wouldn't think so if you have known very many of them, though), so I figured the system would have room for me. The Finns were snoring, all right — I was doing the only search on the system.

You can see the first part of the search results near the bottom of the figure. In 23 seconds, as advertised by the FUNET system, Archie found 200 sites with files on MacTCP (the other sites take 20 pages).

Figure 5-4 demonstrates two key points. Once again, you get into another network with telnet. That's what I meant when I said that telnet is really the fundamental Internet trick. The second point is that Archie by itself is a bit cryptic. It can manage all kinds of fancy searches, but it's not easy to use. That's why I'm going to tell you about Gopher.

```
OK : telnet archie.funet.fi
Trying 128.214.6.102 ...
Connected to archie.funet.fi.
Escape character is '^]'.

SunOS UNIX (archie.funet.fi)
      Finnish University and Research Network FUNET
                 Information Service
Select service (gopher/www/wais/archie/exit) ? archie
Starting Archie ..

archie> set search sub
archie> prog MacTCP
# Search type: sub.
# Estimated time for completion: 23 seconds.

Host ftp.univ-rennes1.fr   (129.20.128.34)
Last updated 03:30  4 Mar 1994

   Location: /pub/Macintosh
     FILE   -rw-r--r--  51769 bytes  14:46  4 Feb 1994  MacTCP_2.0.2_->_2.0.x
     FILE   -rw-r--r--  68246 bytes  14:47  4 Feb 1994  MacTCP_Guide.sea.hqx
     FILE   -rw-r--r--  87986 bytes  14:47  4 Feb 1994  MacTCP_Watcher_1.1.0x
```

Figure 5-4:
Archie goes
to Europe
looking for
Mac
utilities.

CyberRodents, InfoBurrows, HyperMice, InterSkunks . . .

AAAAAGGHH! Excuse me, please. I really dislike words with capital letters in the middle. And I hate cute names for programs (never fear, Apple will have released a program code-named CyberDog by the time you see this). The one exception is Gopher (as TurboGopher for the Mac), which is so useful that the developers could have called it Mucus and it would still be one of my favorites.

Going pher it

Gopher is a menu system that directs searches at different Archie servers. You connect to a Gopher server and make choices from the menus. That's it. Once again, you see the fundamental scheme in Mac Internet software, which is just writing an attractive interface for time-tested programs oriented towards UNIX systems.

In the background, Gopher furiously telnets to different Archie servers, formulates searches, hauls the results back, and presents them to you. These Gophers are all connected to other Gophers, presumably with tunnels dug right through the earth. The Big Gopher in Minnesota is connected to all of them. If you have to start a search somewhere, telnet to consultant.micro.umn.edu and log in as "Gopher."

In Figure 5-5, I connected to my own Internet host and then telnetted to a Gopher site, this time in Australia. At this point, all I need to know is how to type what I want without misspelling it. In this sense, a Gopher search is better than doing Archie directly yourself. Not only does Gopher require less planning from you, but it also gets in and out of its own Archie connections thousands of times faster than you can, conserving Net resources.

```
OK : telnet info.anu.edu.au
Trying 150.203.84.20 ...
Connected to info.anu.edu.au.
|
|                    |Welcome to ELISA
|
| Welcome to the wonderful world of Gopher!
             Search Gopherspace: Jughead & Veronica

 --> 1. Search GopherSpace: Veronica (AARNet, Australia) <?>
     2. Scope of AARNet Australian Veronica Server.
     3. Search GopherSpace: Veronica & Jughead (Other Servers)/
     4. About using the Veronica databases.
     5. About using the Jughead databases.
     6. FAQ: Frequently-Asked Questions about veronica  (1993-08-23).
     7. Archie (searching anonymous ftp sites) Via Texas A&M/
     8. How to Compose Veronica Queries.

 +--------------Search GopherSpace: Veronica (AARNet, Australia)--------------+
 |
 | Words to search for MacTCP
 |
 |                    [Cancel ^G] [Accept - Enter]
 |
 +---------------------------------------------------------------------------+
```

Figure 5-5:
The friendly, albeit text-based, world of standard Gopher.

Too much fun?

What, you inquire sweetly, am I doing in Australia for this search? On the day I did it, I couldn't get into either the Big Gopher, as it was too busy, or the Gopher at `infopath.ucsd.edu` (my dear old *alma mater*, in fact). Neither could I reach the Gopher at `scilibx.ucsc.edu`, where one logs in as "infoslug" (the sports teams at UC Santa Cruz are inspirationally named after the banana slug — no kidding). The Internet is getting to be a crowded place. If you try to use the Gopher resource inside America Online on a late Monday night, you'll probably find the whole AOL system down.

But think of the snoring Finns and remember: It's always 4 a.m. somewhere, and the main users of a given network are still the locals. Pick a good time and then get in and get out before they wake up!

FTP — Fetch This Phile!

Using Gopher, you can find all sorts of files out there on the Internet. Now you have to get them back to your Macintosh. That's when you use FTP.

Figure 5-6 shows a typical stand-alone FTP session, using a direct-connection service provider. There's really not much to it, but it's unMaclike compared to, say, FTP on eWorld. You issue the FTP command followed by the name of the Internet host that has the files. That gets you connected because, like practically every other Internet function, FTP has its own built-in analog of telnet — you don't need to know this, since the programmer of your FTP program has already figured this out.

On some systems, it's more typical to sign on with this sequence:

```
OK: FTP
FTP> open
(to) archive.wherever.com
```

But your own Internet host is supposed to tell you all that.

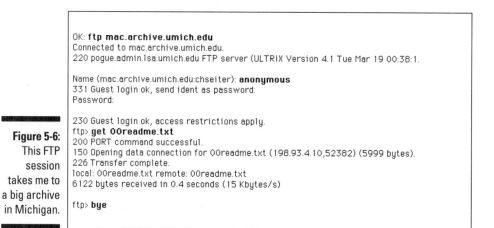

```
OK: ftp mac.archive.umich.edu
Connected to mac.archive.umich.edu.
220 pogue.admin.lsa.umich.edu FTP server (ULTRIX Version 4.1 Tue Mar 19 00:38:1.

Name (mac.archive.umich.edu:chseiter): anonymous
331 Guest login ok, send ident as password.
Password:

230 Guest login ok, access restrictions apply.
ftp> get 00readme.txt
200 PORT command successful.
150 Opening data connection for 00readme.txt (198.93.4.10,52382) (5999 bytes).
226 Transfer complete.
local: 00readme.txt remote: 00readme.txt
6122 bytes received in 0.4 seconds (15 Kbytes/s)

ftp> bye
```

Figure 5-6: This FTP session takes me to a big archive in Michigan.

In this case, I already knew that a plain text file called 00readme.txt was waiting at the Internet host in the main directory. Actually, when you connect to a UNIX host, there's almost always a file with this name waiting for you. If you don't know in advance which file you will be looking for, please read the sidebar on FTP tips and traps and then look at Figure 5-7. Screens like this are the main reason why this edition of *The Internet For Macs For Dummies* is an extended plea for using national online services to get the 500 favorite Mac files. Right now, you and I are treated to the Internet equivalent of a guy with a free airline pass flying to Sydney to buy a Coke. Think globally, act locally (or at least act on your local network, if possible).

Figure 5-7:
Uh-oh.
Internet
logjam
spotted!

```
OK: ftp wuarchive.wustl.edu
Connected to wuarchive.wustl.edu.
220 wuarchive.wustl.edu FTP server (Version wu-2.3(1) Fri Apr 8 14:26:26 CDT
19.
Name (wuarchive.wustl.edu:chseiter): anonymous

530-Sorry, there are too many anonymous FTP users using the system at this
530-time.  Please try again in a few minutes.
530-
530-There is currently a limit of 200 anonymous users.  Yes, there REALLY are
530-that many users on wuarchive -- this message is not the result of a bug.

530 User anonymous access denied.
Login failed.
```

Digging Deeper

Of course, there's more to life than finding and retrieving files. Hey, even *I* think so, and file-hunting and Web indexing is about all I've done for the past six months. You may want some information and not have much idea where it might be stored. The information you want might be stored under a funny filename that doesn't tell much about what's in the file.

As the Internet has expanded to the point where it's barely searchable even by a Gopher, two new tools, described in the following sections, have emerged from the laboratories of various advanced thinkers. Actually, this business is very important — the tools are a model for retrieving electronically-stored information in general. In the next few decades, that will mean practically all information.

Info from everywhere with WAIS

The first tool is WAIS, for *w*ide *a*rea *i*nformation *s*erver. A WAIS database is an index of keywords in the text of its files, so you can search what's *inside* those files. Figure 5-8 shows an edited transcript of a plain-text WAIS search — the main point is that the search turns up lots of sources of information where the keywords turn up in the *description* of the files, rather than just the filenames. Most of the time, when you call up a Gopher server, you see a WAIS option (our

Australian adventure included one). Using WAIS requires no special skills, so if you find yourself with access to a WAIS server, just jump in and start answering the prompts.

FTP tips and traps

Using a standard UNIX interface to navigate at an FTP site is a bit of a pain. Here's what you should know.

The good files usually aren't in the first directory you see (the "top" directory). At the FTP> prompt, type dir.

You see a listing that contains two kinds of entries, such as the following:

```
-rw-r—r— 1 5193    31     5999
    Apr 1 16:27*
    00readme.txt
drwxr-xr-x 3 5193   31     2048
    Feb 3 15:59
            internet
```

You can "get" the entry that starts with -r — it's just a file. The letter *d* that starts the second line means that internet is a directory (the Mac equivalent is a folder). You have to type

FTP>cd internet

FTP>dir

to see what's in the internet directory.

When you see the listing in this directory, you should be aware that most large files will be compressed. You see file types like .sea (self-extracting archive), .sit (compressed with the application StuffIt), and .hqx (stored in a format called binhex), or .bin (a binary file). Sometimes, file transfer works whatever the type, but to be safe you should type

FTP>binary

before you get the file. Then type

FTP>get <filename>

and type bye when you're done.

Files of the type .sea uncompress themselves, and .sit files require UnStuffIt, available free from your own Internet host. For unpacking .hqx files, I recommend a shareware program called HQXer.

Unless you have a direct connection, you have now transferred the file to your own directory on your Internet host, not to your Mac's hard drive. Call up your own host help file and find out how to download using your communications software. At this point, having Microphone or Microphone LT really helps.

```
OK: telnet quake.think.com
Trying 192.31.181.1 ...
Connected to quake.think.com.

login: wais
Welcome to swais.

SWAIS                           Source Selection            Sources:  1
    #           Server                      Source                    Cost
001: * [      quake.think.com]  directory-of-servers                  Free
Keywords: bootstrap   statistics
Found 13 items.
SWAIS                           Search Results              Items: 13
    #   Score   Source                      Title                     Lines
~~~~~~~~~~~~
006:    [ 858] (directory-of-se)  bit.listserv.cdromlan                 22
007:    [ 858] (directory-of-se)  cool                                 108
008:    [ 858] (directory-of-se)  queueing-literature-database         157
009:    [ 858] (directory-of-se)  sas-archive                          14
010:    [ 858] (directory-of-se)  spss-archive                         15
011:    [ 858] (directory-of-se)  statfaqs                             17
~~~~~~~~~~~~
```

Figure 5-8:
WAIS gets
the inside
information
on file
sources.

Hyperactivity: WWW

A very ambitious project called WWW (*World Wide Web*) uses another search technology. WWW is essentially a database made of linked hypertext documents. You call up a starting screen, and some of the words on the screen are highlighted or underlined. Select a word (in the clunky plain-text version, you do this with arrow keys), press Return, and you get a new screen. Of course, to the poor old Netheads who have been using UNIX for years, this technology seems pretty futuristic. If you're a longtime Mac user, you'll be harder to impress.

During 1994, the WWW sphere absolutely exploded. The next chapter covers this fascinating development. If you already know a bit about the Web, you may want to rush right out and get IDG's *Yahoo! Unplugged*, by me and a collection of my jolly colleagues from *Macworld* and elsewhere.

Back to the Mac

So far, I've been using the Mac as if it were just an old-time text-based VT-102 terminal. No Finder, no folders, no icons, no menus, no mouse — you may as well be computing in 1975.

Here is a short preview of Internet navigation with real Macintosh software. Right now, the problem is that you need some kind of direct connection to the Internet to use Mac software: either you're direct-wired to an Internet host at work or at a school, or you have a SLIP account with a service provider. Fortunately, some vendors have smelled money in the business of making this connection easy, so it's much less of a challenge for mere mortals than it used to be. (Chapter 13 has more details.)

Also, merry elves at the major national online services have diligently cannibalized the best features of these Mac products, and you're going to be able to get most of the cool real-Mac features of the programs explained here just by signing up with, for example, AOL. If you're a student at the University of Minnesota, this won't matter much, but if you're an individual Mac user in Dayton, Ohio, it's big news. Meanwhile, compare a few of these screens to what you've seen earlier in this chapter.

Organized Anarchie?

Figure 5-9 shows an Archie search using the brilliant shareware program Anarchie. Send a nice e-mail message to `peter.lewis@info.curtin.edu.au` and ask him for his current mailing address so that you can send him $10 if you've downloaded Anarchie.

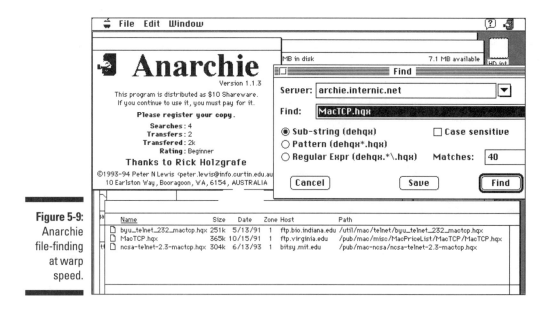

Figure 5-9: Anarchie file-finding at warp speed.

To use Anarchie, type your search terms and click Find. You get a lovely, completely specified list of matching files. Anarchie still uses UNIX search terminology, but it's so fast (and has built-in search limiting) that you can just experiment until you get the hang of it.

TurboGopher

This program, from the University of Minnesota, practically turns the rest of the world into one big directory. TurboGopher is preloaded with the most useful Mac software sites, so it knows the right places to look when you start it.

As Figure 5-10 shows, you can operate this program if you know how to open a folder on your Mac. When it's working, a hilarious little cartoon of a Gopher scampers along on your screen. These people invented Gopher stuff, and this product is king of the Gophers.

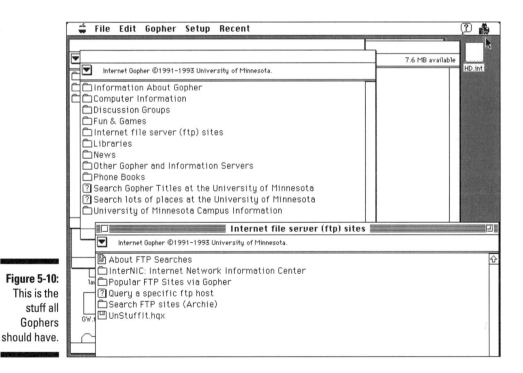

Figure 5-10: This is the stuff all Gophers should have.

Fetch: The super retriever

Fetch, from Dartmouth University, is a Mac replacement for FTP (see Figure 5-11). That's an understatement. If you've ever been stuck poking your way through UNIX directories on remote university machines, Fetch will knock you flat — it brings back everything but a Frisbee. Like TurboGopher, it already knows where to look, so it doesn't have to nose through sites with hundreds of UNIX utilities you'll never need. You click Get File, and you get the file. It was supposed to be that way all along.

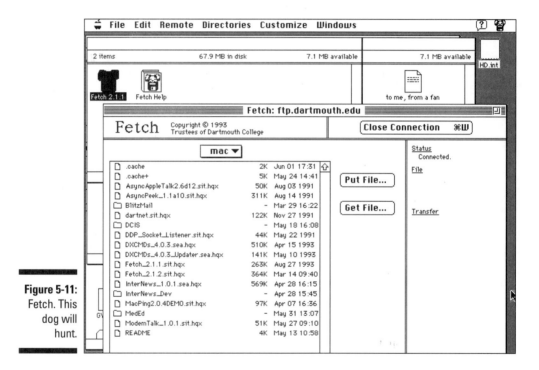

Figure 5-11:
Fetch. This
dog will
hunt.

Something for everyone

You may have noticed that every individual UNIX command seems to have turned into a whole Macintosh program. Is there any way to get most Internet features in a single package?

One way, which I explore in Chapters 6 through 11, is to take online services that already exist and see what combination of Mac features and Internet services you can find on each one. The Internet aspects of most services used to be pretty limited, but, by late 1994, they started to offer what even grudging Net old-timers were forced to admit was the "real thing." People wanted it, and someone delivered — it works for pizza, it works for the Internet. Actually, in many communities you can order pizza on the Internet!

Chapter 6
The Web

● ●

In This Chapter

▶ The new look of the Internet

▶ A bit of surfing

▶ Money talks

▶ Web software and services

▶ Seeking and finding: Yahoo and others

▶ Web pages and HTML

● ●

The Web Invades the Net

In 1995, the World Wide Web changed dramatically. Before 1995, the Web was a fairly specialized service, mostly of interest to people in universities. As late as Autumn 1994, there were perhaps twenty important commercial Web sites. A year later, there were 100,000, with this number doubling every five months or so.

So far, the World Wide Web has proved to be fun to the point of addiction, a major reason for its growth. Most e-mail isn't as entertaining as good television — the Web is actually *more* entertaining than other electronic alternatives. People still talk about a future with 500 channels of TV, although no one knows what to do for decent material with the 50 or so channels available now. But the World Wide Web will effectively have 200,000 channels by the time you read this, and anyone with a computer can be a "broadcaster."

A point of protocol

You need to be aware of a few bits of procedure. In the Internet before 1995, an "Internet address" almost always meant a designation like this

```
chseiter@delphi.com
```

or this

```
topgun@miramarnas.mil
```

with an @ symbol before a letter-designation that fit into a few categories (`.gov`, `.mil`, `.com`, `.edu`, `.net`, and a few special others). Since 1995, an Internet address on a business card is likely to be a Uniform Resource Locator (URL), a so-called *http address*.

Actually, the Web is just one type of Internet service; FTP (file transfer protocol) is another service, and that's why there are computers with Internet addresses like

```
ftp.mich.edu
```

that exist only to support file transfers.

When you see a pointer to a URL like this

```
http://www.netscape.com/
```

you can decode it as follows:

- ✔ `netscape.com` is officially the IP (Internet Protocol) address of the computer (or collection of computers on a network).
- ✔ The `www` designation sends it to the computer in the set that's acting as the Web server.
- ✔ The `http` designation at the very front of the address means that communication will employ hypertext transport protocol, just as an address that starts with FTP means the communication will use a file transport protocol.

There really isn't any particular mystery to Web addresses, except perhaps the mystery of that no one has yet built the "http://" part into the dialog box of common Web browsers.

Unlike the first versions of Internet software, which were really just e-mail and file-search-and-transfer programs, Web software is distinguished by two simple but powerful features:

- ✔ The Web lets you jump from one place to another on the Internet with a clear picture of where you're going.
- ✔ Having mentioned the word "picture," I should mention that the Web is basically the illustrated version of the Internet. You can see pictures immediately rather than downloading them and viewing them later.

A bit of history

Before you plunge into the ins-and-outs of Web navigation, it's time to give credit to some remarkable pioneers of the World Wide Web.

First, the foundations for the World Wide Web were developed by Dr. Tim Berners-Lee, an Englishman living in Switzerland and working at the European physics research facility called CERN.

Around 1989, practically the late Pleistocene in Internet history, Dr. Berners-Lee wrote a modest computer program for his own use in research. It was basically a sort of notepad program, with the interesting feature that individual pages of notes were linked by keywords. You could call up a page about a scientific conference, for example, and click on the title of a particular lecture, and the program would then call up an abstract of the lecture. The abstract itself might contain other links to articles or reference tables.

Dr. Berners-Lee's supervisors thought it would be interesting to develop this idea to become a general-purpose way of exchanging information among the far-flung, big-time physics labs around the globe. If you could dial up a central computer, and if you had one starting-point page with an index, it would be possible to access all the research anywhere, assuming that someone had set up the information and established the links. A group at CERN did just that, and in 1991, the first World Wide Web site was set up at CERN as a service to the world's physicists.

Along the way, Dr. Berners-Lee modified an earlier document-formatting language called *Standard Generalized Markup Language* (SGML), a long-time publishing format scheme for book-length documents. In the new version, he made a formatting language that would support both hypertext links and text formatting (bold, italic, size, fonts, and so forth) and called it *Hypertext Markup Language,* the now famous HTML. HTML, with a few newer extensions over its original version, is still the basis of the World Wide Web. Dr. Berners-Lee is now at MIT trying to define standards for the future of the Web.

The first version of the Web was just text-based, with hypertext links scattered throughout long passages of scientific literature. At the National Center for Supercomputing Applications, however, a student named Marc Andreessen did something amazing.

The amazing thing he did was produce NCSA Mosaic, available for three platforms (UNIX, Mac, and Windows) and then *give it away!* This one act, more than any other, put the Web at the center of Internet computing. Mosaic has an interface that's fun to use; it encourages the use of pictures; and it can be adapted to all styles of Internet access from phone-line dial-up to high-speed direct connection. In fact, when Mosaic was originally developed (some versions were in use in-house at NCSA as early as 1992), it was running on an incredibly fast network direct-connected to the world's biggest supercomputers.

That means that the subsequent programming efforts in developing the off-spring of Mosaic (AIR Mosaic, Spry Mosaic, Spyglass Mosaic, and Andreessen's own Netscape) have focused on making a graphical Web browser work over the 14.4 K-bps modems that most home users still have. Compared to the original software running on the fastest hardware in the world, the new browsers are much, much more efficient because they simply *must* be. Mr. Andreessen is now one of the principals of Netscape Corporation and became a gazillionaire (actually, he got about $50 million) when Netscape made a public stock offering, proving that good deeds are sometimes rewarded.

Surf's Up

If the World Wide Web were just another resource for information retrieval, the Internet universe would have yawned politely and gone about its business, using the Web sometimes, and Gopher at others and various bits of Archie software for other tasks. But the presence of pictures and hyperlinks made the Web different, and Web users posted sites that were more interesting than plain old data. Now you deserve to get a look for yourself.

Fun, games, and info

Here, in no particular order, which is in fact the order you'll find things on the Web itself, is a collection of sites. You will undoubtedly start collecting your own favorite sites in your first few days on the Web yourself since all Web browsing software has some sort of provision for collecting URL (Uniform Resource Locator) addresses of sites in *hot lists.* The sites I show here are just meant to give you a bit of the flavor of "what's out there."

One interesting place to stop is the site called My Virtual Reference Desk, which is a one-stop reference site for Internet information (see Figure 6-1). Like many important and useful sites, this one was assembled and maintained by a single individual. That's one of the great glories of the Web, actually.

And accompanying this reference, here's a site for an online bookstore. I include this with some reluctance — I'm lucky enough to live in a small town with two wonderful, small independent bookstores. They perform a wonderful service and carry all sorts of quirky stuff. They are fighting something of an uphill battle against giant chain stores, and I'm afraid now will face competition from giant online bookstores as well.

Nonetheless, I am putting in this unsolicited plug for Amazon Books because they deliver the goods (see Figure 6-2). Search the million-plus titles, give them a credit card number, and the book shows up in a couple of days. I turned to Amazon to find some obscure archaeology books, and they performed better than the special-order departments of two major university bookstores.

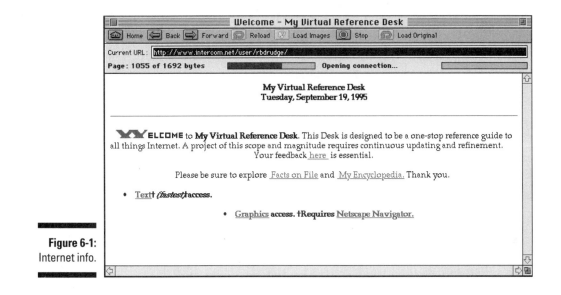

Figure 6-1:
Internet info.

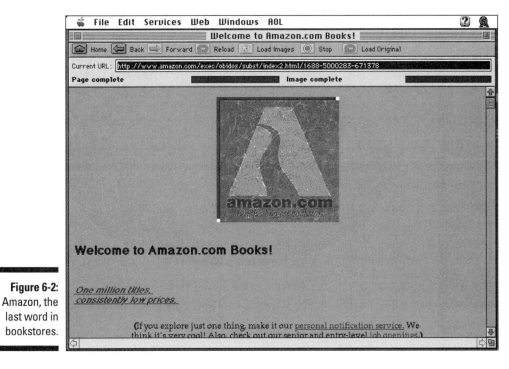

Figure 6-2:
Amazon, the
last word in
bookstores.

Taking a break from these pursuits for a second, look at the Hit List site in Figure 6-3. It's just one reflection of the extreme internationalism of the Web — it's just as easy to find what's on the Top Ten in Bavaria or Kyushu as it is to look up hits in America. Continuing this musical theme, here's the Web site of the fabulous new Rock and Roll Hall of Fame in Cleveland (see Figure 6-4). It's no substitute for the real thing, but it's cheaper than a plane ticket.

Figure 6-3:
More hits
than you
need.

It cannot be said that Rock music is exactly a neglected area of modern society. Teachers (see Figure 6-5) and kids (see Figure 6-6), on the other hand, could probably benefit from a little more attention. Because it costs very little to put a site on the Web, many enterprises that won't meet profit targets can find a home here. It's convenient that, just as public television in the U.S. is running out of official support, a large fraction of what it could and should have been in the first place is appearing in the form of World Wide Web resources.

One particularly valuable site shown in Figure 6-7 contains a collection of the most popular Web tools. Considering the scope of the World Wide Web and its ever-expanding possibilities, it's simply amazing how much of the software that runs this giant enterprise is either freeware or shareware. The people who founded the Web set quite an altruistic tone.

And finally, the reality is that the Web is changing faster than publishers can print books. Therefore, this little supply of cool sites won't be enough. You need a constantly updated directory of cool sites, which you may find at the site in Figure 6-8. If you click through this site, you can also find lists of everything that's been cool over many months as well.

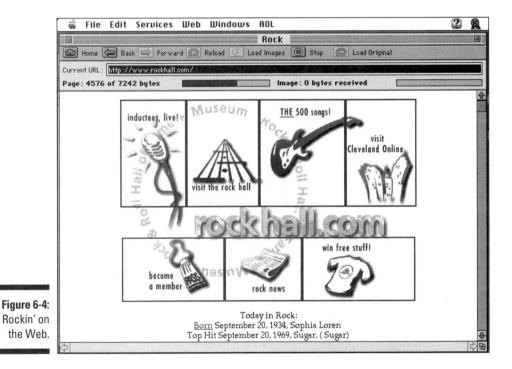

Figure 6-4:
Rockin' on
the Web.

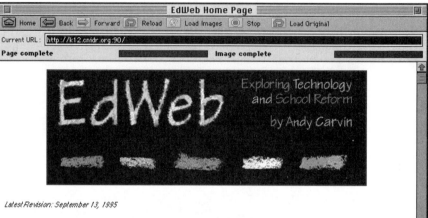

Figure 6-5:
Education
resources,
mostly for
teachers.

Figure 6-6:
Kids,
presumably
kids with
computers.

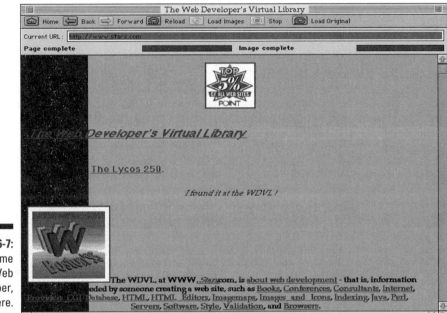

Figure 6-7:
Become
a Web
developer,
right here.

Figure 6-8:
The fountain
of perpetual
hipness.

Business

Some of these Web pages look mighty like advertising. And that's what they are. The combination of links and pictures makes an ideal environment for catalogs, for purchase-order forms, for correspondence through e-mail links, and for files of business data. As I'm writing, it has occurred to many business types interested in the Web that this system could easily replace many kinds of expensive groupware products, such as Lotus Notes. In fact, once some basic security issues get ironed out, offices won't necessarily need their own networks as on-site hardware.

Security on the Web, by the way, is still not a 100% solved issue. Shortly after Netscape issued a browser that was designed to be secure for credit-card transactions, a pair of students at Berkeley found (and reported, bless their hearts) a way to extract credit-card data in supposedly secure transactions. That problem is being fixed, but it's always difficult to prove that a complex system is completely safe. Nonetheless, you can expect money to be flying through the Web with comparative safety through the rest of the 1990s.

I have a big section on business waiting for you in Chapter 15, but here's a little review of three types of business activity that seem like naturals for the Web.

The first type of business is simply the catalog/order-form. You have something to sell, and you set up pages with descriptions and credit-card order processing. Some of these pages and links are quite simple, while others run to hundreds of products. Some of them are successful (flowers, for example, seem to sell pretty well on the Net); some of them barely do enough business to justify setting up a site. There are lots of people eager to help you set up a "storefront" on the Web — the service in Figure 6-9 is a good example.

A second category of company that belongs on the Web consists of businesses that are themselves based on giant computer databases. Besides catalog order companies, the prime example is delivery systems. At the Web site for Federal Express, you can also download software for tracking your FedEx packages yourself. You might not have thought of FedEx as a database, but FedEx's software is the real key to the business — everyone else had trucks and planes years before FedEx started up, but FedEx pioneered a new style of package tracking.

Another type of business that's really a database is a bank. Until someone develops a floppy disk drive slot that will spit out twenty dollar bills, home banking will be lacking a few essentials. But in the meanwhile, most major banks are just salivating at the prospect of doing online banking on *your* computer (and charging you for it). Web designers have been cranking out home pages that look just like the screens on automated teller machines, with clickable buttons just like the real ones that dispense cash.

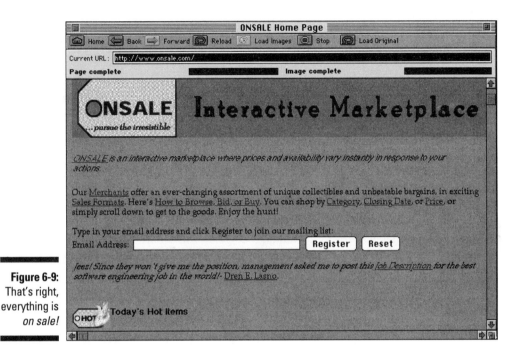

Getting Yourself on the Web

Having seen these glimpses of the future present, you many be asking, "How do I get there?" You really have two alternatives for getting on the Web. There's the easy way, in which you use a Web browser provided by a national online service as part of the software package. This way is pretty foolproof and takes almost no effort on your part. The main drawback is that the way these browsers are usually implemented makes them a bit slower than direct access at the same modem speed.

The Web from the national online companies

At this point, America Online and eWorld have the best-established, built-in Macintosh Web browsers, with CompuServe and Prodigy in hot pursuit (see the next few chapters for details). The AOL and eWorld browsers are nearly identical.

Here's the AOL way (eWorld is identical, and Prodigy and CompuServe have similar tricks): Pull down the Windows menu at a standard AOL Greetings screen, and you find the command **Switch to Browser** (see Figure 6-10). It works. Selecting this command, you get a basic but workable browser, inviting you to load up favorite locations in a hot list (see Figure 6-11). There exists, of course, a lot of fancier software for Web browsing than this, but if you can find the On switch on your Mac, you're cruising the Web.

The Web from service providers

With a national online service, you expect someone to have taken care of the communications software details before releasing their product to the masses. With a service provider, whether a small local firm or a big national outfit like NetCom, things are a little different because you can use all sorts of different software you select yourself. Basically, the service provider guarantees that you will have a SLIP (Serial Line Interface Protocol) or PPP (Point-to-Point Protocol) connection for running any other Internet software you like, with browsers for the Web being a prime example. On America Online, there's a built-in e-mail service, and FTP and Gopher services are integrated into the basic software. In the service provider world, you have different programs for these functions.

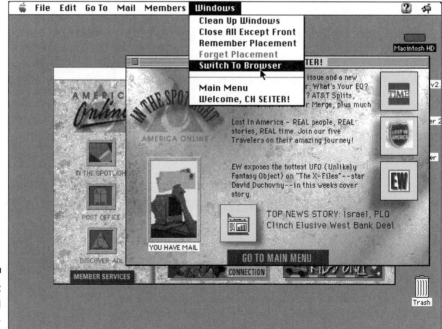

Figure 6-10:
The big switch.

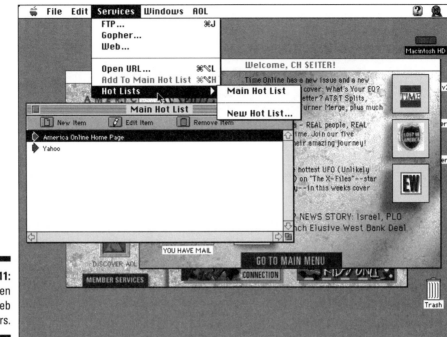

Figure 6-11:
The Bic Pen
of Web
browsers.

The software suite In PSI's Internet Valet is fairly typical, with Eudora Lite for e-mail, Fetch for FTP, TurboGopher for Gopher searching, and a custom, updated version of the venerable Web browser Mosaic. In this streamlined setup (the original, roll-your-own SLIP setups of the last few years were often complex and unreliable), you simply click on a connection icon to get a PPP line to the service provider (see Figure 6-12). Once the PPP connection is established, you can use Mosaic (see Figure 6-13) as a browser (this version has several other functions besides Web browsing).

One argument for having a service provider setup instead of a national online service as your Web resource is that you can use Netscape Navigator, the last word in Web browsers. Navigator 2.0, available by early 1996, is a prime example of the Web swallowing the Net — this one piece of software offers all Net functions and optimized performance on slower modems too. Netscape not only has a top programming staff, but it certainly has the means to pay them after its spectacular stock issue in mid-1995. Those kids have been working nights, and it shows in the software (see Figure 6-14).

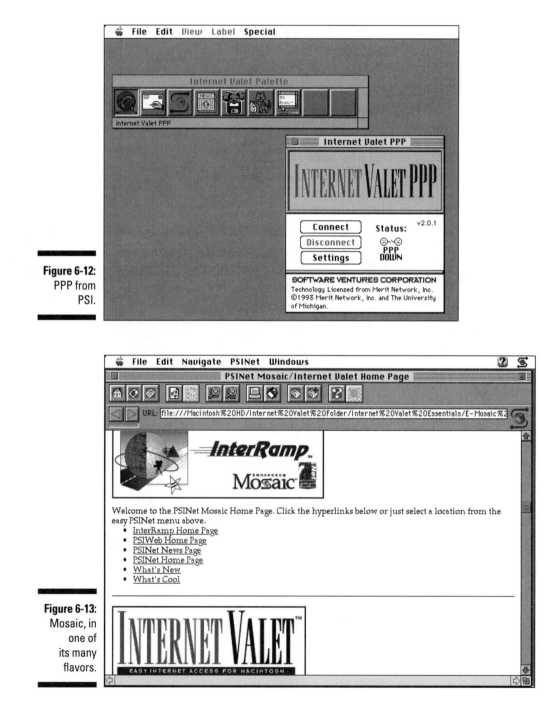

Figure 6-12:
PPP from
PSI.

Figure 6-13:
Mosaic, in
one of
its many
flavors.

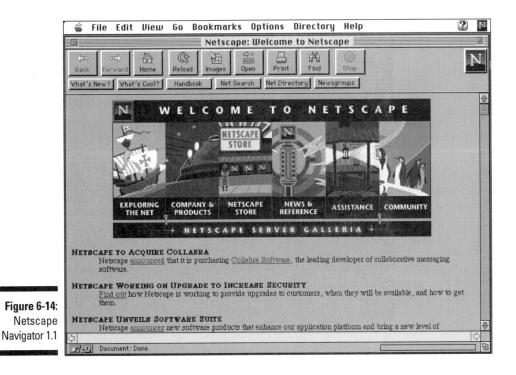

Figure 6-14:
Netscape
Navigator 1.1

Searching, Searching

The Web is a big place, and doubling in size every five or six months. That means finding what you want could be a challenge. Fortunately, however, there's Yahoo (`http://www.yahoo.com`).

Yahoo, which is shown in Figure 6-15, has very efficient menu-based searches, or quick keyword searches, if you prefer. The other search services on the Web are a mixed collection: Some offer menus; others offer keywords; a few offer both. Yahoo offers an Options link to all these other services anyway, so you may as well just try Yahoo first. It's fast, and it's the easiest to use, and it has minimal junk content. If you find some leads on your topic from Yahoo, you can follow up the links on these pages to expand your search. But the main point is that Yahoo won't waste your time. You may need to use other search engines, especially for scholarly topics, but it can't hurt to try Yahoo before doing keyword searches.

For more about Yahoo, take a look at IDG's *Yahoo! Unplugged: Your Discovery Guide to the Web.* Several other services, however, deserve at least an honorable mention.

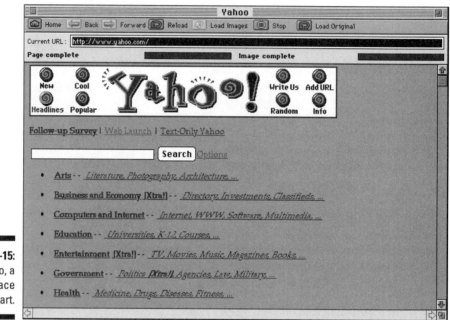

Figure 6-15:
Yahoo, a
good place
to start.

Galaxy, located at `http://www.einet.net/`, was one of the first index services to offer a tree search through the Web. This service is also the home of the software products WinWeb and MacWeb (it's the smallest Mac browser, a serious point if you use a 4 MB laptop or early model of Mac), which are both free at this site. The Galaxy style is somewhat different from the Yahoo style in that it usually presents you with more choices per page.

WebCrawler (`http://www.webcrawler.com/`) doesn't use menus. It is a formidable keyword-based search engine that indexes giant amounts of data on the Web. The indexing is done by a program that automatically searches out URLs and their contents. Because of the scope of WebCrawler's activities, the starting WebCrawler page (see Figure 6-16) gives you a pop-up box for limiting the number of hits it returns. If this feature weren't built in, you could find yourself downloading for hours if you picked a broad enough keyword topic (try "computer" or "America").

WebCrawler uses a computer algorithm that ranks the sites for relevance but often produces relevance scores that may not match a typical human judgement. Despite this potential flaw, WebCrawler is an excellent place to see if there's anything you missed in a Yahoo search. And you almost certainly will miss a few things, partly because Yahoo has screened some of the material that has been automatically indexed elsewhere.

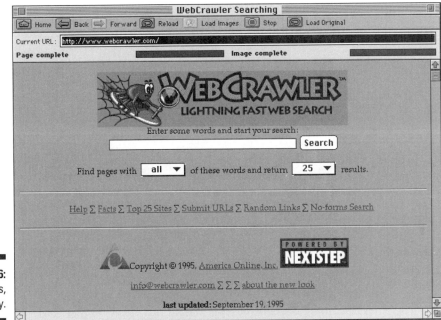

Figure 6-16:
It crawls,
but quickly.

Lycos (http://www.lycos.com/) is like WebCrawler, only bigger. No matter how many sites any other service has indexed, Lycos has more. No matter how many hits you find in a keyword search elsewhere, Lycos can top them. Lycos is maintained by the Computer Science department at Carnegie-Mellon University (see Figure 6-17), and like WebCrawler, it is an automated operation. If you haven't found what you want elsewhere and Lycos doesn't find any search hits, it means that your subject isn't represented on the Web. Yet.

HTML and the Web

Before you proceed, you might as well have a brief look at Dr. Berners-Lee's formatting system, HTML, because it's the basis of everything you see on the Web. The good news is that you aren't going to have to know much about this personally if you just want to browse around on the Web, as everything you see will already have been formatted. At an intermediate level of usage, you can get along with the HTML converters that are now becoming part of standard word processors.

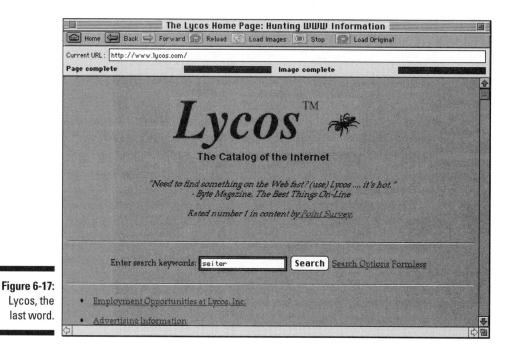

Figure 6-17:
Lycos, the
last word.

If you get interested in this subject, check out a copy of *HTML For Dummies* —
as usual, IDG has every computer topic covered with a suitable *Dummies* book.
Figure 6-18 shows a simple example of a formatted page, and the subsequent
listing shows the HTML codes, or *tags*, that produced it.

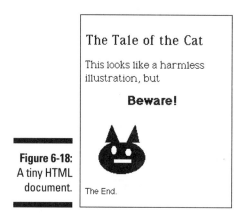

Figure 6-18:
A tiny HTML
document.

The codes for the cat page

```
<HTML>
<HEAD>
<TITLE>cat page</TITLE>
</HEAD>
<BODY>
<BR>
<BR>
The Tale of the Cat<BR>
<BR>
This looks like a harmless illustration, but<BR>
<BR>
<H2>Beware!</H2>
<BR>
<BR>
<IMG SRC="cat_page1.gif"><BR>
The End.
</BODY>
</HTML>
```

What it all means

Interpreting the stuff in brackets < > is really quite simple. In fact, this is how formatting was done on computers before the Macintosh came along and changed everything by displaying formatted text (instead of plain text with formatting codes).

Here's the basic run-down on some common tags. First, the notation HTML at the beginning of the document tells the Web browser that a standard-format Web document is coming (rather than, for example, a file from an FTP server).

Next, the tags <HEAD> and </HEAD> identify the top of the page, which frames the pair of tags <TITLE> and </TITLE>. cat page, which was the name of the original file on the creating computer. Then <BODY> indicates the start of the page you'll see on screen.
, which you'll see a lot, just stands for a line break, and <H2> means a Web level-two heading. </BODY> tells the browser that the end of the page has been reached.

<IMG SRC>, as you might guess, points to an *image source,* here the name of the cat cartoon saved as a GIF document. This style of referencing documents is what allows you to click images On (for full glorious Web stuff) or Off (for much faster, albeit duller, navigation). The image tag actually demonstrates the key

concept of the Web. It refers to another file, the image file, which in this case is presumed to exist in the same subdirectory (or folder) as the original HTML document. If it's located elsewhere, the page designer only has to include a pathname so that the browser can find it. The image file doesn't even have to reside on the same computer as the HTML document as long as there's a way of specifying its location.

And that brings up the idea of links to other documents. As long as you can tell a browser to look up a file, there's no reason the file can't be *another* HTML document. The tag pair <A> and </A> does just that. The link

```
<A HREF ="http://www.macworld.com/">Macworld</A>
```

would take you to the home page at Macworld. There are also special tags for inserting e-mail addresses, and of course <A> tags are used to connect to the rest of the Internet's information servers, such as FTP or Gopher sites. The Web has the big advantage that it evolved after the other services were already in place, so it knows how to handle them. That's why Web browsers, rather than a collection of separate programs, will handle all your Net functions soon.

Part II
Online Services for Internet Access

The 5th Wave   By Rich Tennant

"I'M SORRY, BUT MR. HALLORAN IS BEING CHASED BY SIX MIDGETS WITH POISON BOOMERANGS THROUGH A MAZE IN THE DUNGEON OF A CASTLE. IF HE FINDS HIS WAY OUT AND GETS PAST THE MINOTAUR, HE'LL CALL YOU RIGHT BACK."

In this part...

All the big national online services have figured out that they aren't viable any more without good Internet connections. So they're scrambling as fast as they can to offer Internet services, including Web browsers, with a friendly Mac face to lure you online.

In this part, I'll compare the services from the point of view of their own content and their Internet readiness. This area is rapidly evolving, but it's possible to see what's going to happen. Think of this part as a shopping tour for your Internet connection.

Chapter 7
Internet from America Online

Firstest with the Mostest

In 1993, reading the handwriting on the wall, not to mention the hype in the Wall Street Journal, America Online decided to begin moving into Internet service. Through the first part of 1994, Internet e-mail service was introduced, and then a "toy" version of Gopher, and then a few newsgroups, and by June 1994, America Online users had access to thousands of newsgroups as the system operators gradually added to the list.

AOL operators promised telnet and FTP capabilities for many months and endured heaps of abuse about delays. FTP finally arrived, and it was a great implementation. Then, with a few carefully selected software acquisitions, the World Wide Web, with a simple but effective browser, appeared on AOL in early 1995. It takes these people a while, but they do keep their promises. In fairness to AOL, it was the first service to get real Internet access for the Macintosh in place. Besides this, AOL implemented AOLnet, giving 28.8K-bps access in most big cities (with faster access still to come).The fact is, AOL has a pretty impressive "Internet for Beginners" package.

AOL as an Internet Tool

Yes, the Internet is cool. The Internet contains a huge amount of information and allows easy communication with millions of people. But the fact is *every* large online service provides lots of the same features — AOL itself is so big, with more than 3 million users, that you could spend months just exploring AOL before venturing out onto the Net.

Here's a little Internet tip based on this fact: If you want stock quotes, if you want to chat in real-time with people in Chicago, or if you want to download finance templates to use with a spreadsheet, simply use AOL rather than surf from site to site on the Net. From the standard archives at Stanford and elsewhere, AOL has already retrieved nearly all the Mac-specific shareware you could want. The stock quotes are up to the minute. You can tap into brilliant and idiotic opinions of users who happen to be logged onto the network at the same time as you are. So if you're looking for a job as a historian, by all means use the Internet to look up the academic jobs database at the University of Kansas [listserv@ukanvm.cc.ukans.edu]. But if you're just in a mood to flame about bugs in Microsoft Word 6.0, do it on AOL instead.

Just Do It!

America Online has the best Macintosh interface of any of the national services currently operating (well, eWorld is a close second because Apple bought some of it from the same software people). Place a call to America Online customer service at 800-827-6364, and a few days later you will get in the mail a disk with instructions. Or, every few months, you will find an introductory offer for AOL with some free online time bundled with a copy of *Macworld*. In either case, insert the disk, double-click the installer icon, and you eventually get a screen like the one in Figure 7-1. Note that this software (AOL v. 2.6) is still in development somewhat — the Browser is there, but it's not yet completely integrated into the rest of the AOL
package.

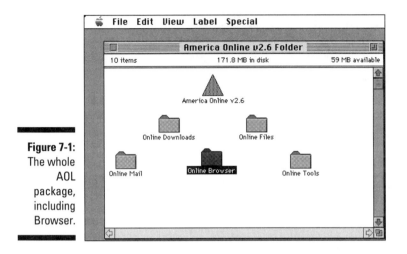

Figure 7-1:
The whole
AOL
package,
including
Browser.

Touring AOL

After you type in your password (AOL assigns you a starter password in its 10-free-hours kit), the software, which has been configured to run your modem at the highest speed available, connects you automatically to AOL. AOL provides you with a local phone number for calls and also a national 800 number with a modest surcharge. About 80 percent of the U.S. has a 28.8K connection point as a local call, and higher-speed-access than this will be available by 1996.

When you sign on, you see the screen in Figure 7-2. The icons at the right are usually topics that AOL management thinks are newsworthy (actually, somebody probably paid for placement). Some of the events billboarded here are truly memorable and bizarre — online sessions with Mick Jagger and Michael Jackson spring to mind. The rest of the action can be called up by a click on the Main Menu tag at the bottom of this screen, which leads you to the picture menu in Figure 7-3.

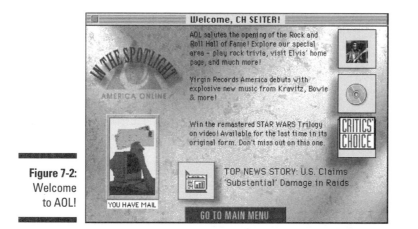

Figure 7-2:
Welcome
to AOL!

Figure 7-3:
The AOL
main menu—
note the
Internet
choice!

AOL has a real Mac interface

In most online services, you have to perform a significant amount of idiotic grunt labor, calling up menus and answering questions. Often you find yourself arguing with the service menus as different commands become available or unavailable, depending on the last menu you were shown. This problem is in direct contradiction to the style of all the other Mac software you use in daily life. If the services want my money, they gotta do better than that!

So AOL did better. Instead of expecting thousands of online users to pound away at their keyboards and scroll through menus, trying to work around the deficiencies built into an interface, AOL hired a handful of programmers to code a proper point-and-click, Apple-interface-guidelines front end for AOL services. There is great efficiency — which saves *you* precious time — in the AOL online screen design. At any point, you can figure out your next move just by inspecting the icons or scrolling the lists presented to you on-screen. You think this would have occurred to somebody else, but it didn't. In fact, the Mac interface on AOL is significantly better than its cluttered and weird Windows interface.

Too much fun!

Even in its currently not-quite-finished form, AOL is one of the few ways to get going on the information superhighway without getting lost in traffic. This list covers some top points in support of AOL:

- ✔ The people at AOL know you're lazy — and they *like* it that way.
- ✔ AOL e-mail is easier than licking stamps.
- ✔ You can use a screen name, such as Zorro or Bambi.
- ✔ AOL people don't censor your flames.
- ✔ AOL's Internet administrator has the patience of Mother Teresa.
- ✔ You can get on the Web with AOL without knowing anything about SLIP or PPP.
- ✔ AOL runs thousands of Usenet groups, even the strange ones!

The icons speak

The first thing you hear is a voice announcing that you have mail. AOL packs some amusing sound files into the interface program it sends you on disk. The message itself isn't sent through your modem; a flag in the sign-on data plays the sound at your end of the connection. At this point, you can read the latest headlines or double-click on some new service — but you're going straight to the Internet.

You can get to the Internet area by clicking the choice on the Main Menu, but it's a bit faster to pull down the Go To menu, pick Keyword from the choices, and type **internet** in the Enter keyword text box in the Go to Keyword dialog box. The screen then changes to the glorious vista presented in Figure 7-4.

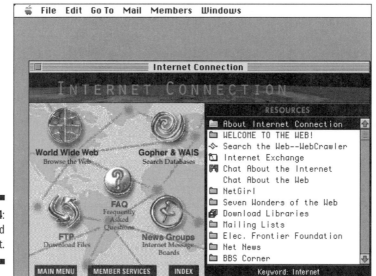

Figure 7-4:
AOL's World
of Internet.

Keyword: Internet

The Resources list at the right of the Internet window in Figure 7-4 contains an amazing amount of material. For example, it contains Zen and the Art of the Internet, Brendan Kehoe's admirable information file, arranged in searchable form. If you don't like my explanations, you can try one of his, although the file is mostly a guide to old-style UNIX telecommunications. The Resources List also gives you immediate access to WebCrawler, probably the best keyword-search tool for the World Wide Web.

You can also get explanations for any Web topic just by double-clicking on the FAQ (Frequently Asked Questions) icon — AOL has pulled these long files off standard sources and they're quite informative and well-edited (see Figure 7-5). Perhaps you will not be surprised to hear that even people who write Internet books have been known to consult them — on various obscure points only, of course.)

Another interesting outfit, reachable through the Resources list, is the Electronic Frontier Foundation, an organization that's trying its best to keep information transfer free and unmonitored. At present, the U.S. government is desperately trying to maintain its right to "wiretap" e-mail when it thinks it's necessary, and the EFF doesn't like this invasion of privacy, to put it mildly.

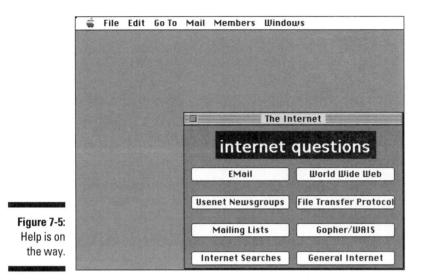

File Edit Go To Mail Members Windows

The Internet

internet questions

EMail	World Wide Web
Usenet Newsgroups	File Transfer Protocol
Mailing Lists	Gopher/WAIS
Internet Searches	General Internet

Figure 7-5:
Help is on
the way.

The Internet Exchange, also on the Resources list, is a good place to post questions for other users. Officially, AOL customer support has the answers to all questions, but you may have non-AOL-related Internet questions. Believe me, somebody out there has had the same experiences on the Net as you have and may have useful tips. In this area, you can also see AOL management being mercilessly slagged by impatient users. (Where's our ISDN? When do you upgrade the Web browser?) To AOL's credit, it doesn't censor any of its online criticism. And these AOL people get flamed plenty.

AOL Mail Gateway

I now leave the flames, change out of my fire-resistant pajamas (decorated, in fact, with little appliqués of spiders), and put on a business suit. Under Mail on the menu bar, I find Post Office as a command, which gets me to the window in Figure 7-6.

While you're in this window, you might want to go into the Internet mail folder and read the Internet Etiquette material. *Etiquette,* in this sense, doesn't really have much to do with Miss Manners; instead, it refers to being careful about addressing messages so that they don't clog up the wrong e-mail mailboxes.

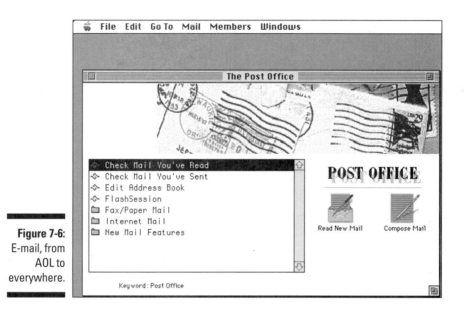

Figure 7-6:
E-mail, from
AOL to
everywhere.

Next, read the Internet Mail document called Your Internet Mail Address. Check this out! You now have your own Internet address, even though you did nothing more than follow a few Mac menus. Sending and receiving mail are handled automatically by AOL, and you can put your new Internet address on your business cards.

If you click the Compose Mail icon, you get a screen like the one in Figure 7-7. Because the America Online software is a real Mac application, you can actually compose your letters in a Macintosh word processor and simply cut and paste text into the message area. Similarly, you can cut sections of messages you receive and paste them into standard documents in other applications. In the To box, at the top of the form, you can list an Internet address in the same way you list an AOL internal address (a screen name, in AOL lingo).

It's hard to see how AOL could be much easier than this. But there are still two problems with AOL Internet mail as it stands today. First, messages are currently limited to 32K (check the New Features folder from time to time, though, since this limitation will be removed fairly soon). Second, the nifty Attach File feature — very useful for sending files of pictures or sound or bits of database to other AOL users — doesn't work for messages to other services.

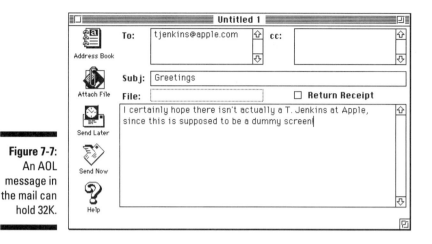

Figure 7-7:
An AOL
message in
the mail can
hold 32K.

Despite these problems, AOL's e-mail messaging system is convenient and inexpensive (you get five online hours per month for your monthly fee, and you can compose your outgoing messages offline). The fax service here, although it invokes a surcharge, is also a great alternative to buying a fax machine if you only need to send an outgoing fax once a month or so.

Newsgroups on AOL

E-mail is certainly useful. It offers a major justification for getting an Internet connection. But it's not all that entertaining, and just using e-mail doesn't make you a "real" Internet user. So it's time to get cool. Close the Post Office window and you're back at the Internet Connection window. If you now click the Newsgroups icon, you get a personal gateway to the thousands of newsgroups on Usenet, BITNET, and WhatNotNet (OK, I made up the last one). Figure 7-8 shows what these newsgroups look like on-screen.

To add to this list, you can find newsgroups by searching or by using the Expert Add icon. To add a newsgroup with Expert Add, you need the exact name of the newsgroup you're joining. I list some groups in Appendix D, and you can join the group news.lists to see the whole list. Actually, using AOL's search procedure is the easiest way.

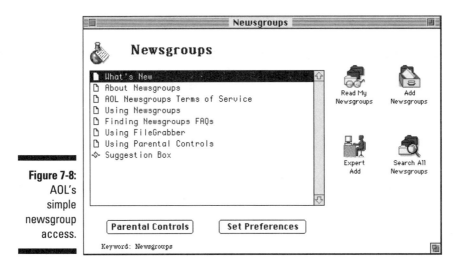

Figure 7-8:
AOL's
simple
newsgroup
access.

A key point to watch is the sheer number of messages that crop up in an active group. The group `Alt-Tv-Mst3k`, for example, discusses Mystery Science Theater 3000, a show that appears on the Comedy Central channel, and it picks up nearly a hundred messages a day! (A lesson from the Internet: the world is big — one percent of millions of people is a lot of people.) You're not going to get around to reading most of the messages unless you feel like spending hours every night online and making AOL ridiculously rich.

Fortunately, AOL shows you the subjects (see Figure 7-9), so you can scan them and pick out a few favorites. Then click the Mark As Read icon. Otherwise, you would drown in a week, even with a rigorously austere list.

All these newsgroup correspondences are conducted in plain text. However, you're going to need to know just a bit of Internet code, such as BTW and IMHO, to read and respond to newsgroup messages. A standard set of abbreviations has been developed over the years; Table 7-1 provides a minimal list of these abbreviations so that you know what's going on when you see them. To convey some sort of accent to the text, symbols that look like cartoon faces soon appeared, too; Table 7-2 contains a smattering of these symbols, called *smileys*, and their interpretations.

```
┌──────────────────── Read My Newsgroups ────────────────────┐
│                                                             │
│           ENGLISH                                           │
│             ▽            📁                                  │
│          NET.NAME       📁                                   │
│        Internet Names   Update All As Read                  │
│                                                             │
│        My Newsgroups                         Unread  Total  │
│   ┌─────────────────────────────────────────────────────┐ │
│   │The (Reposted) Best of the Internet    15   1818    │▲││
│   │Alt-Tv-Mst3k                           95   8729    │ ││
│   │Report America Online Newsgroups Bugs Here  2  518  │ ││
│   │Help with Newsgroups                    2    373    │ ││
│   │AOL Newsgroups Suggestions             13    827    │ ││
│   │Test Messages Go Here                  12    993    │ ││
│   │Comp-Sys-Mac-Misc                      53   6994    │ ││
│   │News-Newusers-Questions                47   4361    │ ││
│   │Rec-Travel                            111  12007    │ ││
│   │Magnetic resonance imaging and spectroscopy. 100 100│▼││
│   └─────────────────────────────────────────────────────┘ │
│                                                             │
│  [ List Unread ]  [ List All ]  [ Remove ]  [ More ] [ ? ] │
└─────────────────────────────────────────────────────────────┘
```

Figure 7-9:
A modest
sample from
an
"alternative"
newsgroup.

Mac Internet interfaces will have improved, probably in 1996, to the point that you can annotate newsgroup messages with sounds and pictures for impact — a sort of smileys-on-steroids. But for now, these abbreviations and smileys are standards, and the pictures and sounds are all on the World Wide Web. If you poke around in the AOL communications forums, you can find whole dictionaries of smileys (various jokers have concocted about 500), which may interest you for cultural anthropological reasons.

Table 7-1	Short Takes
Code	**It Stands For**
IMHO	In my humble opinion
BTW	By the way
FYI	For your information
LOL	Laughing out loud
GMTA	Great minds think alike
RTFM	Read the f*&^% manual

Table 7-2	Keep On Smilin'
On the Keyboard	*What It Says*
:)	Smile
;)	Wink
: *	Kiss
: (	Bummer!
: >	Fiendish grin

Getting Listed

Mailing lists are just collections of Internet e-mail addresses. The mailing list system evolved mainly as a way for researchers at widely separated institutions to keep in touch. The biggest set of mailing lists, in fact, evolved separately from the Internet on an early service called BITNET, although there's considerable crossover. These days, now that businesses are the big news on the Net, mailing lists have emerged as an effective tool for marketing to special interest groups.

The window in Figure 7-10 shows AOL's cool new interface to mailing lists — mailing list service has come a long way from its origins on teletypes with no lower case letters! Find the list you want with the search option, and you can sign up to join any of these discussion groups just by adding your name to the list. You can quit a group just as easily.

These lists are amazingly interesting and entertaining, but there are a few precautions you should be aware of. The first is that when you join a list, you should probably monitor it every day for the first few days to get an idea of the traffic volume. When anyone on your list sends a message to the rest of the list, it appears in your mailbox. If you sign up for lots of active lists, you will find that your AOL mailbox limit (550 messages) can be reached quite rapidly.

The other precaution is that you should read the messages for a week or so to determine whether you really have a contribution to make to the other list members. The Internet gives you, in effect, an introduction to most of the research and special-interest groups in the world. I don't want to sound like too much of an old grump on this point, but please think about whether you'll be wasting your own time and someone else's time by getting involved in an endless series of messages.

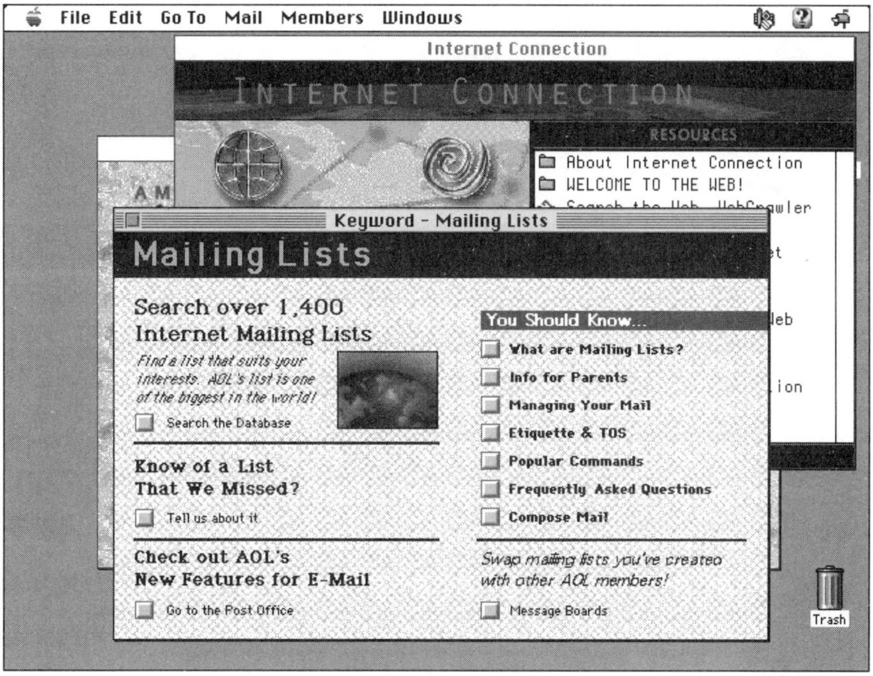

Figure 7-10:
EZ mailing
list access.

Having pointed out the precautions, I still want you to believe that mailing lists are a fantastic way to keep in touch with individuals who share your interests. Somewhere out there in Flatville, Illinois, there's probably someone who's fascinated with Minoan archaeology, and now she can read daily reports from researchers doing field work in Crete. That's wonderful!

Finding Files in the Internet Jungle: Gopher and WAIS

There's so much information available on the Internet that special sets of searching tools (I describe them in Chapter 5) have evolved. One standard tool is Gopher (named for the mascot of the University of Minnesota, home of the Golden Gophers and a pioneer Internet software site). There are hundreds of Gopher sites all over the planet, and they maintain menus of files available on different topics. You give a Gopher some possible file titles of interest, and the Gopher tells you what's available. WAIS, for *wide area information server*, searches the contents of files rather than just file titles. This used to be mostly academic stuff, but as with the rest of the Internet, there's now lots of commercial information.

In standard, old-time (pre-1994) Internet access, you could connect to any Gopher *server*. (A server is just a computer, generally big and fast and set up as a central resource for "client" computers, like yours). To connect to another Gopher server, you find a Gopher list for yourself and Gopher Internet addresses. On AOL, none of these procedures and details really matters.

AOL hides the search details

AOL has done something a bit different. First, it evaluated dozens of Gopher sites for reliability. Most of these are noncommercial sites maintained as a public service, and some of them are as flaky as a basket of crescent rolls. AOL then wrote an interface in which you, the end user, can't always tell whether you're getting information from a Gopher site or a WAIS server. You get the information — you don't get the search path or the Internet details. Unless you're an experienced online searcher, you get better results the AOL way than you get poking around on your own.

From the Internet Connection window, just click the Gopher & WAIS databases icon. Figure 7-11 shows some of the available topics, and in AOL, you can click in these folders to carry out a search. At present, AOL has loaded a large array of topics into what appears to be its own site so that searches are fast and don't usually connect you to other computers.

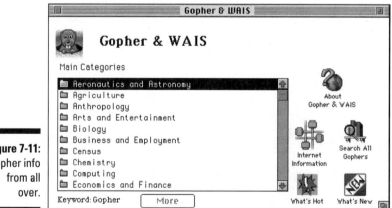

Figure 7-11: Gopher info from all over.

Searching absolutely everything

To find specific subjects, you can also perform a Veronica search over all available Gophers. Just click on the Search All Gophers icon in the Gopher and WAIS window, and you'll see a window like the one in Figure 7-12. I searched on the word *analytical* because I design analytical equipment for biochemistry, so I used this keyword to tell AOL how much material to access. (By the way, I did this search because I already knew what was available from doing searches with full access to all known Gophers and WAIS databases.) At present, my guess is that AOL databases now have between 60 and 70 percent of all text files on this topic that are available worldwide, but the list is expanding fairly quickly as AOL adds behind-the-scenes access to more Gophers.

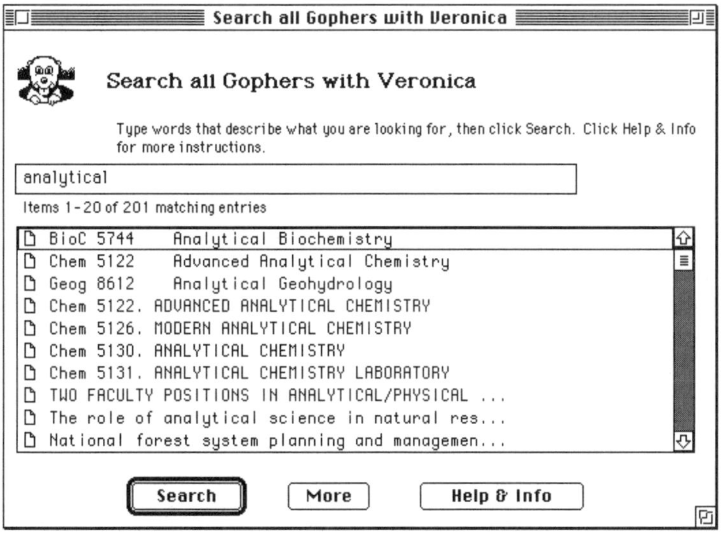

Figure 7-12:
A Veronica
search pulls
out the
details.

Search all Gophers with Veronica

Search all Gophers with Veronica

Type words that describe what you are looking for, then click Search. Click Help & Info for more instructions.

analytical

Items 1-20 of 201 matching entries

```
BioC 5744     Analytical Biochemistry
Chem 5122     Advanced Analytical Chemistry
Geog 8612     Analytical Geohydrology
Chem 5122.  ADVANCED ANALYTICAL CHEMISTRY
Chem 5126.  MODERN ANALYTICAL CHEMISTRY
Chem 5130.  ANALYTICAL CHEMISTRY
Chem 5131.  ANALYTICAL CHEMISTRY LABORATORY
TWO FACULTY POSITIONS IN ANALYTICAL/PHYSICAL ...
The role of analytical science in natural res...
National forest system planning and managemen...
```

[**Search**]   [**More**]   [**Help & Info**]

Whimsy in cyberspace

Archie is a program that lets you search over files that you can find on the Internet and is basically an index of archived software, hence the name. Later, a more powerful search program was named Veronica, for *very easy rodent-oriented netwide index to computerized archives*. *Rodent-oriented* means that the program works with Gophers, but the name Veronica was cooked up as a reference to Archie and Veronica comic books. There is also a program for Archie-searching called Jughead, meaning that a program called Betty can't be too far away. I mention these program names merely because many Internauts are probably too young to have seen any of these harmless relics of a bygone comic-book age (the age cutoff seems to be about 21).

Gossip Hot Line!

To learn more about the direction the Internet is taking, including new kinds of searching systems, you can click back to the main Gopher screen and then click on the Internet Information icon. Figure 7-13 shows the fairly complete set of AOL Internet informational files, including material on InterNIC, a prime resource on Internet operations. At this point, if you want to impress your friends with your totally cool, leading-edge status among Internauts, go and read the items in the Heard on the Net Electronic Newsletter. Even though you haven't spent more than a minute suffering through "real Internet" commands, you'll have all the gossip just as if you were a lifelong UNIX communications hacker. Seems like cheating, doesn't it?

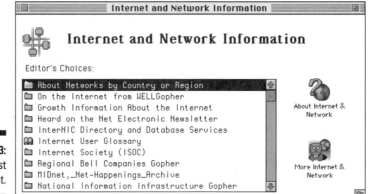

Figure 7-13:
The latest
on the Net.

As Long As You're Here

AOL also has mountains of non-Internet material packed into its own giant system. I'll just show you a few choice bits, and you may find that a lot of what you've been told is out there on the Net is already on AOL.

Buy something

AOL is a commercial service. There is no squeamishness about serving businesses online. The only point you may need to investigate is whether your interests qualify as mere shopping or whether they constitute a lifestyle. If you want to buy airline tickets or roses, for example, you're just an AOL shopper (see Figure 7-14).

Figure 7-14:
Send
somebody
roses.
Really, it's
always a
good idea.

If you are fascinated by gadgets, on the other hand, that's a lifestyle (see Figure 7-15). It's no trouble to find what you want on AOL (you can usually do it with a keyword), but the logic of classification is sometimes quite amusing. I'm sorry to say that nearly everything I do is apparently part of a lifestyle, a humiliating bit of stereotype because I live in the Wine Country in California and remember the ratings of every Chardonnay for the last 20 years. They've got my number, I'm afraid.

Get mellow

Fans of the Grateful Dead have always been one of the best-organized groups, electronically speaking (see Figure 7-16). The brilliant journalist Mary Eisenhart (editor of *MicroTimes*), for example, used to maintain an electronic bulletin board for Deadheads, following them to every concert appearance with a laptop. And she was doing this 12 years ago, when there probably weren't more than a handful of musicians who could identify a modem. The AOL Grateful Dead Forum is a very busy spot — and a whole universe for fans. And for all the users there, I'm really bummed about Jerry, too. I met him a couple of times when he was wandering around the Russian River Jazz Festival, of all places.

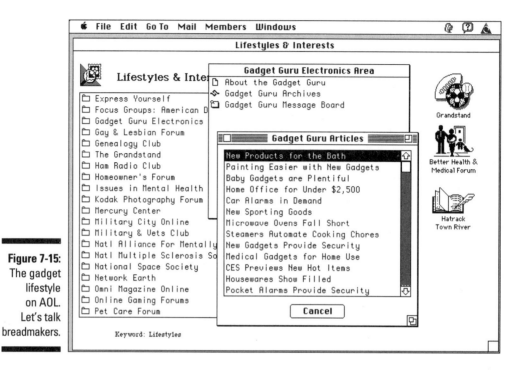

Figure 7-15:
The gadget
lifestyle
on AOL.
Let's talk
breadmakers.

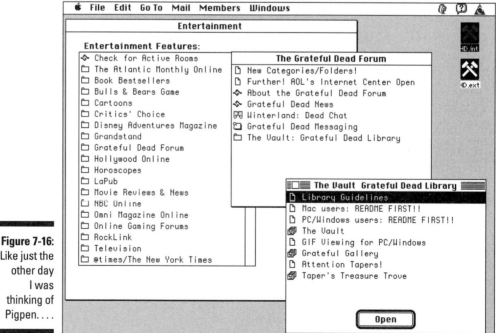

Figure 7-16:
Like just the
other day
I was
thinking of
Pigpen. . . .

Stay informed

Figure 7-17 shows a partial list of online magazines available on AOL. As soon as you start cruising this area, you'll discover that online magazines are better as a way to find specific topics than as a way to browse. There are no ads, and the information is stunningly fresh — I usually see the final version of my own *Macworld* reviews here three weeks before I get the magazine in my mailbox.

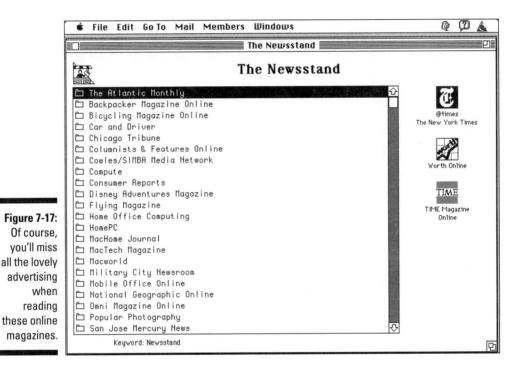

Figure 7-17:
Of course,
you'll miss
all the lovely
advertising
when
reading
these online
magazines.

FTP, For the People

AOL has put its version of FTP on the Internet Connection window, and a jolly good version it is, too. In the bad old days, it was fairly difficult to find files, and even the relatively simple Mac FTP utility called Fetch left something to be desired. Now everything is blissfully simple.

In the FTP area, you get a screen with some choices for explanation of the service and icons for action. The explanations are important because for many AOL users, this will be their first glimpse of FTP.

In Figure 7-18, you also see a bit of AOL cleverness. Rather than telling you to learn the search program Archie and locate files on the Net before starting your FTP session, AOL has built in a proprietary search system, and it runs on an index maintained on AOL's own computers. Technically, this means AOL is its own Archie server, and it uses a custom front end. All you have to know is that it's easier than the traditional way.

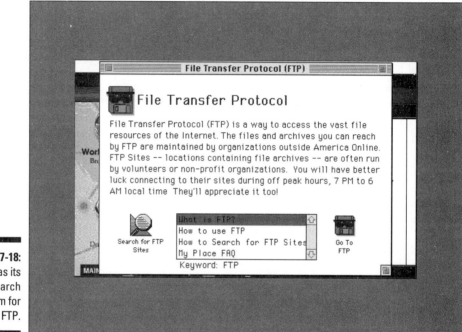

Figure 7-18: AOL has its own search system for FTP.

AOL has preloaded its Gopher service with a bunch of starting points, and the same is true for FTP (see Figure 7-19).

By the way, the note in the previous figure (7-18) strongly encouraging off-peak-time usage of FTP is serious business — AOL users could bring the poor old VAX at Dartmouth to its little electronic knees if they all started jamming on 2:00 p.m. on the same day.

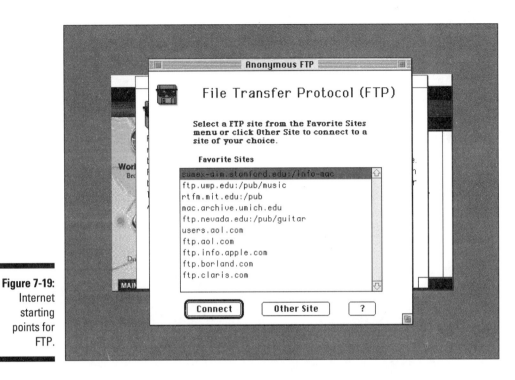

Figure 7-19:
Internet
starting
points for
FTP.

Just for fun, try the White House site (most of its stuff is also available on the White House World Wide Web home page too). You'll find all sorts of briefing papers, the President's daily schedule (with enough detail to give a Secret Service agent security nightmares). Think about it — you can get up every morning and download the President's schedule into your own electronic Day Timer. Pseudo-interactive fantasy adventures like this are a big part of the fascination of the Internet!

WWW, AOL style

By 1995, nobody would take you seriously as an Internet service if you didn't provide WWW access. Back in early 1994, when there weren't many sites worldwide, it wasn't too critical, but when good browsers began to appear, the whole world jammed onto the Web. These days, when someone says "Internet," it's pretty likely he or she actually means Web. So AOL went to another company and bought a custom version of its Internet Browser. In my opinion, they get high marks for this service since it means they had a Mac browser sooner than any other national service, including Apple's own eWorld. As an Internet fun fact, you should know that Macs make up about ⅓ of Internet traffic. You are not alone.

Web basics

You can get to the Web in two ways: through the Web icon on the Internet Connection window or through the Windows option on the menu bar (one choice is Switch to Browser). Click the tiny Home icon, and you see the glorious screen of Figure 7-20.

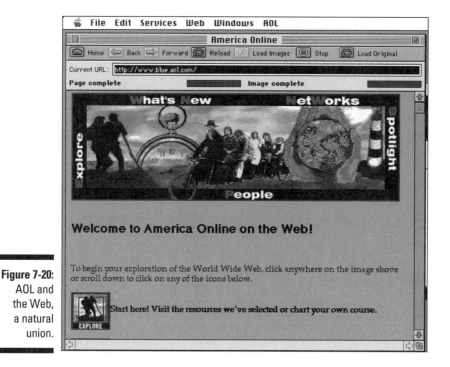

Figure 7-20: AOL and the Web, a natural union.

Now, you have several options as a Web beginner. You can first take AOL's own guided tour (see Figure 7-21). This is not a bad idea at all. AOL has put together some amusing pages and links to other peoples' stuff, and you can navigate the whole system if you know enough to click on an underlined word. That's one of the things people like about the Web — it can really be pretty mindless if that's what you want. Note that from this exploration screen, you can go to a set of directories that then lead elsewhere. Officially, if you are a Web user, you are supposed to be maintaining your own *hot lists* of Uniform Resource Locators (URLs, the basic addresses of Web sites). But the fact is that you can just have AOL's software save URLs you found by cruising the directories, so you could use the service for years without ever typing in a URL address. (You do that under the Services menu.)

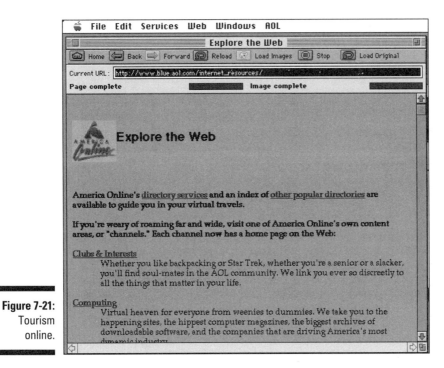

Figure 7-21:
Tourism
online.

But there is one case in which you might as well type in a URL and also use the Services menu to add it to the main Hot List. The URL is

```
http://www.yahoo.com/
```

and it gets you to the Web index service Yahoo, which is shown in Figure 7-22.

Here's the Yahoo story. There are more than a million URLs out there. Probably two-thirds of them are utter junk. Yahoo has a simple directory that will lead you to the non-junk URLs. It's unbelievably easy to use, it has everything of value on the whole Web, and it's updated *every day* by the coolest group of people ever to grace the Internet. AOL is charging you for your online time, so you may as well start finding the good stuff fast. If you take my advice and start every Web search from Yahoo, you'll be a happy little WebSurfer.

With a few clicks, you can find all sorts of amazing stuff through Yahoo. Its tree structure is designed so that you get to the "destination branch" in two or three steps. Here's a search for a photography museum in Arizona that just required a click on Arts on one page and then Museums on another (see Figure 7-23 and Figure 7-24). Just so you know, IDG has a book that's a guide to Yahoo, called *Yahoo! Unplugged* in a burst of editorial creativity, that explains all about searching and reviews hundreds of sites.

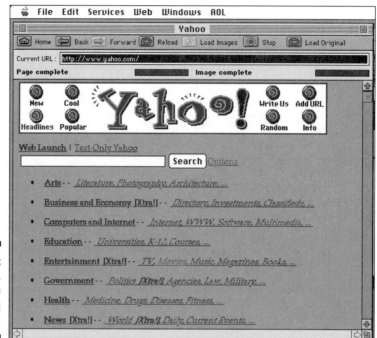

Figure 7-22:
Yahoo.
Where
everything
starts.

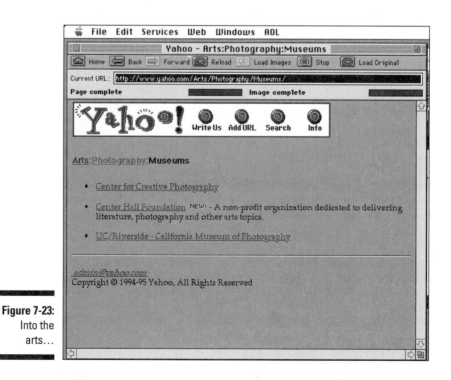

Figure 7-23:
Into the
arts…

 File   Edit   Services   Web   Windows   AOL

Center for Creative Photography Home Page

Home | Back | Forward | Reload | Load Images | Stop | Load Original

Current URL: http://www.ccp.arizona.edu:80/ccp.html

Page complete   Image complete

Welcome to the Center for Creative Photography

The University of Arizona, Tucson, Arizona 85721

The Center for Creative Photography is a museum and research center devoted to photography as an art form. Its collections are among the most accessible in the world. Founded in 1975 from the combined vision of photographer Ansel Adams and then-university-president John P. Schaefer, the Center is a unique institution offering

Figure 7-24:
... and into
museums.

And some tips . . .

For speed in cruising around, you might want to consider clicking off the choice Always Load Images under the Web menu in the AOL Browser (see Figure 7-25). As modem speeds have improved, more producers of Web pages have concluded that you can afford to download their 100K of vanity graphics littering home pages. What you can do is just double click on the image icons after you "get where you're going." If you wade through every picture out there as you surf around, it's going to be slow surfing in small waves. I acted as a Web site consultant to a large firm that at first was happy with a little 15K logo (you could download it a few seconds), and then later decided that its home page deserved a glorious 210K version of the same thing. Fortunately, there is a Stop button on the menu of the Browser to get yourself out of long downloads, but you might as well dodge the bullet in the first place rather than catch it in your teeth.

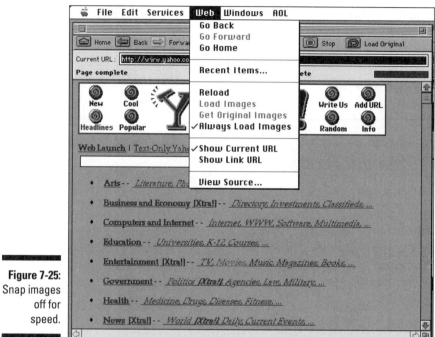

Figure 7-25:
Snap images
off for
speed.

Also, if you use the Add to Main Hot List command under the Services menu
(see Figure 7-26) a lot, it will soon be clogged to the point of uselessness. You
should start thinking in terms of the Main Hot List as a sort of directory page
where you keep a set of URLs that lead to other interesting sites with only a few
clicks. Stash Yahoo here; stash the site for WebCrawler and perhaps ten others.
If you add more, the Main Hot List actually becomes slower to use these items
than to go through AOL's directory link in the guided tour mentioned earlier.

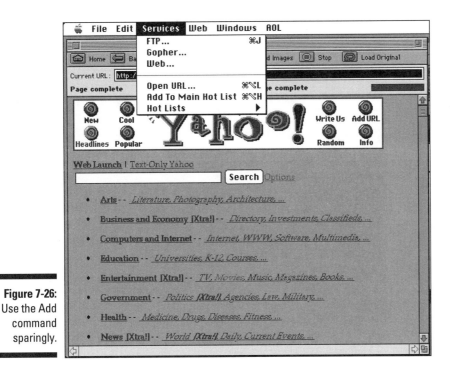

Figure 7-26:
Use the Add command sparingly.

Chapter 8

Internet from CompuServe

· ·

In This Chapter

▶ The new face of CompuServe

▶ Basic Internet services

▶ A different kind of Web service

▶ A big service

· ·

CompuServe has been around for a long time. At a point when the only people with Macintoshes were personal friends of Guy Kawasaki or Steve Jobs, CompuServe was taking care of business at 300 bps for users connected to primitive character-oriented computers.

This gives CompuServe some advantages. Its collection of files you may want to download, for example, is quite impressive. (It should be impressive because CompuServe has been collecting them since the dawn of time, at least in computer terms.) One disadvantage is that lots of things on CompuServe are done in a particular way because that's the way they have always been done. The menu-system design choices were made back in the days of slow computers and even slower networks and compared to newer services, such as America Online, the system looks a little bit old-fashioned.

Its relative antiquity means that CompuServe is a service with more than two million subscribers. CompuServe has also had the time to work out arrangements with the companies (SprintNet, TymNet) that give you local access numbers in a huge variety of cities. Most recently, CompuServe decided to buy more network capacity, to add Point-to-Point Protocol Internet connection in major cities, and to buy a major Web company as well (Spry, developers of Air Mosaic).

Getting into CIS

My CompuServe name is a six-digit number plus a three-digit number. Numbers aren't very exciting — even bulletin boards that are run with freeware on someone's old Mac II in a basement let you log in with a cool name like ZIPPY or AlexBell. But at *CIS* (CompuServe *I*nformation *S*ervices), you have a number that's faintly reminiscent of the number card under your chin when you're being booked for disturbing the peace. The use of screen names is being introduced to CompuServe, but it's progressing slowly among the old-timers.

The passwords assigned to you, however, are almost poetic. I've had six CompuServe passwords over the years, all of them two-word passwords with the words apparently chosen at random. Someone out there probably has the password *free spirit* and relishes every day the irony of having a beautiful password but a number instead of a name.

Managing Information

In traditional CIS-land, you did most of your navigating by picking numbers. The system presented you with a numbered menu, and you responded with the number of your choice. These days, your CompuServe access is mediated by Mac *C*ompuServe *I*nformation *M*anager (MacCIM). MacCIM (shown in Figure 8-1) can be found on a CD-ROM bagged into computer magazines at any newsstand.

Figure 8-2 shows the Connect window that pops up in the MacCIM welcome screen. All you do at this point is click the Connect button, and the program connects you, starting you out with the latest news from CompuServe and elsewhere (see Figure 8-3). If you look at the Browse window, a customary CompuServe starting point, you'll see an icon for "Internet," which is your gateway to services other than the World Wide Web.

Fortunately, CompuServe has been hard at work catching up with other online services — when you click this icon, something actually happens. CompuServe has made a few executive decisions about the way Internet access is going to work. Newsgroups and FTP services, which are actually extensions of e-mail, conceptually, are built into the MacCIM software at present. Web access, as you will see, is handled by a separate program and separate service that may be merged into MacCIM during 1996.

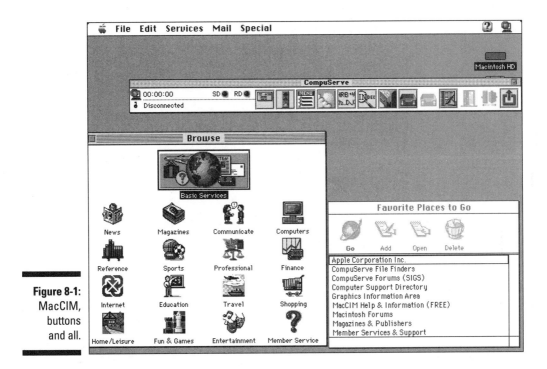

Figure 8-1:
MacCIM,
buttons
and all.

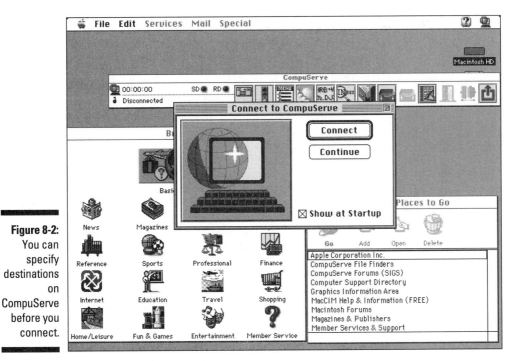

Figure 8-2:
You can
specify
destinations
on
CompuServe
before you
connect.

Figure 8-3:
What's new,
and more.

Newsgroups and FTP

Click on the Internet icon in the Browse window and you are presented with the enticing array of opportunities in Figure 8-4. CompuServe has done something fairly interesting to back up the possibilities. It maintains its own list of newsgroups and its own lists of FTP sites with descriptions of their contents. And because it's CompuServe, you will find that a large percentage of the files you were looking for elsewhere are right here in a CompuServe forum (certainly most games and fun files are here).

Newsgroup fun

CompuServe, like the other national services, has some decisions to make about newsgroups. Some alt. newsgroups consist almost exclusively of picture files of pornography that goes beyond anything you could get at a newsstand. Hard to believe but true. These kinds of newsgroups represent only a tiny fraction of all newsgroups, which tend toward seriousness, zealous fandom, or sheer whimsy, but they do exist. So what does CompuServe do about this situation?

Figure 8-4:
The
overhauled
CompuServe
Internet
center.

It does something a bit tricky. With a simple click of the Newsgroups icon, you are out of CompuServe's somewhat half-hearted attempt at a graphical interface and into plain-vanilla newsgroup access (see Figure 8-5). Double-click the USENET news reader topic (CIM version) and you are led through a series of dialog boxes that let you select newsgroups to join and then review the newsgroups' content. The trick is that CompuServe has trimmed down the list of newsgroups so that your choices don't include anything that will get parents upset if their kids join. You *can* add very odd groups, and CompuServe won't censor the choice (at least for the ten or so I tried as an experiment), but it certainly won't help you find them. By the way, the list-editing extends beyond porn to topics that are merely controversial, such as abortion or other contentious political topics.

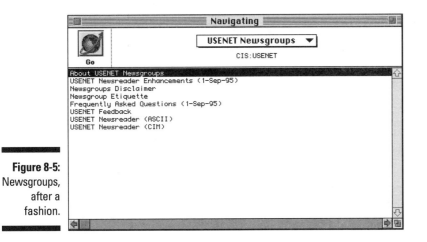

Figure 8-5:
Newsgroups,
after a
fashion.

File city

File transfer protocol services, similarly, are a "managed" service here, although it's not so much an effort at censorship as an attempt to organize the vast universe of files in a way that's easy to use. Double click the FTP icon back in the Internet services window, and you find the main FTP choices (see Figure 8-6). This is a pretty convenient system, and it's fast too, since the screens here are all coming from CompuServe's own computers rather than a third-party remote site.

A good place to start, if you haven't done much of this (FTP searching, that is) is by double-clicking the Popular Sites button. These sites typically have the best files, the best maintenance, and the easiest directories to understand. One funny little secret of the Internet is that lots of FTP sites are located at universities and other nonprofit organizations, and it isn't always clear who has responsibility for updating stuff in the FTP archives. These sites (the Populars) tend to be up-to-date, and feature the files that are the current hot buzz on the Net. If you are looking for updates of different companies' Internet software, for example, look here first. CompuServe nonetheless lets you access a huge list of sites without requiring that you know any specific FTP Internet addresses (see Figure 8-7).

If you do have a favorite FTP site, found in this book or elsewhere, you can enter it directly using the Access a Specific Site button. This button is shown in Figure 8-6. The window it opens is shown in Figure 8-8. Note that the service here has already filled in the little bits of information you need to access anonymous FTP services (the services merely use these to track statistics). You need to know the site name exactly (often these are amusing or confusing or both — `ftp.apple.com` is a relative rarity for clarity). Also, as you can surmise from the "Directories" entry in this window, you can often find yourself out in hostile Unix or Windows territories. It's great that there's full FTP access here on CompuServe, but you may find that the Mac-specific forums on CompuServe are worth checking also for interesting materials.

Another point about the FTP service here is that you may want to download the Mac FTP sites file from the CompuServe Mac Communications Forum. Although this area offers description of the FTP sites, they tend not to be overwhelmingly detailed. I bet the description of the Apple site in Figure 8-9 doesn't strike you as comprehensive.

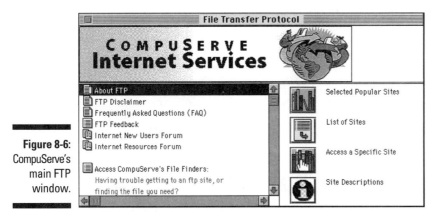

Figure 8-6:
CompuServe's
main FTP
window.

Figure 8-7:
Almost
everybody
in FTP.

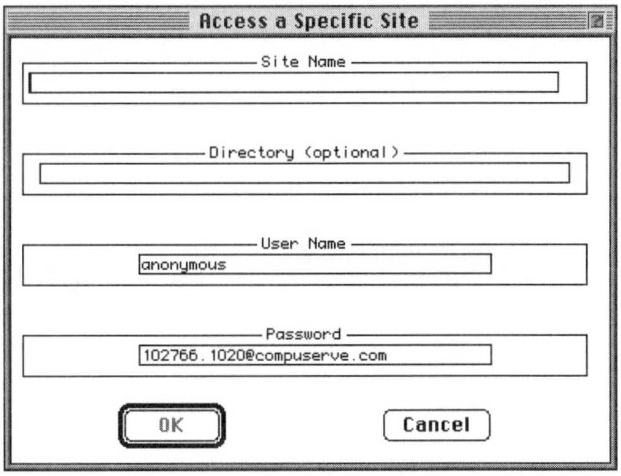

Figure 8-8:
If you know
the site, it
will all
be right.

File   Forward   Continue

COMPUSERVE
Internet Services

Apple publishes support information, including Apple software updates to the Apple ftp site.

This site provides a wide range of services, including:

Apple Software Updates

Apple Information

Top Apple Assistance Center Questions

Figure 8-9:
A rather
concise
description
of the
Apple site.

. . . and More!

The main Internet window also supports telnet, which was once a principal method for floating around the Internet but which has now been eclipsed as an access method by the success of the World Wide Web (it's easier for sites to manage Web activities than full-tilt telnet access). Also, although this is easy access (see Figure 8-10), you may find as a Mac user that most of the computers you can reach through telnet expect you to know a little UNIX syntax to make something happen.

On a more encouraging note, CompuServe has collected tons of background material for you to study — you click the Internet Resources topic back in window shown in Figure 8-4. That brings you the list of subjects in Figure 8-11, which includes most of the online information resources collected over many years by the diligent CompuServe folks in Ohio. Clicking on Internet Resources forum, you are brought to the screen in Figure 8-12. And at last, you're in a position to Browse Libraries, and as you can see from the list of libraries there is a wealth of Mac-specific Internet files. If you used this book to lead you here and then used these libraries for most of the rest of your Internet education (I assume you probably buy an IDG book once a month out of force of habit anyway), you would be a qualified Internet expert in a few months.

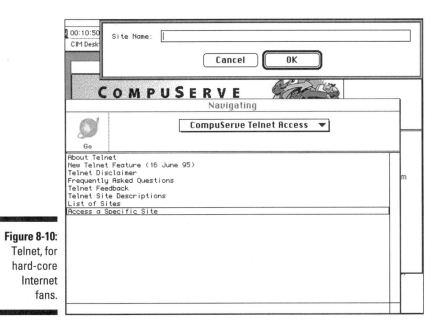

Figure 8-10:
Telnet, for
hard-core
Internet
fans.

Figure 8-11:
Internet
info . . .

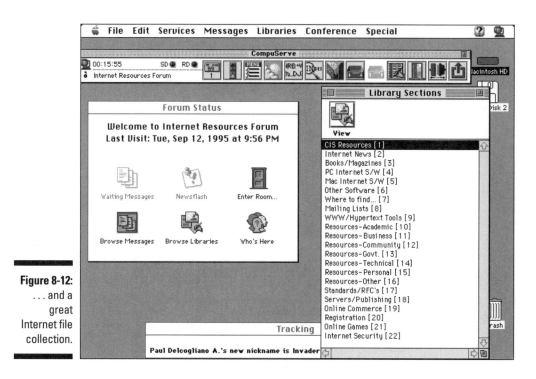

Big Plans for the Web

On the other national services, the business approach has been to buy a Web browser and more or less tack it onto the existing software. CompuServe did something a little more dramatic. It concluded that users who were really interested in Web access were more sophisticated than the rest, and thus ready for something a little fancier.

It set up its own national network of PPP access points and bought the rights to Mosaic-In-A-Box from a company called Spry, which is now part of CompuServe (the business, not the service). The idea here is that you use Mosaic and other software in the Box kit to establish a "real" Internet connection, and you then use a special version of MacCIM that works with this software. In other words, CompuServe itself becomes one other part of Internet access, like Web access or FTP. Think of CompuServe itself as a giant, somewhat strangely organized Web site, and you have the idea.

As this book was written, the Mac software was being tested for release in late 1995. But it works nicely (it's fast and virtually glitchless) and is based on incremental improvements in Mosaic, so it's got a few more features than AOL or eWorld Web access (see Figure 8-13). This approach, combined with new lower CompuServe rates, makes it a real contender for Mac attention.

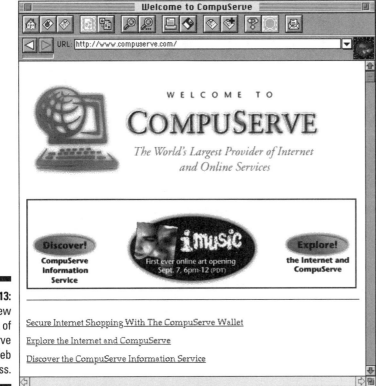

Figure 8-13:
The new
look of
CompuServe
Web
access.

As Long As You're Here

CompuServe has accumulated some unique online information resources over the years, many of which replace standard household or library reference books. For example, rather than buy a copy of the *Physician's Desk Reference* every year, you can look up background information on your prescriptions in CompuServe's drug database.

Assuming that you are the sort of person who plans vacations carefully, you can use CompuServe to find yourself golf courses everywhere you go. This service would be more helpful if you could download color pictures of difficult holes, along with weather reports, but you can't have everything (at least not yet). It would be nice if the golf database pointed out, for example, which of the California courses shown here are flat as a billiard table and 115° F most of the summer.

The golf course database may be missing some crucial notations, but you can't complain about CompuServe's movie reviews. I had the system search on "Peter O'Toole" and it popped up Roger Ebert's reviews of the celebrated Irish thespian's greatest hits.

I regard it as a public service that CompuServe doesn't carry reviews of some of Mr. O'Toole's less fortunate outings (*The Seventh Coin, Foxtrot*) although the lack of a review of *The Stuntman* is an odd omission. In any case, these examples just scratch the surface of the CompuServe databases. As I said above, a large fraction of what people expect to find on the Internet is here on CIS already.

You may want to go through the new user orientation (see Figure 8-14) to get an idea of the scope of CompuServe itself. The service has not only expanded the quality of many options (online magazines now have much more graphic content, as Figure 8-15 illustrates) but has greatly extended the number of services grouped under individual options, such as the Electronic Mall (see Figure 8-16).

Figure 8-14:
You'll save time by taking the tour.

Figure 8-15:
Not bad
looking,
really.

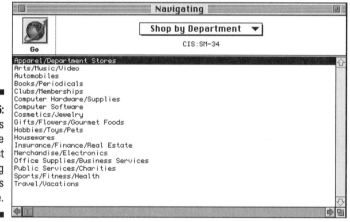

Figure 8-16:
The Mall is
one of the
biggest
shopping
services
online.

Chapter 9

Internet from Prodigy

• •

• •

*I*t will be clear to you in a page or two that I don't think Prodigy is the ideal choice for Macintosh Internet access. Nonetheless, it's a very distinctive type of service. If you like Prodigy, I can tell you right now that there is no substitute for it. It is the only source of Prodigy-type stuff, that's for sure.

Some Good Things about Prodigy

Prodigy has many exceptional features and services, which I will discuss on the next few pages.

Prodigy is big

Prodigy has more than two million users — about as big as the Internet was itself a few years ago. Most of these users have computers at work and computers in a home office as well, meaning that they are chosen from the same general demographic as the readership of this book.

Prodigy is big enough to generate its own discussion groups on herpetology or coin collecting, and its designers put lots of work into reaching the home market. All you do is double-click the Prodigy icon (on the software Prodigy sends you) to get to the screen in Figure 9-1. Click on the View Highlights button, and you are signed on and ready to sort through piles of information (see Figure 9-2).

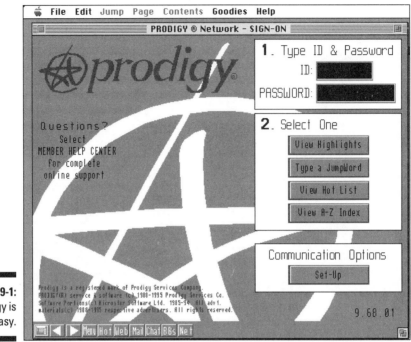

Figure 9-1:
Prodigy is
easy.

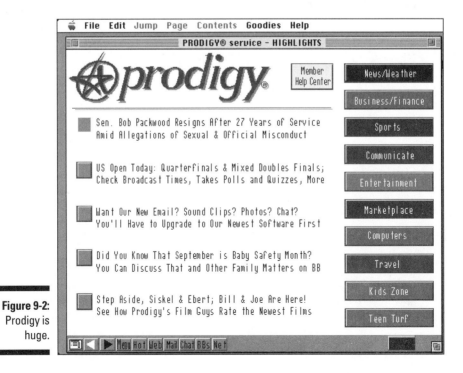

Figure 9-2:
Prodigy is
huge.

Prodigy means business

The Internet is still setting up and defining its relationship with business. Prodigy has been a for-profit enterprise since day one, with ads, shopping specials, and hundreds of signed-up national firms.

And every now and then you *want* to shop. On Prodigy, you can't avoid it. There are ads and promotions at the bottom of most screens on the system (see Figure 9-3). I, for example, have had an out-of-control fountain-pen-buying problem for years. In making up the Internet screens for this book, I found myself wandering off through the menus and ordering a pen from a dealer in Los Angeles. You just about *can't* log on to this service without having some potentially red-hot deal waved under your nose, and often the deals are genuinely good (see Figure 9-4).

You may find yourself ordering discount airline tickets to Hawaii! This, of course, is the aspect of the information superhighway that has all the businesses drooling. You will either love or hate this aspect of Prodigy, but it's a fact of life.

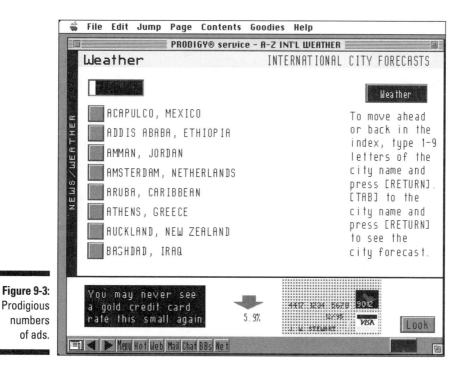

Figure 9-3: Prodigious numbers of ads.

Figure 9-4:
Land's End
clearance?
Let's do it!

Prodigy cares

Some longtime Internet users might snicker about this, but Prodigy has put a lot of administrative time and software engineering into making this a service that eight-year olds can use. Suitably armed with key URLs, of course, a young person whose parents haven't done a Parental Control lockout could find all sorts of strange stuff out there on the Web. But Prodigy has done something more positive than mere censorship by setting up large collections of age-appropriate material, both for very little kids and for teens, as Figure 9-5 demonstrates. AOL and other services have some of this material, but the kids and teens stuff is really billboarded on Prodigy.

There are more good things about Prodigy (see the section "As Long As You're Here" at the end of this chapter), but these features are particularly important.

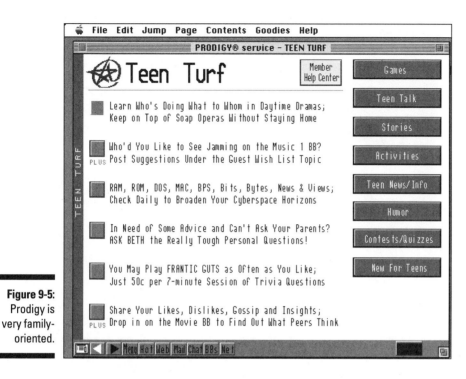

Figure 9-5:
Prodigy is
very family-
oriented.

Some Bad Things about Prodigy

Now I am obliged to give you the bad news for Mac Prodigy users.

Prodigy is slow

Every time you pick a menu item, Prodigy has to write you a new, full-color screen. Even at 14.4K bps, it takes a long time to ship these big files. It's too bad that you can't see the vivid (close to garish, actually) color interface in this book. Text files move fast; black-and-white graphics move reasonably fast; but color takes forever. As of late 1995, only major cities had 14.4K access (see Figure 9-6), and plans for 28.8K and ISDN were still being formulated.

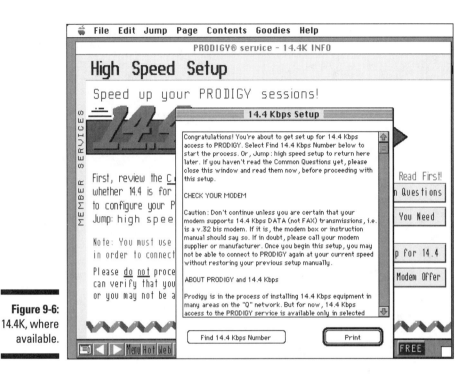

Prodigy is not, at heart, a Mac-oriented system

Another example of non-Macness is the e-mail system. For online message entry, you use the little pencil icon as the text insertion point (see Figure 9-7). You have to click to get to the next screen when you have a few hundred characters in this frame (it doesn't scroll), and you can see for yourself that the fonts are pretty stringy by Mac standards. Everywhere you turn on Prodigy, you encounter PC-specific touches — a frequent feature of Prodigy screens is a Windows-style close box (as shown in Figure 9-8) and often navigation on Prodigy follows a confusing non-Mac style. Prodigy has been a joint venture of Sears and IBM, and you can confidently predict that Apple's latest gyrations don't loom large in Prodigy's planning. Prodigy does get around to giving its Mac users most of the same features as it provides for Windows, but you can expect serious lags in delivery.

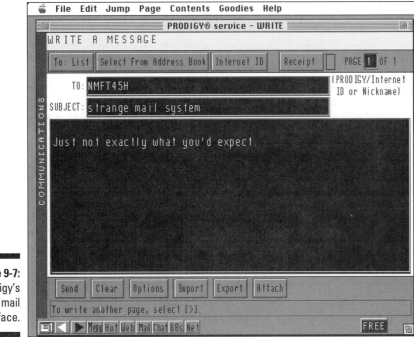

Figure 9-7:
Prodigy's
unusual mail
interface.

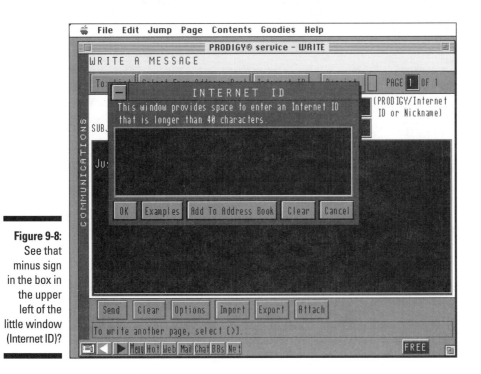

Figure 9-8:
See that
minus sign
in the box in
the upper
left of the
little window
(Internet ID)?

Prodigy-based Internet is a bit odd

Prodigy is the most controlled online environment on the planet. The Internet is, by contrast and for all practical purposes, not controlled at all. Prodigy was notorious a few years back for censoring complaints on its bulletin boards — not just complaints about Prodigy service but about all IBM products. Most networking pioneers believe in free information exchange. They found this censorship despicable and flamed Prodigy to the point where you might have expected IBM to develop fireproof pinstriped suits for its Prodigy staff.

But there was simply no way to resist the massive pressure for true Internet access, and that means giving up a certain amount of control. There are some obvious potential throttle-points, such as parental control that lets parents lock kids out of USENET newsgroups (see Figure 9-9), and Prodigy is gamely trying to maintain both a "clean" channel and a wide-open channel through the Internet. The upshot, though, is that Internet access through Prodigy is distinctly different in tone from, say, Internet access with PSInet and a Web browser.

Blue moves

As long as Prodigy has raised the subject in its warning to parents, I want to make a few reluctant points here as a public service. First, there is text material flying around on the Internet, particularly in Internet Relay Chat, that qualifies easily as "beyond adult." The fellows who wrote the First Amendment probably weren't thinking about this stuff explicitly, but these messages are, I guess, made up of Constitutionally-protected electrons.

The second point, for the curious, is that, despite hysterical articles in the popular press, the Internet is not generally a viable source of pornographic pictures. There are, in fact, not all that many of these pictures out there, and those that are out there are not very spectacular. The really hard-core graphics files are all on private computer bulletin boards, which you can look up in local computer publications. The fancier grade of this material is found on commercial CD-ROMs. Do yourself a favor by not trying to find color graphics files like this to download from the Internet. The data transmission rate involved in buying a copy of *Penthouse* or *Playgirl* is multiple gigabytes of graphics over the counter in a few seconds. That's better than the fastest modems on the drawing board, and it's the appropriate technology for the job (if that's what you want).

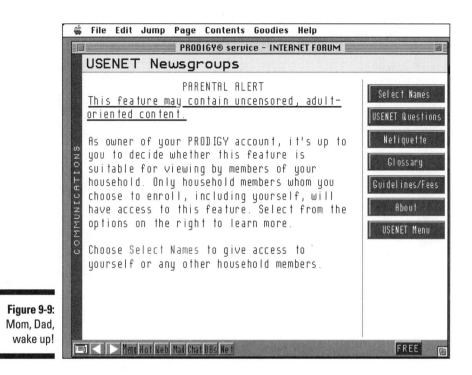

Figure 9-9:
Mom, Dad,
wake up!

The Elements of Internet, Prodigy Style

E-mail connection to other Internet users is simple (although the weird mail system requires the special dialog box in Figure 9-8 to accommodate the frequently long Internet service addresses. In fact, in the old days, Prodigy tried to route e-mail access through its e-mail service, using the old-fashioned work-arounds called *FTP-by-mail* and *Archie-by-mail*. You could get along this way, within limits, but Prodigy found that it couldn't easily attract new users with this clumsy set-up.

The Web

If you look at the bottom of the start-up screen back in Figure 9-2, you will find a tiny button labeled Web. It appeared there in late 1995, and after a few months of frustrating eager Mac users who would click this button in the quite normal expectation that it should do something, Prodigy delivered its own Web browser. As with everything else on Prodigy, it's quite distinctive. A click on the Web button leads you to a glorious splash page (see Figure 9-10) that leads to a simple browser that's nonetheless well integrated with Prodigy (see Figure 9-11). Actually, since a Web browser has to work with information that's already out there at different sites, the text becomes refreshingly normal — the Prodigy font disappears.

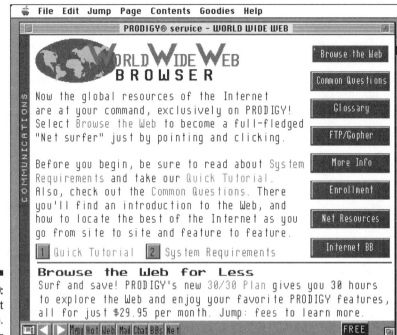

Figure 9-10:
Starting out
on the Web.

Figure 9-11:
The Web
from Prodigy
(an early
version
of the
Browser).

FTP and Gopher

Having gone to the trouble of programming a Web browser, it naturally occurred to the hard-working Prodigy staff that they had also thereby accom-
plished everything necessary for easy FTP and Gopher access. These earlier
services have for all practical purposes been absorbed into the blob-like bulk of
the Web, since to reach, for example, an FTP site you just type **ftp:** instead of
http: with the intended location. And that's all you do on Prodigy (see
Figure 9-12) — enter a Gopher or FTP address in the Web browser. Note that the
example information has that good old IBM flavor — were you particularly
looking for the latest on IBM's 6000 AIX system?

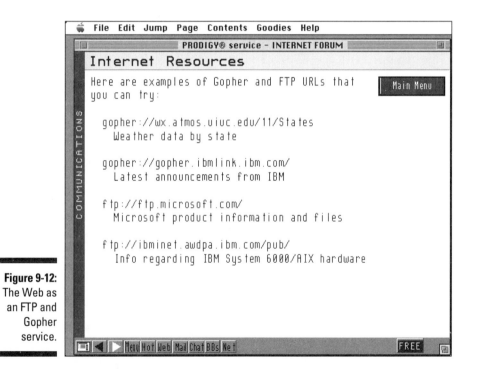

Figure 9-12:
The Web as
an FTP and
Gopher
service.

Prodigy and newsgroups

The Web browser takes care of Internet FTP and Gopher services, but what about the rest of the Net? You use the Prodigy "Jumpword" **Internet** to get to the interesting screen shown in Figure 9-13, which acts as a sort of Internet Central for other services. The Internet help function on Prodigy is mainly handled through the Internet Bulletin Board, which also contains both endearingly naïve files of users' questions about Internet basics (see Figure 9-14) and invitations to peculiar adults-only parties across the length and breadth of American swingerdom.

The other main function of the "Internet on Prodigy" screen is access to USENET newsgroups. From a control standpoint, you either have access to newsgroups or you don't — they can't be blocked by name one at a time, and few parents would have the expertise or the patience to sort through the newsgroups (see Figure 9-15) one by one. As a result, if you are an adult and have your own account, you have access to everything percolating out there. Most of it, to tell the truth, is either a bit silly, like the fan newsgroups for the old Monty Python show, or quite serious, like the mathematical economics newsgroups.

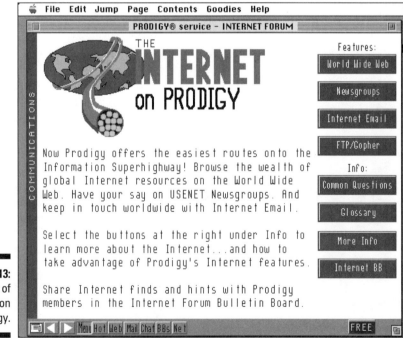

Figure 9-13:
The rest of the Net on Prodigy.

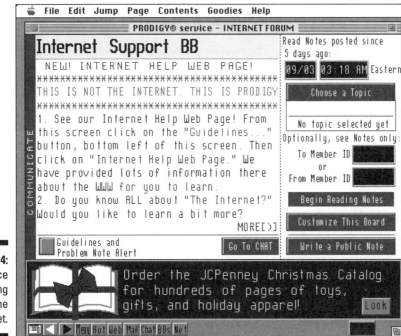

Figure 9-14:
A resource for learning about the Net.

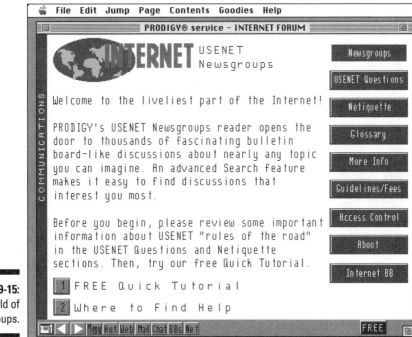

Figure 9-15:
The world of newsgroups.

As Long As You're Here

Prodigy is one of the richest as-long-as-you're-here online service. It's a complete, if somewhat carefully edited, universe of its own. Its own news services collect everything instantly, reformat it into Prodigy's font, and put it online. I have it on good authority that this font is used on the equipment found in disabled alien spacecraft. That's why you, as a Mac user, probably can't identify it — the font is called Zartron, after the home planet of the big aliens (who control the little aliens most often pictured with big black insect-like eyes). OK, I made that up. But it might be true anyway.

Well, it may be weird by Mac standards, but this service has the goods. It's the only service, for example, that has a built-in macro recorder (see Figure 9-16). If you typically want to log on, collect a bunch of information on particular stocks, write it to a file, and then log off as fast as possible, you can do it with a Prodigy macro.

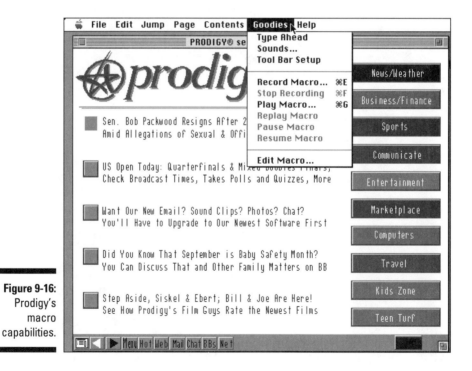

Figure 9-16:
Prodigy's
macro
capabilities.

If you are obsessed with entertainment trivia (see Figure 9-17), you can find the ripest collection on the whole Net right here without leaving Prodigy.

If you want to make travel arrangements, Prodigy has the most highly evolved set of services of the major national online companies, as Figure 9-18 illustrates.

Finally, you can discover here that two to three million people is a lot of people, and therefore, that Chat groups on Prodigy cover every type of opinion and personality type (see Figure 9-19). There's a bit more monitoring on Prodigy than some other services, but given that the main problem in chat groups is frequently boorish imbeciles, such interference is not invariably unwelcome.

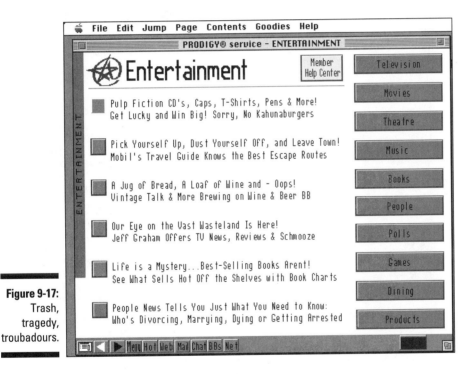

Figure 9-17:
Trash,
tragedy,
troubadours.

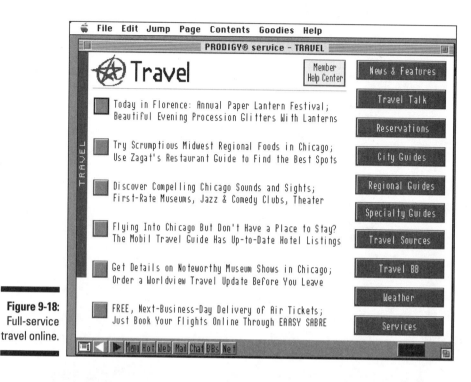

Figure 9-18:
Full-service
travel online.

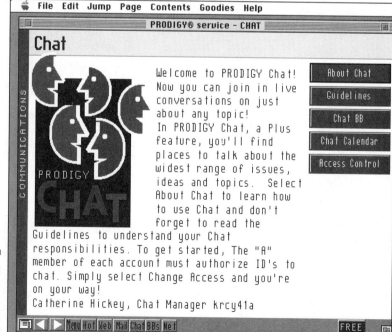

Figure 9-19:
Mostly polite
chat on
Prodigy.

Chapter 10
Internet from eWorld

· ·

· ·

*I*n Apple's eWorld online service, started in the summer of 1994, you can see the most extreme contrast between the old world of character-oriented computing and the new world based on the Macintosh graphical interface.

In the traditional Internet, tiny little packets of characters went zinging down the wires of the networks. If you wanted to make the Internet do anything for you, you had to master a large set of commands. If you wanted to connect with any interesting place, you had to get a list somehow and know where you were going in advance. If you made a typing mistake in a command, you were out of luck. Of course, the old Internet was very thrifty with computing resources: you could sign on by using only a terminal program (some as small as 20K!), and the text file you were likely to download was still small compared to a run-of-the-mill color picture or sound file.

A Very Friendly Interface

The Macintosh interface arrived in 1984; by 1994, it had taken over the world. It may appear in parts of the world in the form of Microsoft's Windows 95, a rather clumsy copy of the Mac interface, but there's no denying that the Mac way is now *the* way, even on non-Mac machines.

Flying over the net

Look at the little screen in Figure 10-1, which is rendered in the real application in lovely pastels instead of the dull grays of book publishing (users frequently ask why the eWorld images of people look like bowling pins wearing overcoats). You get to this screen by clicking on a Connect button in the program Apple sets up for you. Within 20 seconds or so, you're in eWorld (see Figure 10-2), a mythical electronic online paradise, with an interface that looks like the map they give you on the way into Disney World.

Figure 10-1:
Apple's strange little man in the overcoat represents you.

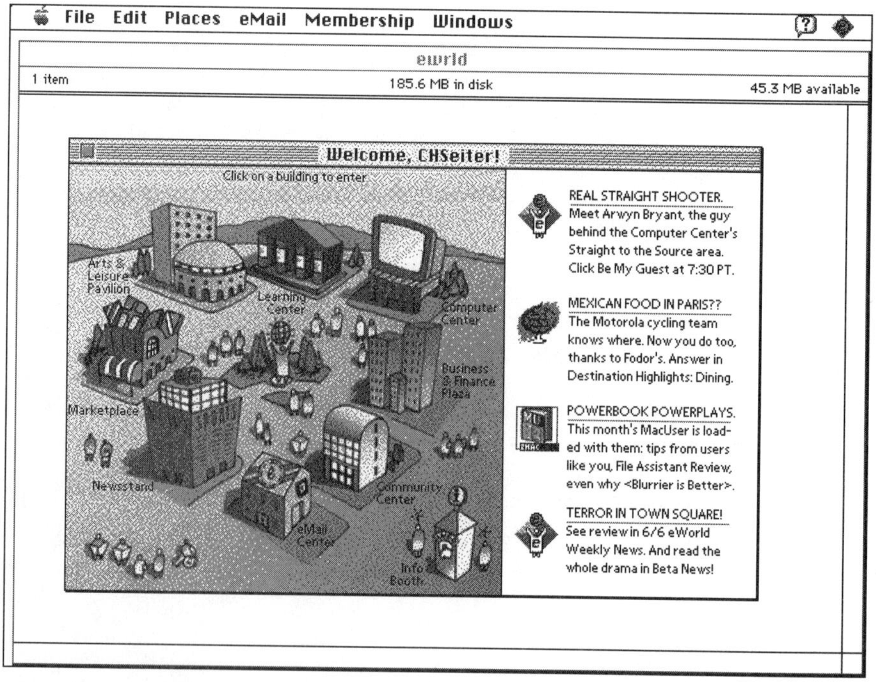

Figure 10-2:
Knock on any door in this eTown.

In eWorld, you click on the buildings (that's right, the buildings!) to get where you're going. This seems very far away from the electronic network universe of commands, such as

```
%telnet archie.techno.whatzis.org
```

It's not really. In the Macintosh-style graphical interface, every time you click on some spot on-screen, the program looks up the location that you clicked, finds the piece of code that corresponds to that spot, and sends the code to another part of the program that translates it to Mac instructions. If you click on the Computer Center building shown in Figure 10-2, the program translates the click into a Mac instruction to open the window in Figure 10-3.

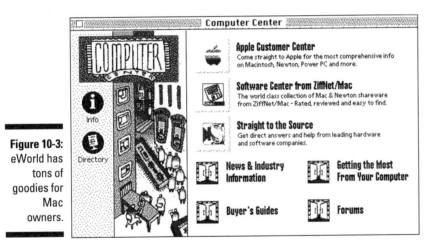

Figure 10-3: eWorld has tons of goodies for Mac owners.

Computer Center

Apple Customer Center
Come straight to Apple for the most comprehensive info on Macintosh, Newton, Power PC and more.

Software Center from ZiffNet/Mac
The world class collection of Mac & Newton shareware from ZiffNet/Mac – Rated, reviewed and easy to find.

Straight to the Source
Get direct answers and help from leading hardware and software companies.

News & Industry Information

Getting the Most From Your Computer

Buyer's Guides

Forums

Info

Directory

Pictures take time

One way or another, you pay for convenience most of the time, and eWorld is no exception. In this case, you pay for the program's size and speed. The version of eWorld that I used for these figures contains 8MB of color graphic files to present these attractive screens. On an older Mac, the screen shuffling with these big files is noticeably slower.

Apple has designed this service to be a jump or two ahead of the other online services, and it has landed itself a jump ahead of the current-state of telecommunications, too. 9600 bps is the minimum modem speed for using eWorld conveniently, and a higher speed than this would be lots better. During the beta phase of eWorld development, it frequently took *two hours* to download the latest version of the program at 14.4K bps. And following the Iron Law of Software, programs never get smaller.

eWorld: It's Got the Goods

If you've made it this far in the book, you've seen me make the following point at least five times in earlier chapters. *Use the Internet for files and services you can get only from the Internet.* Some of the most famous Internet sites were already starting to clog up by mid-1994 just because most of the first-generation Internet books recommended the same handful of sites, over and over, as places to collect the coolest stuff.

Imagine giving everyone in the U.S. a free airline pass. Now picture yourself at O'Hare International Airport in Chicago on Christmas Eve. See what I mean? Don't call up the Internet file server at poor old Stanford just to see if it has a blackjack game for you. Absolutely every national online service has a choice of blackjack games, including the same games they have at Stanford. Use the site at Stanford for Greek language fonts and programmers' utilities.

Time out for games

eWorld so far is doing a very good job of finding the most-accessed files and posting them right. In the fabulous Arts and Leisure Pavilion, shown in Figure 10-4, you can find a selection of games that is about as good as it gets (the eWorld staff has weeded out the duds). Besides standard computer games (see the list in Figure 10-5), eWorld has online interactive multiplayer games that are a giant improvement on the plain-text dungeon games of the traditional Internet. And because eWorld members tend to be "into this kind of stuff," the level of play is great.

Easy files

There's another advantage to using a cozy Apple-based service for collecting programs and files. Out on the Internet, it's pretty typical to find files both compressed and then *binhexed* — converted from a binary to an ASCII (character) file. After you find a file, you get to rewash it with the program HQXer or the equivalent and then uncompress it with another program. This process is a hassle. In even worse cases, the file is processed with a UNIX utility first so that you have to have a copy of UUTool or one of the ghastly and confusing programs for dealing with .tar and .z files. (Check the Glossary for the lowdown on these beasts.)

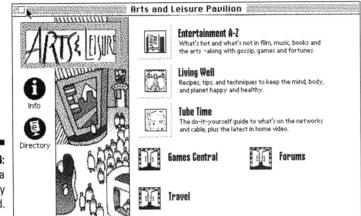

Figure 10-4:
eWorld in a
leisurely
mood.

Because all the files on eWorld were put there by Apple, getting a file from this service is easy. When you see the file you want, click on the Download button, and eWorld does the rest. After you sign off, eWorld automatically uncompresses the file (if it was compressed). All you do is pick the file, and it appears on your Macintosh in working order. That, folks, is how it should be. It's supposed to be someone else's job to do file manipulations.

So in terms of my glorious self-appointed mission to keep the Internet open for real Internet jobs, I would encourage you to look on eWorld first if you've heard of a hot file. Honest, it's easier.

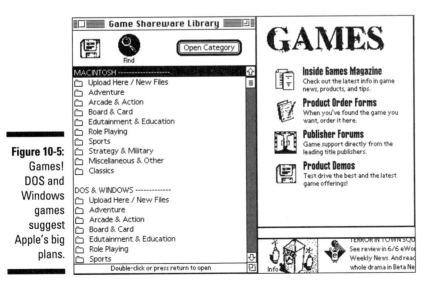

Figure 10-5:
Games!
DOS and
Windows
games
suggest
Apple's big
plans.

E-Mail for the Rest of Us

If you can't use the eMail Center, shown in Figure 10-6, you probably can't operate stamps either. Everything means just what it says. There are, however, a few wrinkles that may not be obvious.

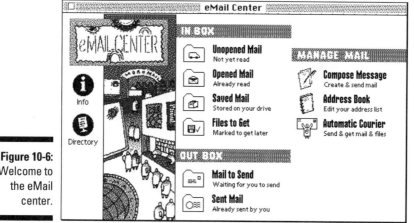

Figure 10-6:
Welcome to
the eMail
center.

Time-delayed transfers

When you use the Files to Get option for file transfers, you can mark files to get later. Simply find the files you like, mark them all, leave your computer and modem on overnight, and set eWorld to download them all at 4:15 a.m. (when, presumably, you are otherwise engaged). In the mail system, using the Automatic Courier option works in a similar way — you can choose times to send and deliver mail and files. One obvious use of this feature is making up lots of letters to people offline and then sending them out while you go to work on something else.

Getting from eWorld to reality

eWorld is still small enough that you usually will be sending lots of e-mail on the Internet to people outside of eWorld. Communicating outside of eWorld is easy. Click on the eMail Center icon and you get to the standard eWorld e-mail window. As you can see in Figure 10-7, you just type out a standard Internet address in the address space (click the little Internet button in the mail window to get this message).

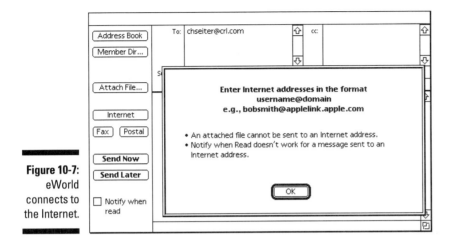

Figure 10-7:
eWorld
connects to
the Internet.

Because of the ease of connecting to the Internet, you may think that you can use all sorts of Internet e-mail services, such as Archie and FTP by e-mail. As it stands now, however, eWorld e-mail was originally set up to accommodate both Macintoshes and Newtons. Files bigger than 8K tend to blow the Newton's tiny hand-held mind. This means that in the first issue of eWorld, there is a file size limitation of 8 Kbytes. This, in turn, means that unless you are willing to put yourself through all sorts of contortions (stitching together binhexed 8K file fragments by hand and using a text editor), you can't collect much useful stuff through the old e-mail tricks. eWorld needs to get the rest of its Internet act together.

As Long As You're Here

There's plenty to do in Apple's jolly little online playground. These are just a few examples of unique-to-eWorld activities.

About money

You can make money, you can spend it, and eWorld will help you do both. Figure 10-8 shows the stock-quotation system, one of the most sophisticated online systems available, that's built into eWorld. I used it to track Microsoft stock while Microsoft went through all sorts of antitrust investigations by the Justice Department. If you like to believe that crime doesn't pay, this was not an encouraging spectacle.

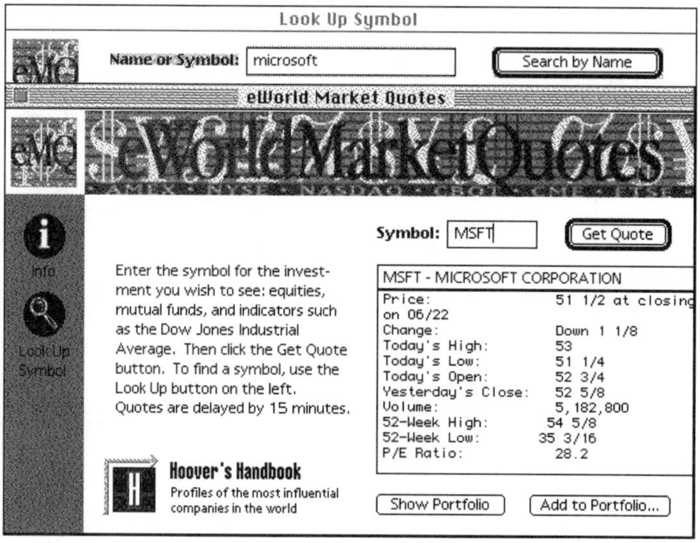

Figure 10-8:
Checking
up on
Microsoft
stock.

Now that you realize you've made money in your speculations, you may as well spend it, upgrading your Mac. (I mean, really, what other use is there for money? Food? House payments?) Figure 10-9 shows the screen for the online version of MacZone, one of the largest Macintosh discount mail-order houses. These guys are very hard to beat for price or delivery, and while writing this, I found myself absentmindedly ordering more memory for my rapidly aging Quadra. What I really need is a source of snap-in memory modules for my own head — as far as I can tell, the Quadra's doing better than I am.

Figure 10-9:
Click-based
eWorld
shopping.

About information

Speaking of my once-fine mind disintegrating under the impact of reading too many press releases from Apple, eWorld lets you take intellectual decay further or attempt to reverse it. It's your choice.

For example, if you want to see an application of technology at its finest, you can join a discussion group about the TV show *Melrose Place*. It's really quite remarkable — think of Shockley inventing the transistor, and the brilliant work of Turing and von Neumann on computers, and Apple's pioneering computer interface developments — 40 years of dazzling technical ingenuity making it possible to discuss Heather Locklear online (see Figure 10-10). Kind of makes you wonder what virtual reality products will really emerge some day.

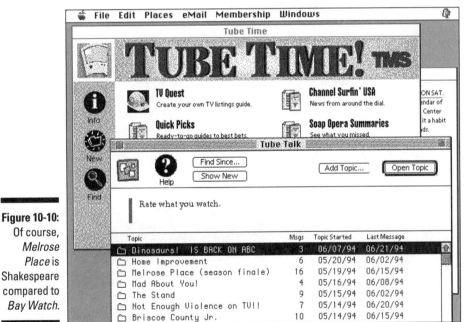

Figure 10-10:
Of course, *Melrose Place* is Shakespeare compared to *Bay Watch*.

On a more elevated intellectual plane, eWorld has libraries stocked with electronic equivalents of magazines, newspapers, and encyclopedias.

To avoid a transition shock upon leaving *Melrose Place*, I could start by leafing through the online edition of *USA Today*, sometimes nastily characterized as the paper for people who don't have the time for TV news (see Figure 10-11). Actually, this is a sort of business edition of *USA Today*, and the news is about eight hours ahead of anything you can find in print.

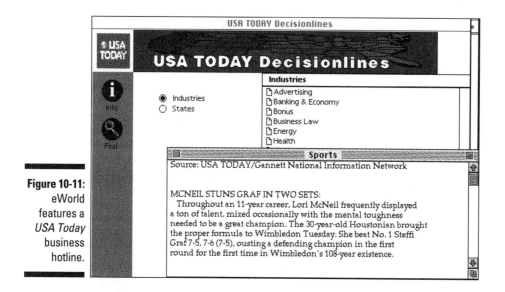

Figure 10-11:
eWorld
features a
USA Today
business
hotline.

eWorld also has some of the standard online magazines (computer and business magazines, mostly), but the encyclopedia feature in eWorld is a standout. When you search for a term in the eWorld Grolier's, you get an easy-to-use file of related topics (see Figure 10-12). This feature makes the eWorld encyclopedia much more like a paper version, in which you often find things that are more interesting than your original topic. The only problem is that online encyclopedias don't offer nearly as many illustrations as the print variety (see Figure 10-13).

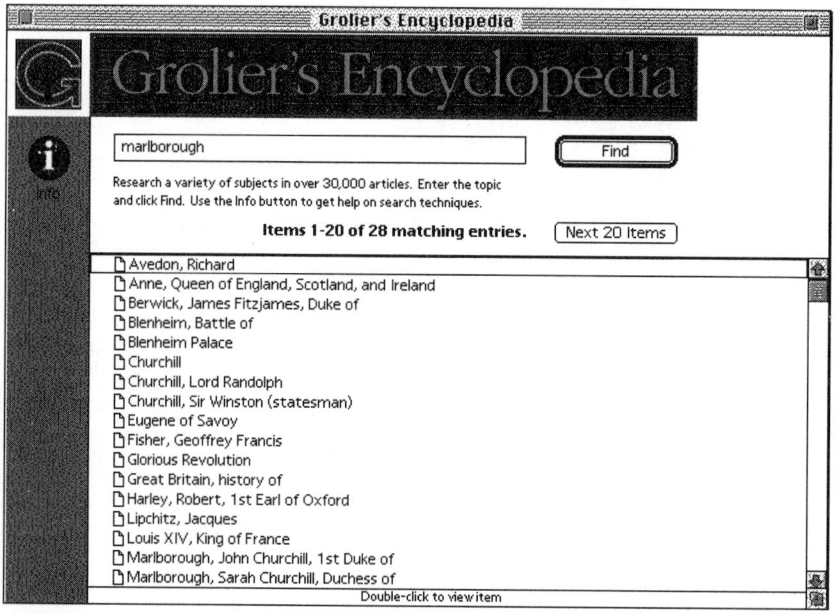

Figure 10-12:
Grolier's via
eWorld:
simply the
best.

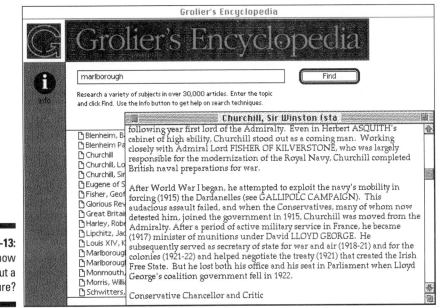

Figure 10-13:
Hey, how
about a
picture?

Grolier's Encyclopedia

Grolier's Encyclopedia

marlborough   Find

Info

Research a variety of subjects in over 30,000 articles. Enter the topic
and click Find. Use the Info button to get help on search techniques.

Churchill, Sir Winston [sta

following year first lord of the Admiralty. Even in Herbert ASQUITH's
cabinet of high ability, Churchill stood out as a coming man. Working
closely with Admiral Lord FISHER OF KILVERSTONE, who was largely
responsible for the modernization of the Royal Navy, Churchill completed
British naval preparations for war.

After World War I began, he attempted to exploit the navy's mobility in
forcing (1915) the Dardanelles (see GALLIPOLC CAMPAIGN). This
audacious assault failed, and when the Conservatives, many of whom now
detested him, joined the government in 1915, Churchill was moved from the
Admiralty. After a period of active military service in France, he became
(1917) minister of munitions under David LLOYD GEORGE. He
subsequently served as secretary of state for war and air (1918-21) and for the
colonies (1921-22) and helped negotiate the treaty (1921) that created the Irish
Free State. But he lost both his office and his seat in Parliament when Lloyd
George's coalition government fell in 1922.

Conservative Chancellor and Critic

- Blenheim, B
- Blenheim Pa
- Churchill
- Churchill, Lo
- Churchill, Sir
- Eugene of S
- Fisher, Geof
- Glorious Rev
- Great Britai
- Harley, Robe
- Lipchitz, Jac
- Louis XIV, K
- Marlborough
- Marlborough
- Monmouth,
- Morris, Willia
- Schwitters,

Junior-high-school confidential

This online stuff looks like the answer for every research assignment you could have in seventh grade. It's good, but it's not the last word. Here are some points for concerned students and worried parents.

1. The dog *can't* eat your homework any more. It's online in Cupertino and you can download it again.

2. You've *got* to use more than one source. The teacher has already seen everything you can find on eWorld.

3. With a little cut-and-paste and a thesaurus on the big words, you can make an encyclopedia entry sound like your own work.

4. The class can chip in and pay someone's older sister to do all the online searching.

5. You can't meet your friends at the eWorld library, so you may actually learn something.

6. "The dog ate my modem" may work as an excuse. "Dad reformatted my floppy by accident" could also fly.

Real Internet

Apple is a funny company. It was finally more or less *shamed* into offering complete Internet access because of its role in supporting the summer 1995 hit *The Net*. By the way, if you look closely at the very last scene in the movie, you can see a copy of this book (first edition) next to Sandra Bullock's Macintosh.

It took them a while, but they did it right, even to the odd touch of buying InterCon's Web Browser (just like AOL did). You can navigate to it from the Computer Center or directly with a keyword, but basically, a few simple clicks get you to the glorious spectacle in Figure 10-14. And when you get there, if you are just starting out on the Internet, Apple has stocked this private trout lake with almost every piece of useful public-domain information about the Internet you could find in a month of collecting (see Figure 10-15).

Figure 10-14:
eWorld's
shiny new
Internet
center.

Figure 10-15:
eWorld's
wealth of
Internet
resources.

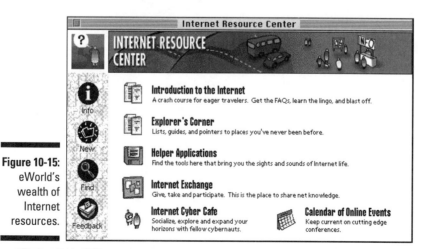

Now superficially, this service looks a lot like America Online, but there's a serious difference behind the interfaces. America Online has been adding users so fast that the service is very often hopelessly clogged. eWorld has been growing at such a leisurely rate (it's almost Apple's private e-mail service) that it has plenty of hardware capability to handle everyone who's connected. When I was working on *Yahoo! Unplugged* for IDG in summer 1995, I found that eWorld's Web access was always working, even when independent service providers (Netcom, PSI) and nationals like AOL were punking out every five minutes.

A hearty welcome

You might want to spend some time checking out the resources Apple has collected. The Helper Application section (see Figure 10-16) includes everything you need to set up your own Web site, become a master of HTML, and start a career as an Internet consultant. In fact, many people in wired cities like Boston and San Francisco have found jobs at advertising agencies with no more background than you could gather right here in a few days.

And if you find some of this material baffling, just click on over to the Explorer's Corner, where you can not only look up any info you need, but you can also post questions to well-intentioned Net experts. The Internet Insider material is especially valuable (see Figure 10-17).

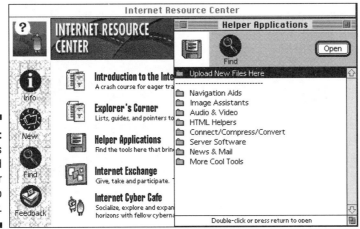

Figure 10-16:
All the tools
you need
for your
own Web
development.

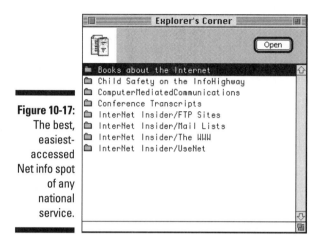

Figure 10-17:
The best,
easiest-
accessed
Net info spot
of any
national
service.

Newsgroups and mailing lists

These features are remarkably simple and delightful. To sign up for newsgroups, you just click the Newsgroup button, and you get to the screen in Figure 10-18. At this point, you can either scroll through the newsgroup lists for the ones you want, or you can use the button to "Add a Known Newsgroup." The difference between these is that scrolling down the browsing list (see Figure 10-19), you will find that various newsgroups Apple doesn't want kids to find have been neatly excised from the lists. If you know the name of the group you want (and it's not much trouble finding it, really) you can add it specifically by name.

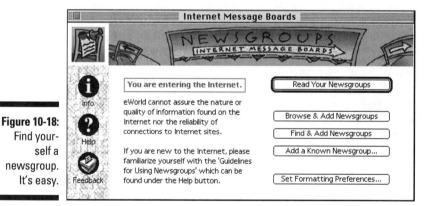

Figure 10-18:
Find your-
self a
newsgroup.
It's easy.

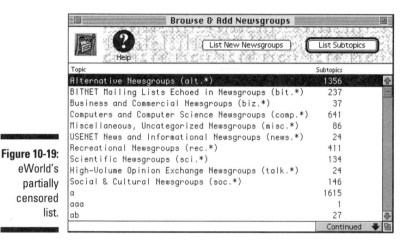

Figure 10-19:
eWorld's
partially
censored
list.

Mailing lists, although they are mostly concerned with academic or professional information, are really one of the richest resources on the Net. I understand perfectly that Web sites are cool and that everyone wants pictures, but for serious information as opposed to personal goofing around, there's still a lot to be said for plain old mailing lists (see Figure 10-20).

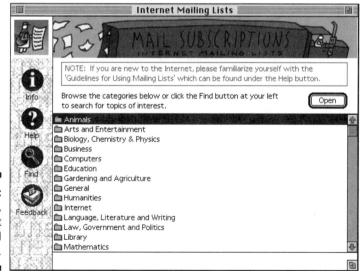

Figure 10-20:
Mailing lists,
still worth it
after all
these years.

File express

As a Mac owner, you are a registered member of a minority group in the world of computing. There is a ton of great free and shareware software out there for you, but most of it is collected into a relatively small number of big archives. Realizing this, Apple has preloaded eWorld's FTP service with not just a slick interface (see Figure 10-21) but also all the right connections.

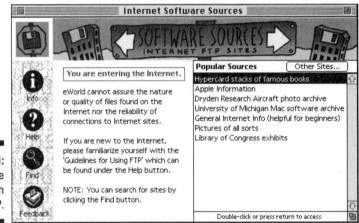

Figure 10-21: True Macintosh FTP.

The "Pictures of all sorts" site mentioned here is a good first place to look for pictures, since this file is maintained at eWorld itself and there's no transfer slowdown. Figure 10-22 shows that this collection is complete enough to have a couple of pictures by Jan Vermeer (although the titles aren't particularly evocative). Vermeer is not only interesting in his own right, but pictures by Vermeer figure in both the biggest forgery case and the biggest unsolved art theft in the 20th century.

For more conventional files, you can proceed directly to a mirror site of the great University of Michigan collection (see Figure 10-23). If they don't have it here, you may not need it after all.

The Web

Beats me why the people who run Apple didn't get Web service going in the first edition of the service, instead of waiting for a million or so Mac owners to run off to AOL. It's especially puzzling since they just bought the same Web browser AOL uses, at the same not-particularly-superb level of integration.

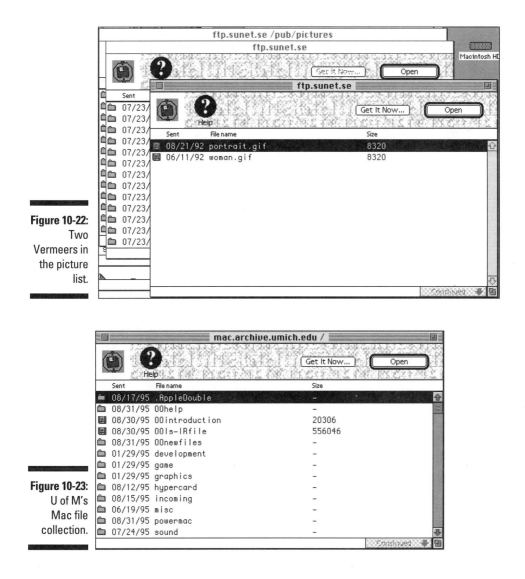

Figure 10-22:
Two
Vermeers in
the picture
list.

Figure 10-23:
U of M's
Mac file
collection.

You can reach the Web (see Figure 10-24) with a simple click on the Internet access screen — the click fires up what's essentially a separate program that's fired up when you call for it, rather than a part of eWorld. There are, however, a couple of nice features of this particular browser. The first feature is that it's easy to turn off image downloads with a command under the Web menu. Yes, yes, I know pictures are the whole point here, but if you are cruising around looking for sites of interest, you will find a number of cases in which someone has loaded a 159K graphic as the first item that appears. You can always click Load Images if you like the site.

The second nice feature is that the Edit menu has a command "Copy Current URL" that lets you stash the URL for a site in a standard Mac program (word processor, for example). I think this feature beats hot lists by a lot, especially if you are searching with a directory service like Yahoo since you can bring more methods of classification to bear on your results.

It took these people forever, but I must say that Apple finally put together an Internet service that's a model for everyone else. And the usage is so light, compared to eWorld's installed server base, that you just never get the "busy signals" or glitches that plague other services.

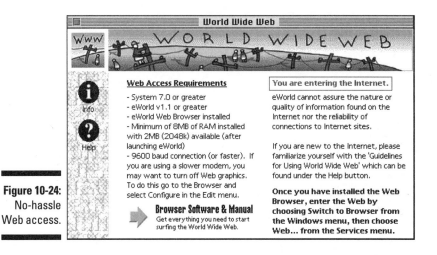

Figure 10-24:
No-hassle
Web access.

World Wide Web

Web Access Requirements

- System 7.0 or greater
- eWorld v1.1 or greater
- eWorld Web Browser installed
- Minimum of 8MB of RAM installed with 2MB (2048k) available (after launching eWorld)
- 9600 baud connection (or faster). If you are using a slower modem, you may want to turn off Web graphics. To do this go to the Browser and select Configure in the Edit menu.

Browser Software & Manual
Get everything you need to start surfing the World Wide Web.

You are entering the Internet.

eWorld cannot assure the nature or quality of information found on the Internet nor the reliability of connections to Internet sites.

If you are new to the Internet, please familiarize yourself with the 'Guidelines for Using World Wide Web' which can be found under the Help button.

Once you have installed the Web Browser, enter the Web by choosing Switch to Browser from the Windows menu, then choose Web... from the Services menu.

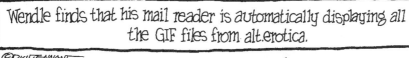

Chapter 11
Three Special Services

$\bullet$ $\bullet$

In This Chapter

▶ Small is beautiful (uh, sometimes)

▶ Pipeline and its relatives

▶ The mysterious GEnie

▶ Delphi grows up

$\bullet$ $\bullet$

I have a fatal weakness for underdogs. I've been following the Chicago Cubs for decades, knowing perfectly well that if they ever do well throughout the season they'll manage to blow the playoffs (only Boston Red Sox fans really understand this situation). I learned Portuguese before I learned Spanish, Ukrainian before Russian, and Dutch before German. I'm the guy who adopts the legendary three-legged blind dog named "Lucky."

That's why I am now going to take you on a tour of three national online services that, for one reason or another, got pushed aside in the big Net explosion of 1995. CompuServe, Prodigy, and America Online all have users numbering in the millions — each of the services in this chapter has a few hundred thousand members. But, just as some people would rather live, say, in Honolulu rather than in Houston, you may find yourself charmed by one of the smaller nationals.

Pipeline

Somewhat ironically, Pipeline was actually the *first* service to provide easy access through a Web command, implementing a browser in May 1995 when AOL was still making excuses. Based on a fast, efficient front end, Pipeline service is one of the few Internet connections that really works well at 9600 bps or less.

Pipeline has been bought by PSINet, and will be available as a national-oriented Mac-ready operation in early 1996. There have been nationally accessible versions of Mac Pipeline for some time (the Starter Kit version of this book includes a free Pipeline trial), but they have been available in distinctly localized versions. Let me explain.

Pipeline these days is mostly Pipeline NY, a Big-Apple-centric service that is readily characterized as Internet for New Yorkers. You start it up, and the first screen you see has News as a clickable category (see Figure 11-1). Another distinctive feature of Pipeline NY is the amount of space it gives to cultural matters, art museums, and the like. It's a sharp contrast to the level of chat on the big national services, which often has the wit and panache of CB conversations at truck stops.

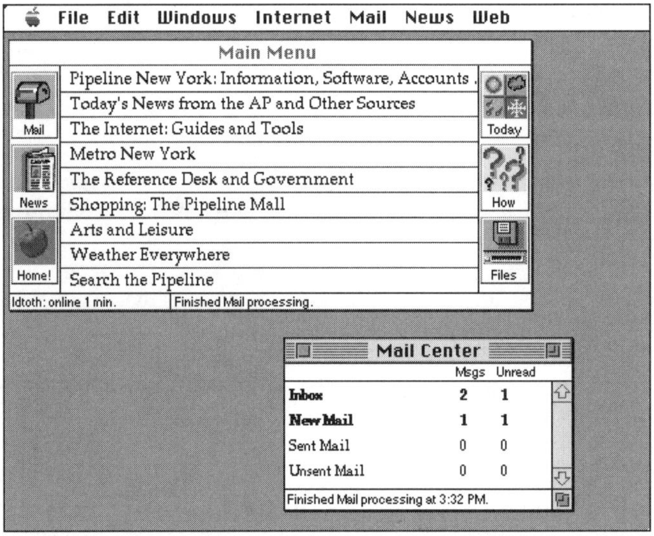

Figure 11-1:
New York
online.

Similarly, the news (see Figure 11-2) presented on Pipeline assumes you have a basic level of smarts. This service was founded by science writer James Gleick, who works mostly for *The New York Times,* and the material has a sort of Timesy flavor. There's none of the "Hey, Kids! Talk to Drew Barrymore online now!" cheerleading that characterizes AOL. Even its West Coast relative, Hooked (415-343-1233), which licensed the basic Pipeline software, has a distinctive San Francisco South-of-Market hipster feel to it. These big-city services are not trying to make everyone in Gun Barrel, TX necessarily feel right at home.

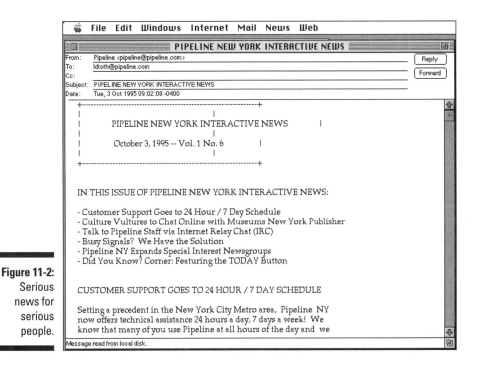

Figure 11-2:
Serious
news for
serious
people.

Internet connectivity is excellent, partly because the relatively compact software doesn't place extraneous demands on your Mac. Straightforward Archie and FTP services (see Figure 11-3) cover the old-time Internet, and an integrated but spartan Web browser (see Figure 11-4) takes you out to all the new stuff. Combined with Pipeline's relatively low access rates, this service has a lot to recommend it, particularly if you're among the 10 percent of Americans in the geographic orbit of NYC (see the sidebar "At home on the range").

At home on the range

Here's a little-known vacation fun fact. Out here in Wine Country (and in other rural locations), innkeepers at cute little country B&Bs will often claim that they have no vacancy if they recognize your area code as part of the metro New York area. As one innkeeper told me "Look. My inn is at the end of a dirt road in a winery outside Calistoga. *No,* we can't get the Sunday Times. Our knishes, Chinese food, pastrami, and bagels in town probably would qualify as garbage in Manhattan. I *don't* know

what happened to the Jets this Sunday. And I hate disappointing these people!"

But now you have the option of carrying your own little Manhattan inside a modem-equipped PowerBook (Pipeline has local numbers everywhere). The food is still going to be a problem when you travel (I mean, try to find decent caviar outside the Russian Tea Room — just try), but with Pipeline, you can at least get your information fix even in the middle of nowhere.

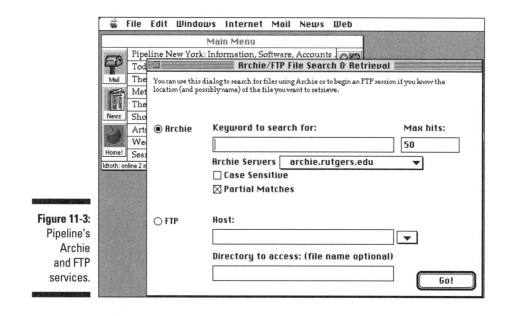

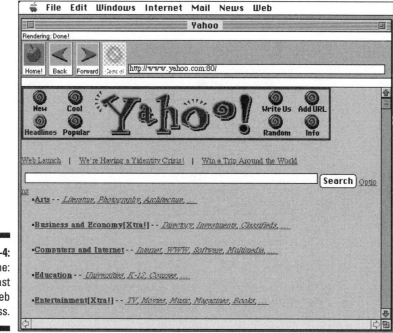

GEnie: Still in the Bottle

Earlier, I said I like underdogs, but it's stretching the point a bit with GEnie. After all, it's backed by General Electric, and while that great firm has occasionally had problems with bad PR and lawsuits, it's not exactly on the ropes. What seems to have happened to GEnie is that the whole Web phenomenon blew up faster than this service could respond. The GEnie strategy was to assume that users would need a lot of hand-holding with basics such as FTP and e-mail, and it set up lots of online help and provision for slower modems. In the meantime, everyone decided to get a fast modem and head out onto the Web independently. So GEnie didn't exactly get its Web act together as fast as its competitors, but it's a pretty conGEnial place anyway.

Parts of the GEnie interface (see Figure 11-5) may look familiar to long-time Mac heads because of this services's association with AppleLink; General Electric Information Services (GEIS) was the backbone of AppleLink until recently.

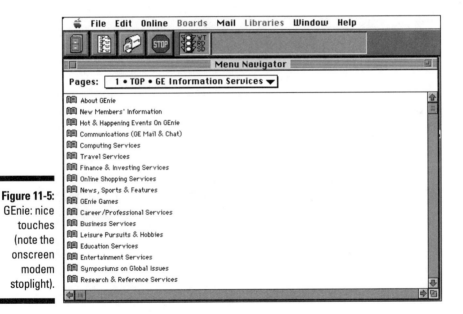

Figure 11-5:
GEnie: nice touches (note the onscreen modem stoplight).

To navigate through GEnie you simply click folders or pages as they are presented to you, or try keywords in a dialog box. On this service, one keyword particulary worth trying is Games. From the beginning, GEnie has specialized in multiuser and arcade-type games (see Figure 11-6). There are interest groups for Nintendo, Atari, and Sega, among others. In fact, GEnie market research indicated, in the pre-Web days, that games was what most users wanted in an online service.

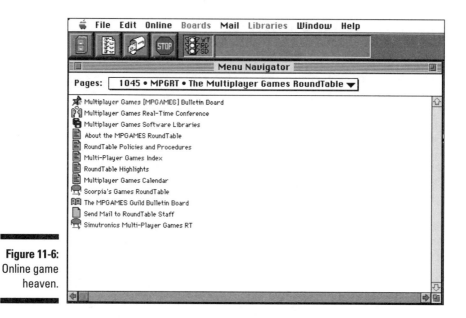

Figure 11-6:
Online game
heaven.

Internet access is going to be different by early 1996. For now, if you find the Internet bewildering, GEnie has the comforting feature that you can simply send requests for files by e-mail to the system operator and get the files sent back to you (see Figure 11-7). As a way of getting started, this feature has some advantages, although the point-and-click interfaces now available from AOL and others encourage direct experimentation.

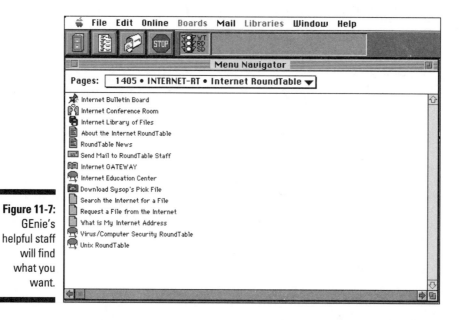

Figure 11-7:
GEnie's
helpful staff
will find
what you
want.

Where the original form of GEnie fails to impress the discerning modern Internaut is that Web access still depends on the text-only browser called Lynx (see Figure 11-8). If you're stuck with a 2400-bps modem (maybe you got a Performa or PowerBook with a 2400-bps modem built in), you're actually better off with Lynx than with Netscape. At low speeds, the last thing you need to see is some company's 120K logo crawling down your screen a millimeter at a time. But nobody is going to accept a service that doesn't have a graphical Web browser, and GEnie's choices are to fix this situation pronto or be relegated to the online backwaters. Don't worry, though — the executives at GE certainly know how to buy a browser.

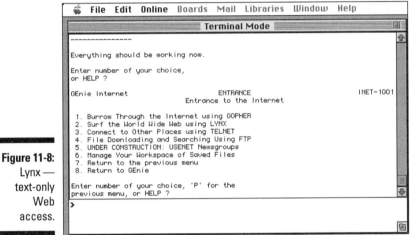

Figure 11-8:
Lynx —
text-only
Web
access.

Delphi

I'm very sorry to file Delphi here among "others." It was an Internet pioneer, and it was the only place (except for do-it-yourself "real" access) to get uncensored newsgroups and Internet Relay Chat in the old days. Although it was text-based, the original Delphi service gave users access to the whole Internet (see Figure 11-9).

```
Internet SIG Menu:


About the Internet      Help
Conference              Exit
Databases (Files)
EMail                   FTP
Forum (Messages)        Gopher
Guides (Books)          IRC-Internet Relay Chat
Register/Cancel         Telnet
Who's Here              Utilities (finger, traceroute, ping)
Workspace               Usenet Newsgroups
```

Figure 11-9:
Delphi —
Internet in
letters.

Needless to say, a text interface is just radio in a TV world, relegated to secondary information-transfer roles. Delphi, therefore, got itself acquired by a backer with deep pockets, MCI, to finance its transformation. As you read this, Delphi should be reincarnated as an all-Web service, perhaps the only really modern way to go. They are going to overhaul Delphi, and they want your business. So why are you supposed to switch to the new Delphi? The pitch will be that MCI will have all sorts of news and entertainment services that are *not* simply open to anyone with a browser (you'll have to be a member), and that these services will be so attractive that you'll sign up.

What's Next?

Beats me. The pace of change online has no parallels elsewhere. Planning a service would be like running a chain of grocery stores in a country where everyone might decide to go vegan at the drop of a hat. Given the Web as a giant sponge blotting up all interesting content, it remains to be seen whether *any* smaller services are economically viable. For that matter, it's not clear that the biggest services are viable either. It's a dirty little financial secret that no online service has ever made as much money as its business plan hoped, and, in fact, all the major nationals lost money for years and years. A year ago, you couldn't post advertising on the Web; a year from now, you'll see advertising every time you log on. Will large social gulfs emerge between Webbed and non-Webbed people? Will specialized online services in areas like medicine or education emerge? Can anyone figure out how to make a fortune when users expect the software to be free and connect charges to be minimal? Nobody knows, but we're all in this wacky adventure together.

Part III
Big Business, High Speeds

The 5th Wave   By Rich Tennant

KYLE AND TODDS SOFTWARE Co.

"WE'D LIKE TO TALK TO YOU BOYS ABOUT COMMERCIALIZING YOUR INTERNET FREEWARE APPLICATION."

In this part...

1 f you're an adventurous spirit, you may want to strike out
and get your own Internet connection rather than use a
national online service.

Frankly, a roll-your-own connection is harder to do, but this
book still brings it within reach. I'll tell you all about the
dazzling Mac software you can use to surf the Net.

Chapter 13, my personal favorite, is the only guide to SLIP
connection for your Mac that gets down to the real what-
next details of a direct-connect SLIP Internet account.

I also cover a topic that a lot of you have probably been
wondering about: business on the Internet, specifically
the Web.

Chapter 12

Bulletin Boards — The Local Electronic Community

*A*nyone who can afford to leave a computer running all the time can operate a *bulletin board*, or its grander cousin, a *conferencing system*. Both terms really just mean a computer with incoming lines and a filing system for messages. A national online service like Delphi, for example, consists of big computers that carry hundreds of specialized message areas and thousands of files. A bulletin board may consist of a single Mac with only one or two incoming lines. But in both cases, you get to rummage around the files and see what's there, post messages, or join a discussion group.

The biggest urban bulletin boards can have tens of thousands of paying members and carry all the latest Mac files — some big boards are, in effect, mini-Delphis. Other smaller boards flourish by specialization. Specialty bulletin boards cater to people interested in steam locomotives, 18th-century antiques, phenomenally kinky sex, multiuser online games, chess, astronomy, and any other topic you can — or can't — imagine. The big boards are quite stable (the WELL in San Francisco was operating before most national services), whereas small boards require monthly reading of *Boardwatch Magazine* just to see who's still there and who's not.

Ten reasons to use bulletin boards

1. If you find a date, you both live in the same area code.

2. You can find cheap, used Macs.

3. You're a hard-core nerd (EMS 301-924-3594 voice).

4. You're a Buddhist (Mt. Kailas 617-252-9988 modem).

5. You hunt elk (Vacation Source 800-868-7555 modem).

6. You hunt dragons (ONIX 215-879-6616 modem).

7. You're gay (Eye Contact 415-703-8200 modem).

8. You want to join Throbnet, Kinknet, and Wildnet. (I'm not making this up! Blues Cafe 214-638-1186 modem.)

9. All your credit cards are maxed out and Prodigy won't let you on.

10. You believe that the national online services are simply fronts for a giant market-research firm (I'm not sure that I don't believe this myself).

In the past, bulletin boards rarely had Internet connections, but now it's becoming typical. A board that is free (or charges a few dollars a month) and has an Internet connection can be an attractive alternative to national services. A local call for your modem is the cheapest connection you're likely to get, unless, of course, you're a Stanford student, where your $20,000-per-year tuition includes absolutely *free* access to `sumex-aim.stanford.edu` (I vaguely remember some proverb about free lunches . . .). In this chapter, I give you a couple of examples of bulletin board access to the Internet and then send you out looking for these local on-ramps to the information highway. All you need is a modem to dial the service and a willingness to use (most of the time) a plain text-based interface.

The WELL: It's Swell

Almost every big city has a bulletin board that's been a hangout for Macintosh fans for a decade now, and most of these boards are now Internet-ready. Some states have their own statewide boards: in Hawaii, it's Hawaii FYI; in Montana, it's Big Sky Telegraph; and in Michigan, it's NovaLink.

Deluxe hand-holding

The San Francisco area's WELL (Internet name is `well.sf.ca.us`, voice phone 415-332-4335) is an excellent example of a community bulletin board with Internet links. The name stands for Whole Earth 'Lectronic Link, as this bulletin board was founded by the crew of jolly, futurist pirates who published the wildly successful "Whole Earth Catalog," a mild dose of counterculture during the 1980s. They took the profits from the catalog and used some of the money to start the bulletin board. With its foundation as a nonprofit, electronic-freedom pioneer, the WELL is similar to many other bulletin boards from a computing point of view, but it has a rather high-minded internal Net culture. Even now, it reminds one of the altruistic Net, back in the days before Web pages full of advertising were a key component of the Internet.

Figure 12-1 shows you what happens when the wireheads meet the hippies. The WELL is a UNIX system, but instead of leaving you with a one-character prompt, it at least gives you chatty little menus and live, online help.

```
UNIX(r) System V Release 4.0 (well)

This is the WELL

Type    newuser   to sign up.
Type    trouble   if you are having trouble logging in.
Type    guest     to learn about the WELL.

login: chseiter
Password:
    May 17   Intermediate Tutorial (g wellcome ; s 93)         <== TOMORROW!
    May 20   WELL Office Party #92 (g news ; s 1541)           <== Friday
    Jul 23   Annual WELL Picnic (g news ; s 1515)

                Welcome to The WELLcome Conference!

Gotta question? Ask away over in topic 118: type    s 118 nor    then type    r
Introduce yourself in topic 119:             type    s 119 nor    then type    r
For immediate help from a real person:       type    helpers
For the WELLcome Conference menu:            type    wellcome
```

Figure 12-1: Wherever you go, there you are — WELL help covers it.

I don't know how they do it, but they have people around to answer your questions at 4:17 a.m. The whole system is as friendly as a Yorkshire terrier snoozing in your lap.

Real Internet, plus help

But, you may ask, where's the Internet? It's all here, and for a text-based system, it's pretty amazing. You type the following:

```
g inet
```

and you're in the Internet conference. Then type

```
netmenu
```

and you see the choices shown in Figure 12-2. On the WELL, you don't really need to know these commands because you can ask for options or help at any point and the system gives you your choices.

```
OK (type a command or type  opt  for Options): netmenu


        The   Internet   Conference   Menu

type  1   for Introductory Readings

type  2   for Rules and Regulations on the use of the Internet from the WELL

type  3   for Cheat-sheets on how to use Internet tools

type  4   for Information on Libraries online

type  5   for Information on FTP (File transfer protocol)

type  6   for Information on Internet Services

type  7   to look for an Internet site near you

type  8   for the Miscellaneous files
```

Figure 12-2:
Detailed
WELL
menus start
you on the
Internet.

Gopher on the WELL

You get online cheat sheets for help with old-time Internet standards Archie, FTP, and telnet and also online versions of the standard Internet beginner's documents. Where this bulletin board really passes up other BBS systems, however, is in its own Gopher, called, appropriately, *wellgopher* (see Figure 12-3). Because it's a real Gopher, this menu lets you automatically sail out into all the other computers on the Net, searching for the elusive wonder-file. And because it's the WELL, "Cyberpunk and Postmodern Culture" is one of the busiest topics.

```
OK (type a command or type  opt  for Options): wellgopher
Welcome to the wonderful world of Gopher!
Press ? for Help, q to Quit
Root gopher server: gopher.well.sf.ca.us

--> 1.   About this gopherspace (including a quick "How To" guide)/
    2.   See the latest additions to this gopherspace/
    3.   Search all menus on the WELLgopher <?>
    4.   Internet Outbound (*New!*)/
    5.   Art, Music, Film, Cultural works, etc/
    6.   Authors, Books, Periodicals, Zines (Factsheet Five lives here!)/
    7.   Business in Cyberspace: Commercial Ventures on the Matrix/
    8.   Communications and Media/
    9.   Community/
    10.  Cyberpunk and Postmodern Culture/
    11.  Environmental Issues and Ideas/
    12.  Hacking/
    13.  K-12 Education/
    14.  The Matrix (information about the global networks)/
    15.  The Military, its People, Policies, and Practices/
    16.  Politics/
    17.  Science/
    18.  The WELL itself/
```

Figure 12-3:
Do you
feel lucky,
cyberpunk?

Going down a more sedate wellgopher hole (see Figure 12-4), you find yourself ready to scan the latest from the Advanced X-ray Astrophysics facility. (If this facility is advanced, is there a Beginner's X-ray Astrophysics site in a high school somewhere?) The wellgopher keeps telnetting to other Gophers until you're satisfied.

```
         Internet Gopher Information Client 2.0 pl11

                  SCIENCE, MATH, STATISTICS

    1.   ASCinfo (Info. relating to Advanced XRay Astrophy. Facility) <TEL>

    2.   E-Math (Am. Math. Soc. bbs w/ software and reviews) <TEL>

    3.   Math Gopher (Math archives (software, teaching materials, other go../

    4.   Nuclear Data Center (National nuclear data) <TEL>

    5.   Particle Information (Lookup information on any particle!) <TEL>

    6.   Periodic Table (electronic periodic table of elements) <TEL>

   >7.   STIS (Science & Technology Information System) <TEL>

   |8.   The Scientist (Biweekly paper targeted at science professionals)/
```

Figure 12-4:
Serious
information
from around
the globe.

Fun and games

Some day, weary at last of advanced X-ray astrophysics, you may want to play an online game. The people at the WELL are so concerned for your happiness that they not only equip this bulletin board with plenty of interactive games, but they also include tip files (see Figure 12-5) so that you don't wander into a simulation as a "clueless newbie" and get killed off in 12 seconds. A bulletin board that defends you against your own cluelessness is a treasure indeed.

Figure 12-5:
Tip files
keep your
cluelessness
from making
you lose
games too
quickly.

```
People gather treasure, slay monsters (and each other), gain experience
points, and thereby become wizards, with powers that are useful in
playing the game. In a variety of MUD known as a Muse (Multi User
Simulation Environment), communication and education and worldbuilding
are the goal of the exercise, rather than gaining points in a game.

Some MUDs can be brutal. If other players can gain points by killing
off "clueless newbies" (which is what you will be until you learn the
ropes), you might find that the first action someone in a new world
takes is to slash at you with a virtual broadsword.

Other MUDs are entirely nonviolent. One good example is Cyberion City.
You can get there by telnetting (see topic #7 in the Internet
conference) to michael.ai.mit.edu, registering as guest, and connecting
as guest. If you decide that you want to get a character, follow the
instructions in the guest login screen.
```

Power to the Public

The WELL is a private, nonprofit bulletin board that charges a monthly fee (basic fee is $12.50 a month). There are also private, for-profit bulletin boards, some of which justify their membership fees by providing harder-core stuff than the Internet, and some of which are very specialized and charge something just to make sure that you're really interested.

The Internet invades the library

Yet another type of bulletin board with Internet connection has appeared lately — the community information service. Typically, this service is organized by a library network, because once a library commits to the horrendous expense of replacing card catalogs with an online system using a big computer and terminals, the extra effort of joining the Net is negligible.

Library networks tend to have limited message systems and limited or no e-mail. After all, the library is supposed to serve up information for you, not run your errands. Figure 12-6 shows a typical sign-on screen from the local branch of a countywide library system. I can tell you with confidence that a community information service is coming to your town, if it's not there already, because the vendors have all the parts in place and are lobbying the librarians like crazy. They may not buy enough new books any more, but libraries are buying terminals like there's no tomorrow.

```
16 JUNE 94              Healdsburg Library              10:45pm
                 PUBLIC ACCESS (402 , ttyd4p6)

                 Welcome to the online catalog.
           Please type the number and press the key labeled RETURN.

                 1.  TITLE
                 2.  AUTHOR
                 3.  SUBJECT
                 4.  MAIN WORDS IN TITLE
                 5.  MAIN WORDS IN SUBJECT
                 6.  SERIES
                 7.  CONTENTS (Plays, short stories, etc.)
                 8.  COMMUNITY RESOURCES
                 9.  PERIODICAL INDEXES
                 10. Search Your Holds and Fines
                 11. Bulletin Board
                 12. Print Saved Bibliography
                 13. Other Searches (INTERNET)
                 14. Logoff
```

Figure 12-6:
The library on the corner gets wired to the universe.

Moving out of the stacks

So there's the usual stuff you expect from a library, and then there's choice 13 on the menu in Figure 12-6, which is your gateway to the Internet. What the system does when you pick number 13 is fairly simple. A script behind the choice telnets you to a bigger computer — in this case, the main library at Sonoma State University (see Figure 12-7). Then *that* computer presents you with a menu that telnets you to other sites if necessary (refer to Figure 12-8).

```
Connecting to ADMVAX.SONOMA.EDU on account OPAC -- PLEASE
WAIT
Password:
      SONOMA STATE UNIVERSITY     RUBEN SALAZAR LIBRARY     MERLIN SYSTEM

                          == MAIN MENU ==

      1    SSU Catalog -- Books, Media, Gov. Doc., Other Index/Full Text...

      2    SSU Library Information; Reserve Book Room; Tips on Using This System;
           Suggestion Box, etc...

      3    Indexes, Abstracts & Full-Text Databases--periodicals, encyclopedias,
           book reviews, company profiles, etc...   (Password Required)

      4    Additional Libraries and Online Information Services...

      5    Quick Access to All Resources

      6    Exit
```

Figure 12-7:
If the book you want is not at the local library, you can check the nearest college.

```
      SONOMA STATE UNIVERSITY     RUBEN SALAZAR LIBRARY     MERLIN SYSTEM

                          === RESOURCE MENU ===

      RESOURCES REQUIRING PASSWORD:          PUBLIC ACCESS RESOURCES:
        11 CARL (CL)                           21 CTP (CTP)
        12 Chronicle of higher educ. (CH)      22 LIBS (LIBS)
        13 Dow Jones info service (DJ)         23 LOCIS (LC)
        14 DowQuest (DQ)                       24 MELVYL (MVL)
        15 Eureka (EU)                         25 Sonoma Co Lib (SCL)
        16 InfoTrac (IT)                       26 SRJC Lib (JC)
        17 Lexis/Nexis (LN)                    27 Open Access CARL (OAC)
        18 CD-RomNet (CD)

      TRIAL PRODUCTS:
        31 Eureka (TEU)
        32 Full Text CARL (TCL)
        33 SSU OPAC (SSU)
```

Figure 12-8:
Casting the info-net even wider.

Once you get out onto the Net, the choices keep expanding. The library system, you may have noticed, is really just a specialized Gopher in which all the other Gopher Internet sites happen to be libraries or online databases. Nonetheless, in the next few years, this system will be offering a large portion of the print material stored in traditional libraries.

The Internet in Your Backyard

People in my small town are often startled to discover that the Internet they've been reading about in the newspapers is the same Internet they can reach from terminals in the library. Our library system lets you dial it from home as well. It's worth checking in your town — if a system is in place, you can practice Internet navigating on the library system before you start shelling out $2 per hour online to get lost. When you get a perspective on the contents on the Net for free, you can then think about what service you want that includes a Web browser and so forth.

You should also make an effort to find local computer publications — you can usually find them in big-city newsracks. Not only do new private and public bulletin boards appear all the time, but lately, an amazing number of boards have decided to stop charging fees. An Internet-connected board with a decent system operator is as good an introduction to the Net as you're likely to find.

Some bulletin boards now have a provision, using a piece of software called TIA (The Interface Adapter), for connecting you to all services on the Internet, including graphical World Wide Web browsers. If you can find one of these bulletin boards that's a high-speed (28.8K) local phone call away, it's worth checking out. As the big national services succeed, their contents are becoming more bland and in many cases less relevant to the action in your own corner of the world.

Chapter 13

Really Wired — Direct Connection

*I*f you have read this far, I'm assuming you haven't been completely seduced by the comforts of America Online or eWorld. Instead, you want to be able to use any software you like, including the latest Web browsers, without waiting for a national service to get its act slowly together.

Now, here's a way to tell whether direct Internet is easy as AOL or not. Look up every book on the Internet you can find in your local library. (Remember, you're supposed to *buy* IDG books, but you're allowed to read the other ones for free if necessary.) Look up the section on MacTCP, if the book has one.

You will find that every last one of the authors says something like, "Um, when you get to the part where you actually have to install the Internet connection, you better find a hotshot Mac guru to do it for you." Or "Find a net buddy." Or "Talk to your system administrator." That's not encouraging. But things changed a bit in 1995, so now there are ways to get MacTCP running without being a real wirehead yourself.

I'll tell you exactly how to get your own Internet connection. I'll cover the classic SLIP connection with a service provider and then give an example of a newer kind of connection with PPP. And while it may not be the good ol' *Dummies* easy reading song-and-dance exactly, it's the most detailed (and demystifying) explanation of SLIP connection you're going to see in print.

For PPP connection, I'll be using Internet Valet ($39.99 from Software Ventures) as an example — it's a product of the wave of Net mergers that occurred when Performance Systems International swept through the Mac market and bought half the stuff worth having. If you don't want to spring the forty bucks for this product, look around in the bookstore where you bought this book for IDG's *Mac Essential Web Secrets* (by myself and *Macworld's* Tom Negrino). We're including a disk with a quick-installation suite from Quarterdeck Software (who licensed it from Spyglass, who licensed it from the original Mosaic Web-meisters at NCSA).

Getting on the Internet

There are a few different ways to get an Internet account that let you use Mac software. If you already have a Macintosh at a university that is directly connected to a network or you have a Mac on an office network, you are entitled to make someone else do all your setup work (a net administrator at work or school). This discussion is for individuals who are willing to find a service provider independently that offers SLIP accounts and who will be contacting the service with a modem. That's a *dial-up SLIP account*, in case your friends ask you. Back in Chapter 5, I told you that SLIP means *Serial Line Interface Protocol* without giving many technical details. Here come the details.

Step one: Collect the tools

Don't take any of the following steps as your introduction to the Internet. Instead, take one of the free introductory offers from a national online service (you know — those bagged copies of computer magazines in the supermarket that include an America Online disk). In the five to ten hours of connect time you get free, you can not only orient yourself, but you can also get the software and files that you need.

Go to the Macintosh software archives on the national service and get your own copies of InterSLIP, Fetch, TurboGopher, and Mosaic (most versions of Mosaic are now commercial but the original is still distributed as freeware). You might also want to collect the information files on MacTCP, too (MacTCP is part of System 7.5, so you either have to upgrade your system or buy this software from Apple). Check to make sure you're running your modem at its highest speed also, because these files take a while to download.

Step two: Call a SLIP provider

How do you find your own SLIP account provider? The service runs ads that have the word *SLIP* in them. Alternatively, find *Boardwatch Magazine* or *Online Access* and leaf through the ads; new players appear in this game almost weekly. A local version (different cities produce different editions) of the tabloid computer monthly *Microtimes* is another good place to look; you can find it free at newsstands in big cities. By the way, the same considerations apply to PPP accounts — it's just that more organizations started out with SLIP, so you'll still see it more commonly.

Expect a setup fee and monthly fees between $15 and $25, but it's also typical *not* to have a per-hour charge. In the conversation about getting an account, ask for the customer-support number. Call the number and ask the person you reach at customer support if he or she is familiar with MacTCP and InterSLIP. Some services do ten Mac setups a day, and some can't be bothered. You want one that will bother. And get a fax number because you'll need it in a bit.

Step three: Setting up

After you get MacTCP, you put it in the Control Panels folder of your System folder. InterSLIP has a Control Panel too, called InterSLIP Control, and it goes in your System folder, too. When you drag the icons for the MacTCP and InterSLIP Control panels to your System Folder icon, the system itself asks you whether you want to put these icons inside the Control Panels folder.

Now take this book to a photocopier and make copies of Figures 13-1, 13-2, 13-3, and 13-4.

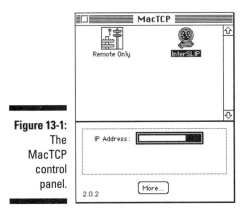

Figure 13-1:
The
MacTCP
control
panel.

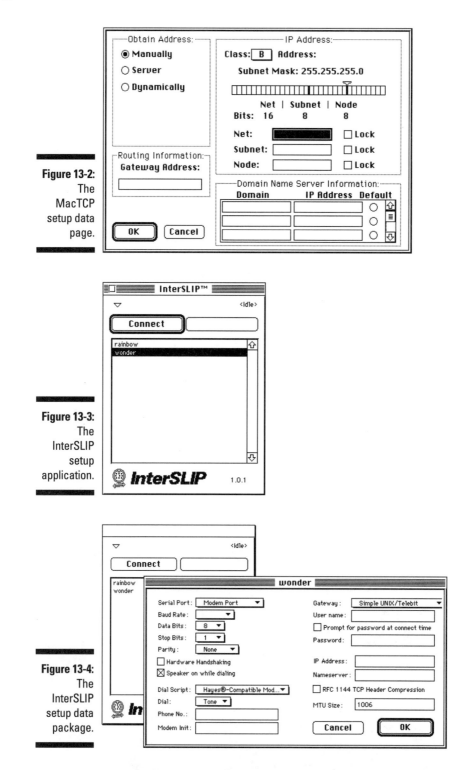

Figure 13-2:
The
MacTCP
setup data
page.

Figure 13-3:
The
InterSLIP
setup
application.

Figure 13-4:
The
InterSLIP
setup data
package.

I'm serious about this step. You should do the following tasks to save yourself and the customer support at the service untold agony:

1. **Fax these figures to customer support at the service.**

2. **Tell support to fill in the right numbers in the blank spaces.**

3. **Ask the support people to show you where to set the little slider for Subnet Mask setting in Figure 13-2.**

4. **Have the support people fax the whole set of figures back to you with this information marked.**

With this information, you'll be in great shape. I don't know why, but it's typical for Internet service providers to have their own forms, developed a few years ago, that are almost uniquely confusing. Insist that the service show you what to enter in these software screens. You're paying a setup charge to get a SLIP account, and any service worth having will be glad to consider this step as part of the setup.

Countdown before Launch

I want to make sure you're all checked out before you press the InterSLIP Connect button. Watch for the following points.

MacTCP

1. **Find Control Panels folder under the Apple menu and select it to open it.**

2. **Find the MacTCP icon and double-click on it.**

If your screen doesn't show an InterSLIP icon like the one in Figure 13-1, you haven't put the InterSLIP parts (Control Panel and Extension) in the right places. Fix this problem now (get the InterSLIP Control Panel in the Control Panels folder and the InterSLIP Extension into the Extensions folder) and then come back and type the IP Address.

More MacTCP

1. **Double-click on the More button in the MacTCP window.**

2. **Fill in the information the service gave you for Figure 13-2.**

3. **Make sure that you have the Obtain Address radio button set properly according to the fax from your service.**

4. **Move the Subnet Mask slider to the position the service recommended.**

5. **Fill in the Domain Name Server data at the lower-right of the window.**

6. **Pick the default.**

SLIP

You may have downloaded a version of SLIP that shows nothing in the scrolling list area in the InterSLIP window yet. To enter the information about your SLIP service provider, just pick New from the File menu and fill in a name in the dialog box. When you're done, click back to the window in Figure 13-3 and then double-click on your new file name. You get to a screen that looks like the one in Figure 13-4.

And more SLIP

In the Gateway option on the wonder window, choose Simple UNIX/Telebit because you're not a direct connection. In the Dial Script option, choose Hayes and pick your modem's speed. Every other bit of information should be on the fax of Figure 13-4 that you receive from the support people.

Launch!

When you have filled in every last scrap of data provided to you, double-click on the InterSLIP Setup icon (in the InterSLIP folder) to get to an InterSLIP window like the one in Figure 13-3. Click on the Connect button, and InterSLIP makes your connection.

Watch the top of the window. You see the message change from Idle, to Dialing, to Signing In, to Connected. Sometimes you'll see it pop back to Idle.

It's a good idea to check the Speaker on while dialing box in Figure 13-4 so that you can hear whether your dial-up number is busy or whether (as often happens) there just isn't a line. If you have problems for more than two days, call customer support. You'd be amazed at how often the service itself has made setup mistakes that it needs to fix (your password is wrong, for example).

The Big Payoff

I know this has been a tiresome section, but hey, if you think this is tiresome, you ought to try figuring out TCP/IP setups from scratch. I couldn't think of any other way to give you enough information to make this connection work. It was a slow news day on rec.humor.funny when I wrote this, too.

Your reward for being patient is that if you get a dial-up SLIP connection, you can use Fetch, TurboGopher, and Mosaic. There are other amazing Mac programs, and now that you can use Fetch, you can find them all in a few days, but these are worth mastering.

Fetch

You've seen the rest; now try the best. For FTP, at least, this is a reasonable statement about Fetch, the lovable mascot from Dartmouth. Fetch is the premiere Macintosh utility for Internet file retrieval.

When the message in the InterSLIP window says you're connected, double-click on the Fetch icon. The wonder-pooch leaps into action, and you see the equivalent of Figure 13-5. I've clicked the little black triangle next to Shortcuts in the Open Connection window, and this action lets me pick any of the top Mac sites.

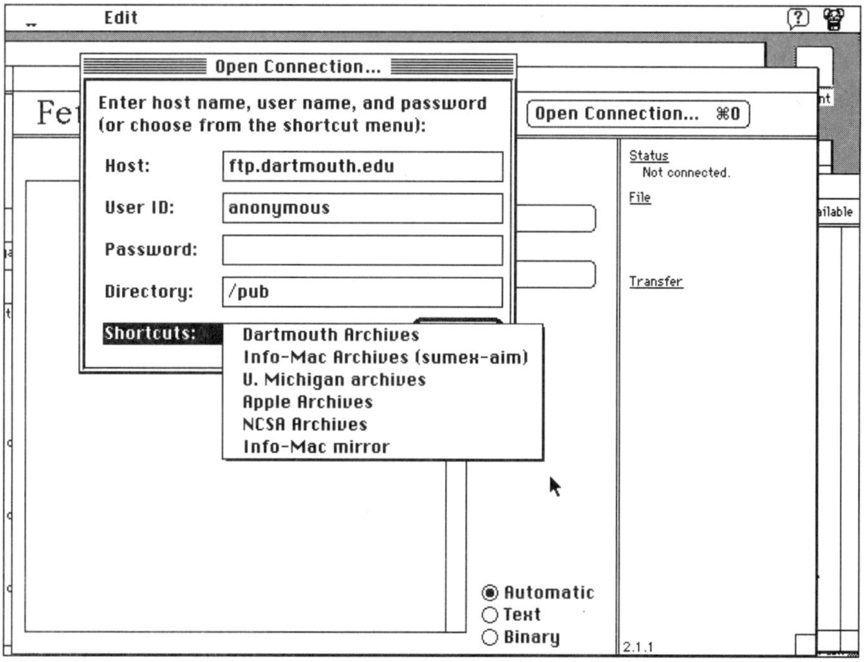

Figure 13-5:
You want
it; Fetch
gets it.

As a good citizen, you should fill in an assortment of Mac software collection sites (see "The Part of Tens" in this book for ten good examples) in the short-cuts. You can, of course, just type any site in the world you may want to visit anyway. Fetch logs you onto the site, and you can look through the available files just as if you were connected directly to a big hard drive. When you see a file you like, click the file to highlight it and click Fetch's Get button.

TurboGopher

Unless you get a commercial product called SLIPper ($95, Sysnet Corp., 800-683-5515), you can only run one of these programs at a time. Quit Fetch and double-click on TurboGopher. If you're calling at a nonpeak time, you'll usually find yourself connected to the Gopher server faster than you were connected to your service provider. That's because TurboGopher works with one computer direct-connecting to another over a fast network, instead of a modem connecting to a computer.

Good old TurboGopher. This animal has saved me from certain doom many times. The diligent creature has links to all the other Gophers in the world, so if you're looking simply to explore, this is an excellent place to start.

All you do is open these folders as if they were folders on your own Macintosh, and you can highlight files and tell Gopher to download them. The difference between Fetch and TurboGopher is that TurboGopher lets you search for files by title rather than having to page through the files yourself.

Mosaic and its brethren

You already know about Mosaic from way back in Chapter 6. What I want to tell you here is to watch out for new versions of Mosaic and other Web browsers. When you FTP to familiar sites, check the version numbers of the available types of browsers against your own.

Software advances in compression (and design advances in the balance of screen-structure-stored-on-your-computer vs. structure-sent-over-the-wire) will result in much faster Web browsers for SLIP modem connections. The Macintosh version (2.0) of Mosaic introduced back in summer 1994 was a revolution in its day, but new versions that don't assume you have a fiber-optic line to a supercomputer are going to revolutionize Mosaic itself for individuals.

WARNING!

What about e-mail?

A dial-up SLIP account can, in principle, be used for e-mail. In the software libraries of the national online services, you can find early versions of Eudora (now a commercial program) and LeeMail, a very nice shareware program.

A dial-up SLIP account has a problem in the way it gets to e-mail, however. You are now your own Internet address (a number). If you're not connected, your mailbox is not available. Some service providers have a mail-forwarding plan

worked out, in which they take your mail on a big computer that is connected 24 hours each day and then notify you when you dial up with your SLIP connection. Other providers don't provide this service. The convenience of e-mail on a big system is one reason the national online services are so popular. I get mail at America Online but I use a direct connection at PSINet when I have to do lots of Web surfing. This combination lets me pick the best way to accomplish any given online task.

Being Cool

A dial-up SLIP account will probably cost you more than an account at a national online service. But SLIP gives you direct access to some of the best Mac software available, so if you're serious about the Internet, it's worth the trouble and expense.

Alternatives to traditional SLIP that will let you run Mosaic over a shell account have recently started to appear. These alternatives assign a sort of "dynamic dummy" Internet numerical address when you sign on, so you don't have a four-part-number address of your own, and installation is simplified for the service provider.

One program called TIA (The Internet Adapter, from `tiasales@marketplace.com`) has been accepted by some service providers, although there are complaints about slowness compared to stock SLIP. Nonetheless, some services (Pipeline, for example) have been successful at running TIA connections to the Web for their users.

A "Package Deal"

An easier way to make a direct connection is through one of the bundled deals now provided by Internet network service providers. My favorite so far is Internet Valet from Software Ventures (510-644-3232). I have read every piece of feedback from the first edition of this book (IDG forwards your comments to the authors) and I can tell you that I greatly value software that works the first time without much fuss. Internet Valet works.

You get a newsgroup reader, an enhanced version of Mosaic, Eudora for e-mail and an e-mail account, our old pals Fetch and TurboGopher, a slick version of telnet, and MacTCP and MacPPP. What the program has to recommend it, however, is that you can get fired up and online without configuring the TCP or PPP sections yourself. At installation, you are responsible for knowing your own name and credit card number. That's about it.

Once you complete the registration, a process that takes about ten minues, you can double-click the Internet Valet icon, and you get the little toolbar palette shown in Figure 13-6. Double-click the icon on the far left, and you get the PPP connection (see Figure 13-7) window (don't worry about settings — they were established back during registration). Once the little PPP faces go "happy," meaning that a connection is established, you can click any other icon on the palette to start up that form of Internet service.

Figure 13-6:
Buttoning up
the Internet
with Internet
Valet.

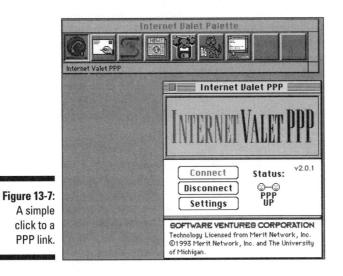

Figure 13-7:
A simple
click to a
PPP link.

The advantages of this kind of Internet connection over, say, America Online, show up in the Web browser and newsgroup access. The Web browser (see Figure 13-8) is a customized version of Spyglass Mosaic, and it's simply faster and richer in features than the basic browsers AOL and eWorld licensed from InterCon (now a division of PSI itself, ironically enough). With respect to newsgroups, you get a decent facility for managing them, but direct access to all. If you look at Figure 13-9 and gaze down the list, you will be allowed to marvel at its completeness. You will have a hard time finding some of these newsgroups on a national online service. And my own blushing modesty causes me to present you with this almost-harmless list — if I were to scroll down a bit, I would have a screen shot containing newsgroup titles that IDG almost certainly would not be willing to print.

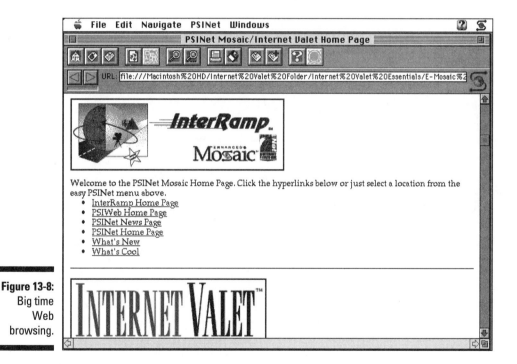

Figure 13-8:
Big time
Web
browsing.

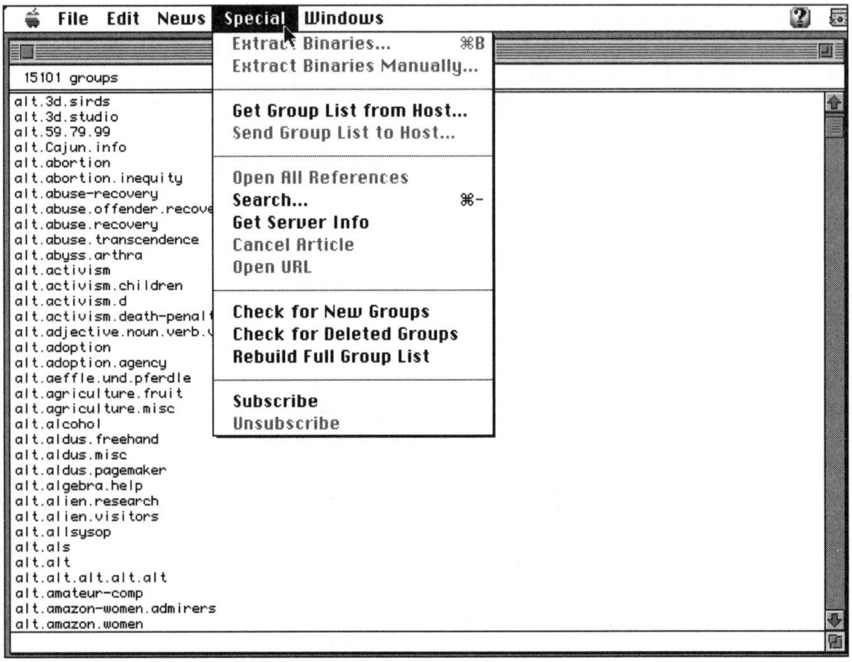

Figure 13-9:
All the newsgroups, and I do mean all.

Apple Gets into the Act, Finally

Sometime in late 1994, Apple, a company with the finest products and the most bone-headed marketing staff in the world (these are the people who ordered about half as many PowerPC chips as they needed to keep up with worldwide demand) could have set up convenient Internet access for all Macs. In fact, it would have been a lot easier to implement Internet access than to implement PowerTalk, a system facility that even now is barely used.

Instead, Apple spent a critical year-and-a-half giving away the Internet to everyone else, and only the fierce determination of Mac users to be cool ahead of everyone else prevailed. Macs are in fact about 25 to 30 percent of all Internet clients, amazingly enough, and no thanks to Apple. But Apple has now cobbled together a software collection like Internet Valet, with a quick-registration scheme with a choice of service providers. Presumably, if you buy a Performa at an electronics discounter some time in early 1996, this Apple Internet Connection Kit will be bundled as part of the deal.

At least you get a decent bundle of stuff. The list is as follows:

- Apple Internet Dialer, online Internet service registration and connection software
- Netscape Navigator
- Apple Guide
- Claris Emailer Lite
- Fetch and Anarchie
- Aladdin Stuffit Expander
- NewsWatcher
- NCSA Telnet
- QuickTime VR Movie Player
- Adobe Acrobat Reader
- RealAudio Player

The only thing missing is TurboGopher, which you don't need, as Gopher services are built into Netscape. A very nice touch is the inclusion of Claris Emailer Lite. If you get e-mail at more than one service, Emailer will collect all your e-mail from all sources and present it to you in one convenient lump. One can only wish, as a Mac loyalist, that Apple succeeds in this venture. But, given that nearly every piece of this package has been available for more than a year, one can only wonder what time-warp the folks in Cupertino inhabit.

Netscape

Another argument for direct connection rather than online service connection is that you get to use Netscape as a browser — it's the browser in Apple's package. The Netscape people started out at NCSA and then went on to take over a large chunk of Web activity. The key feature of Netscape (see Figure 13-10) is no single feature at all, but rather the assurance that Netscape will always have more functions than any other browser. It's very common to come across Web sites that depend on the latest features of Netscape, so you can't see graphics or tables or some other aspect of the site if you don't have the latest version of Netscape Navigator (2.0 at least, by early 1996). With an Internet connection and Netscape, you can manage e-mail, read newgroups, conduct searches of FTP sites, and cruise through Gopherspace (see Figure 13-11). Because Netscape Corporation went public and has all the financial resources imaginable, you can confidently look to Netscape to be the only *necessary* software in the near future of the Web.

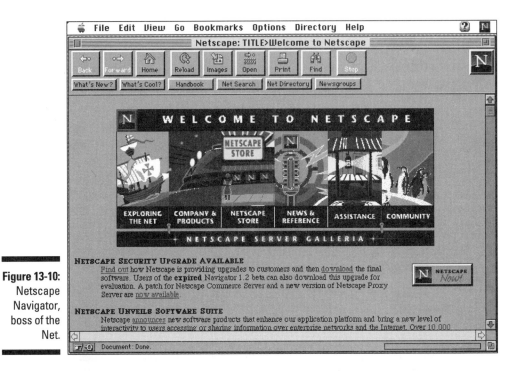

Figure 13-10:
Netscape
Navigator,
boss of the
Net.

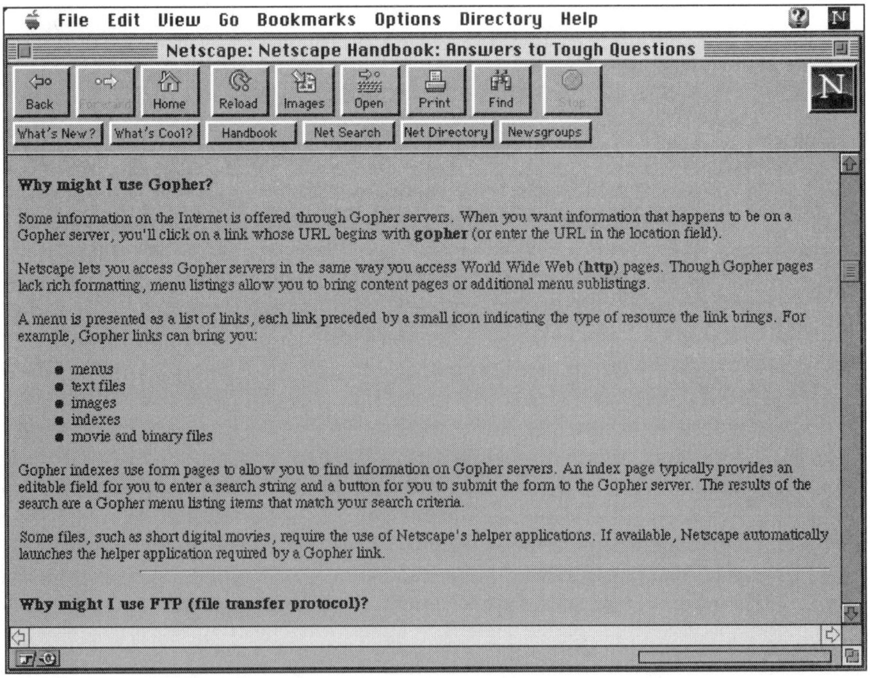

Figure 13-11:
All Net
functions
will be
swept into
Netscape's
package.

Chapter 14

You Mean Business

The Party Has Started

As late as March 1994, large parts of the Internet were a sort of electronic party for computer graduate students. I used to give Internet talks where business topics were handled in the question session at the end! Then I had to add a twenty-minute section on business, and now weekend seminars on Internet business would be the appropriate forum. Whether there's gold out there or not, the Gold Rush is definitely happening.

As a word of advice from Northern California, home of the original American Gold Rush, think about this: Levi Strauss is still making money and no one knows what happened to the fortunes of even the most successful 49ers. I don't know about you, but when I read that eggs sold for a dollar a piece in Sacramento in 1850, it makes me think about owning chickens instead of buying a pick and shovel. There may be more money to be made *assisting* the Web revolution than leading it.

Getting Webbed

It's not much trouble making up a page, even if you don't know HTML. If you make up a text-plus-pictures document about your business in ClarisWorks 4.0 or WordPerfect 3.5, you can convert it to an HTML document. Microsoft Word 6.01 for the Macintosh will similarly generate Web pages automatically by early 1996. You still have to put in links for e-mail, and you will probably have to learn a bit about HTML forms, but picking up this knowledge isn't difficult, and there are dozens of firms near you just dying to help you in this endeavor (just pick up your regional version of *MicroTimes* or *Computer Currents*). If you are inclined to do the groundwork yourself (and it can't hurt to experiment a bit even if you are ultimately going to hire a consulting firm), you can order a whole do-a-Mac-Web-site package from StarNine at `http://www.starnine.com` (see Figure 14-1).

Once you have anything worth looking at, there are several kinds of Web-page services to consult. Global Entrepreneurs Network (`http://www.entrepreneurs.net/info/dom-reg1.htm`), for example, will get your site registered as an official Internet name (see Figure 14-2), managing the registration process and passing on the standard (since late 1995) fees with a small surcharge.

But lots of large private organizations want to help you find your place on the World Wide Web. One of the largest is MCI (at `http://www.internetmci.com/marketplace/`), which has been snapping up Internet-related businesses (see Figure 14-3) to complete different pieces of the Web puzzle. You can click your way through this site to a number of e-mail addresses where helpful MCI staffers will guide you onto the Web if you don't know HTML from a hot stove (see Figure 14-4).

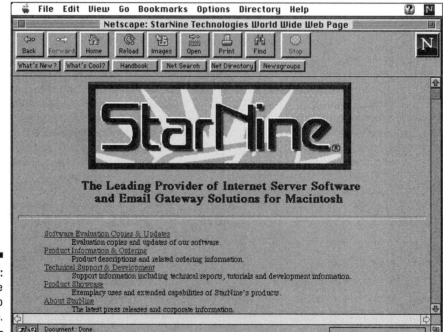

Figure 14-1:
StarNine
wants to
help.

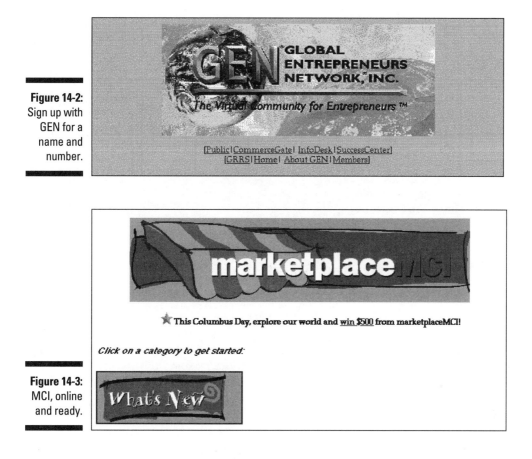

Figure 14-2:
Sign up with
GEN for a
name and
number.

Figure 14-3:
MCI, online
and ready.

If you want to hire a combination service provider who will design a Web site
for you, and post it, and provide you with traffic statistics on "hits" and so forth,
I must tell you that 10 to 20 new firms enter this busy arena every week. Here's
what to do after you finish this chapter: Go to the URL www.yahoo.com with
your Web browser and search on

```
business Internet (name of your state)
```

The Yahoo search function automatically links these terms with a logical AND.
What you will get, as a starting point in putting your business on the Web, is a
list of Web service providers in your state. Call them all up and have a little
chat. Services that used to cost $200/hr for a discussion and $1000 per month
to post your site have recently gone to $75/hr and $50 per month for a site.
From a business standpoint, you don't need to be in a do-it-this-week hurry to
get on the Web, to tell you the truth.

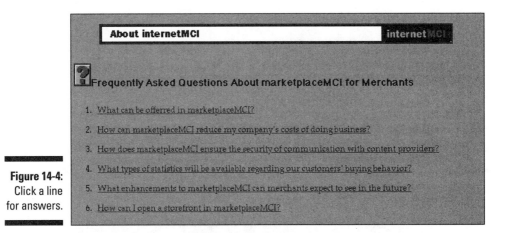

Figure 14-4:
Click a line
for answers.

A Bit of Hardware Info

Sticking an old Quadra on a phone line as a Web server is a relatively straight-forward matter. Getting a company LAN (local area network) properly connected to the Internet is another issue altogether. I hope that you have a net administrator to handle the details of this operation for you (presumably your business is paying someone a generous salary for this function, if you have a big collection of Macs, or, more challenging yet, a mixed-platform network). If you are obliged to find someone to tell you how to connect an in-house network to the Web, you might want to try the merry crew at `http://www.tic.net/` (see Figure 14-5).

In the first edition of this book, I listed hardware connection sources directly, but the feedback collected by IDG from the cards in the back of the book suggests to me that it's a pretty daunting experience to debug Routers and Bridges and Gateways (oh, my!, as Dorothy would say on her way to Net-Oz) yourself. Just so you can keep up with the jargon the consultants are going to sling around, you might want to consult the "NetBits" sidebar, but generally linking your net to the Internet is a kids!-don't-try-this-at-home situation, where a judicious expenditure on outside help is appropriate.

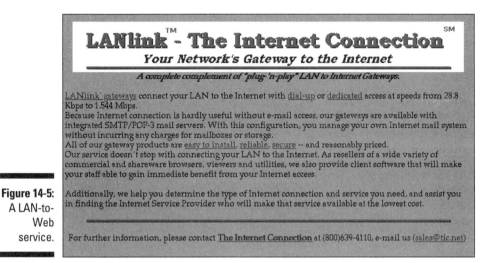

Figure 14-5:
A LAN-to-
Web
service.

Getting Noticed

Having gone through the agony of working on a Web-site index book, something like a Yellow Pages but more coherent (IDG's *Yahoo! Unplugged*), I can tell you that there's no problem getting a site. Doing the index on specific areas (mail-order vitamin vendors, for example), I would return to the topic two days later and find that the number of sites had doubled. So please understand that getting a site isn't the big challenge.

NetBits

This is just a little digression on terminology. If you have to discuss Mac Internet possibilities with the higher-ups at work, you don't want to sound like a dummy.

A *gateway* lets you connect two different kinds of network. The typical Macintosh network runs along rules specified by the AppleTalk standard, and the Internet uses, appropriately, Internet protocol (IP). You need software to translate messages designed for one network into messages that can be read properly by the other network. That's a gateway.

A *bridge* is typically hardware and software that connects two local networks of the same

kind. You might have two different AppleTalk networks in different parts of a building or in different departments. If you want the two networks to look like one big network to users, you have to buy a bridge, usually from the company that sold you the two networks.

A *router*, for Internet purposes, sends IP messages from one Internet network host to another. Most commercial routers also know how to translate messages coming from other kinds (non-IP) of networks. There are zillions of tricks involved in making routers efficient, and if you're reading this sidebar, it's somebody else's job to learn them.

THE BIG CHALLENGE ON THE WEB IS GETTING NOTICED.

Think for a moment what it means that the number of commercial sites on the Web is doubling every five months. It means that several hundred thousand other eager firms got themselves posted in roughly the same time interval as you did, if you only recently joined the group. How do you make sure that people actually find you? Just getting posted would be like telling someone to find you at Woodstock with the instructions, "Uh, I'll be the guy in a T-shirt."

Well, for every problem on the Web, someone will offer a solution in two clock ticks of a RISC processor, and services have appeared that will help you get the word out about yourself. One of the simplest ways to get noticed is to sign up for the Yahoo service called WebLaunch (see Figure 14-6). For a fee ($750 in late 1995), Yahoo will billboard your site at the busiest crossroads on the Web for a week and then give you a high-profile place in the Yahoo Web index.

If people can't find you after this treatment, it means they don't want to know about you, as hundreds of thousands of people per day will nearly be forced to recognize your home-page URL. Another Web-publicity service called AAA Internet Promotions (`http://www.west.net/~solution/`) makes sure that your site is available through the large (more than 50) collection of indexes currently available on the Web (see Figure 14-7), so that if someone looks for your custom doll-clothes manufacturing business, they'll find it on any plausible combination of keywords.

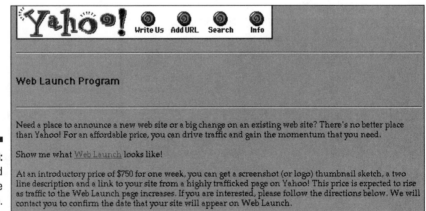

Figure 14-6:
Billboard
your site
on Yahoo.

Figure 14-7:
Get yourself
indexed all
over.

One of the most important parts of running a Web site is to make sure that people can find you. You want to be sure that you are reaching your total potential audience or target market. It really doesn't matter how great your page is or how many people are interested in the subject matter, if no one can find it.

Making It Work

Technically, it's not much of a challenge getting some sort of Web page together and having it posted somewhere online. At this point, dozens of firms stand ready to help you with network connections, server support, and page design. Just to make the design point vivid, one service vendor called Right Angle Design at `http://www.rightangle.com` (see Figure 14-8) shows before-and-after Web pages to illustrate its prowess in visuals (see Figure 14-9).

Figure 14-8:
Like this
page?

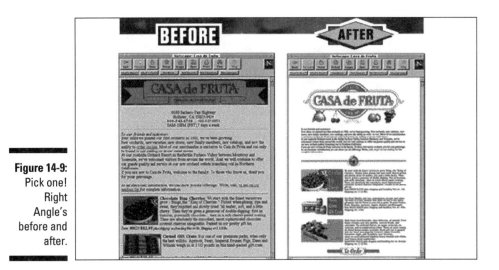

Figure 14-9:
Pick one!
Right
Angle's
before and
after.

What the service vendors can't do, necessarily, is tell you what to say in the text blocks on your page to make something happen (an order for your products, for example). For the best advice that there has ever been on this exact topic, I'm going to refer you to three books, written well before the development of the World Wide Web. As it happens, I have done tons of advertising copywriting, with record-breaking response rates for both direct mail and magazine print ads, simply by slavishly following the advice in these books.

The first book is David Ogilvy's *On Advertising* (Vintage Books, 1985). The reason Ogilvy's book is worth reading is that it's based on several decades of research, rather than an opinion about last-year's-fad-that-worked. The issue clearly highlighted by Ogilvy is "How do you keep someone's attention long enough to get your message across?" I should also tell you that Ogilvy's book is about a hundred times more entertaining reading than any of the dozens or so "Make Money with a Hot Web Page" books currently cluttering the shelves at a mall near you.

If you read Ogilvy, you will notice that practically every third page or so he acknowledges his debt to Claude Hopkins and his books *My Life in Advertising* and *Scientific Advertising* (NTC Business Books, 1993). These works were actually written in the 1920s by the man generally acknowledged as the all-time advertising copy-writing champion. You might imagine that a book from the Roaring '20s wouldn't have much to say to the Internet generation. But human nature has not changed much (it hasn't had enough time, genetically), and coffeehouse Gen-X hipsters turn out to have hopes, dreams, and insecurities remarkably similar to those of the wild youth after World War I (or World War II, or World War III), and playing to these emotions (along with a hard-hitting emphasis on product benefits) is by all accounts what actually sells products.

Finally, NTC Business Books puts out another slender volume that will allow you to determine whether you have a reasonable judgement of ad effectiveness before sinking your ad funds into the Web. It's called *Which Ad Pulled Best?* (by Philip Burton and Scott Purvis, and updated almost yearly) and consists of 50 matched ads that, to the untrained eye, look fairly similar. But in each pair, one ad was a whopping success and the other one was a dud. The authors carefully point out the key features responsible for the difference in response. The people who manage Web index sites (Yahoo, for example) have done enough research to show that some business Web home pages can get 20,000 to 25,000 hits per day with no sales at all, while some other pages with the same hit rate get hundreds of sales.

All the principles underlying this difference were thoroughly understood decades ago, and you can find them out in the work of Drs. Burton and Purvis. Steal a march on your competitors — while they're all reading the latest dorky book on the Web, you can read this trio of classics and find out how to make your own Web page bring in results!

A Natural Marketing Area

The Internet business scene is changing every few weeks as new vendors try to stake out claims in the Great Online Gold Rush of the late '90s, but a few principles have become clear already. The first principle is that people are reasonably willing to order from a Web page things that they are used to ordering by phone anyway. The site for 1-800-FLOWERS is a prime example, being a rip-snorting success, even to the point of offering consulting services for online businesses. The second principle is that residents of the Web are by definition in the vanguard of computer users. That means that computer hardware and software are going to sell better than, say, garden supplies.

Software in particular is a natural, because

- ✔ You already know the products. You can read a review of Microsoft Excel 5, and if you're using version 4.1, you can decide if you would like to upgrade. The vendor doesn't have a big selling job to do.

- ✔ If you find yourself looking at a Mosaic screen for Internet Shopping Network, you're among Web pioneers and are likely the kind of person who does buy upgrades.

- ✔ Software purchasing is pretty straightforward. There aren't different sizes or colors. An Internet shopping service can give you the same level of service as a paper catalog, only faster.

Taking advantage of this knowledge, of course, there's a service called SoftSell at http://www.softsell.com (see Figure 14-10), specifically set up to help you market your software on the Internet. Makes sense, doesn't it?

Marketing your own product on the Web, whether it's a natural like software or not, is clearly an evolving art. One thing you might want to do is assemble a special hotlist of twenty sites or so that you feel did an impressive job of selling to *you*. If you go check them a few months later and they are still there and unchanged, you may have found yourself some models for your own Web pages.

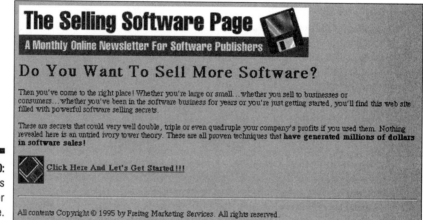

Figure 14-10:
Selling 1s
and 0s over
a wire.

Chapter 15

The Web Means Business

S o the great Internet Web stampede is well underway, and it's hard to name a large business without a Web site. Every week, if you like, you can look for the Web index in Business Week, listing the Web sites of all the advertisers. That's why, when I talk about business, I will generally mean business on the Web, since I assume that you have e-mail and other more pedestrian Internet uses well under control. All through 1996, you should be able to overhear conversations about the fabulous business opportunities on the Web. Keep in mind that, although it may be possible to make a breakthrough of your own, all the same big companies that owned most of the economy when you woke up this morning are crowding onto the Web as fast as anyone, and the nature of the opportunities is not necessarily clear.

Connections Everywhere

When I agreed to do the first version book in 1994, the generally accepted figure was that there were fewer than 100 URL addresses on the World Wide Web. As I finish the second edition in October 1995, I've seen quotes from 100,000 to 300,000 *business* sites alone, not to mention the millions of colorful individual home pages. It also turns out to be the case that the Mac is a big presence on the Web — somewhere between 25 and 30 percent of Web traffic originates on Macs. One reason is that, despite Apple's original flailing around and near-hopeless marketing, the Mac as a system is easier to set up as a Web client or server than any other hardware platform. And Apple now wants to help.

Apple and the Web

If you haven't done so by now, you should visit Apple's Web site (see Figure 15-1) at www.apple.com. The reason you should visit the site is that, under products and services, you can find all the software you need to set up your business as a Web site. You can collect the elements elsewhere a piece at a time, but Apple has collected either the software or links to the software in one place. It also used to be the case that a book like this would need a directory of Mac shareware sites (there's one in the back anyway). But if you follow the links at this Apple site, you'll find every Mac archive of any importance. Seems like the least they could do, actually.

Figure 15-1:
One call to
Apple gets it
done.

A Web solution for the rest of us

Now, cozy as things are at Apple, you still have to have some technical savvy to roll your own business Web site using standard HTML software and Apple hardware for a server setup. You may want to make your life easier, and for that matter, do the job a little cheaper. Because thousands of organizations have the same desire, other organizations have sprung up to service that wish. One of the easiest paths to Web site creation is through Navisoft (see Figure 15-2), a company owned by America Online. Navisoft lets you download free software for creating a Web page (www.navisoft.com) and post the Web page for a free trial. (You get to pick your own individual or business name, too.)

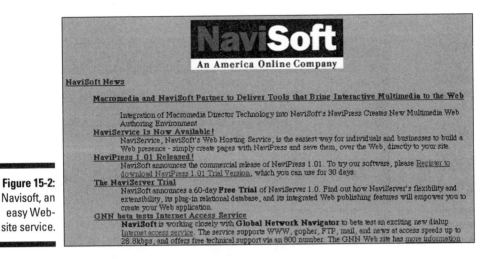

NaviSoft
An America Online Company

NaviSoft News

Macromedia and NaviSoft Partner to Deliver Tools that Bring Interactive Multimedia to the Web

Integration of Macromedia Director Technology into NaviSoft's NaviPress Creates New Multimedia Web Authoring Environment
NaviService Is Now Available!
NaviService, NaviSoft's Web Hosting Service, is the easiest way for individuals and businesses to build a Web presence - simply create pages with NaviPress and save them, over the Web, directly to your site.
NaviPress 1.01 Released!
NaviSoft announces the commercial release of NaviPress 1.01. To try our software, please Register to download NaviPress 1.01 Trial Version, which you can use for 30 days.
The NaviServer Trial
NaviSoft announces a 60-day Free Trial of NaviServer 1.0. Find out how NaviServer's flexibility and extensibility, its plug-in relational database, and its integrated Web publishing features will empower you to create your Web application.
GNN beta tests Internet Access Service
NaviSoft is working closely with Global Network Navigator to beta test an exciting new dialup Internet access service. The service supports WWW, gopher, FTP, mail, and news at access speeds up to 28.8kbps, and offers free technical support via an 800 number. The GNN Web site has more information

Figure 15-2:
Navisoft, an
easy Web-
site service.

If you like your handiwork and are getting an interesting number of hits, you can choose individual, business, or dedicated (hardware is reserved just for you) service, at a range of monthly payments that range from less than twenty dollars per month for individuals up to hundreds of dollars per month for serious business service. If your organization doesn't already have a network staff that knows how to keep servers and routers and gateways humming, Navisoft may be what you need.

If you want a little more organization and business guidance, another easy-access route to the world of Web sites is found at www.industry.net (see Figure 15-3). This service is a set of storefronts and businesses that offers a free temporary membership so that you can see what it offers, and it offers a lot (see Figure 15-4). One of the advantages of this service is that it has a considerable body of experience in what works and what doesn't work on the Web. Let's face it: The most experience *anyone* can have on the Web is a few years — so every little bit helps.

Big Time Web Stuff

As examples of unbridled enthusiasm (hmm, what would *bridled* enthusiasm be?) for the Web, I'd like to review some Web sites of large businesses. One reason you might want to inspect these is that you can glean some idea of what a professionally-designed Web site looks like before putting your own material on the Web. Also, this little survey is intended to convince you that essentially every major business worldwide put itself on the Web by late 1995.

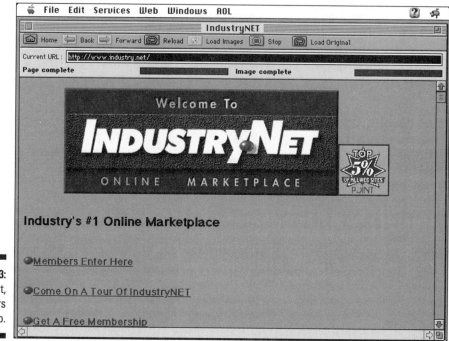

Figure 15-3:
Industry.net,
old-timers
on the Web.

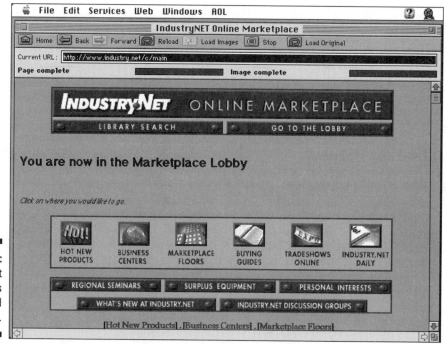

Figure 15-4:
Industry.net
and its
myriad
offerings.

Wires

After all, they *are* they are the phone company, even dismantled and deregu-
lated. AT&T would very much like to use Internet services (see Figure 15-5) as a
way to re-establish the communications dominance it once had. Remarkably,
for an organization that was once perceived as technologically remote and
somewhat hostile, these people offer the absolute friendliest Web site gimmick
in the world (see Figure 15-6). You don't even have to know anything about Web
protocol — you just send documents, as word processor material or even as
paper (!) to the AT&T free trial offer and the AT&T staff (`http:/www.att.com/
gems/samples.html`) will translate it into a Web page, post it, and send you
an e-mail telling you where to look for it. At this rate, people's pets will have
their own home pages, and it's pretty much a given that Ms. Trimble's third
grade class in Winnebago Elementary in Kenosha will be on the Web, with a
clickable class picture.

Figure 15-5:
The Phone
Company
becomes
The Web
Company.

Similarly, IBM at `http://www.ibm.com` (see Figure 15-7) would like your
business. It's something of an odd spectacle, watching all sorts of proud, old,
giant American businesses scrambling all over each other for your low-rent Web
business (wait and see: I predict you will be able to get a Web page posted
through Prodigy at any Sears store in two years), but there's nothing like a
clean-slate growth industry to get the marketing boys at the head office salivating. IBM's site seems to be organized for the benefit of its gigantic internal
machinery for the manufacture of press releases rather than for pumping up
sales, but that's been a characteristic problem at IBM for more than a decade.

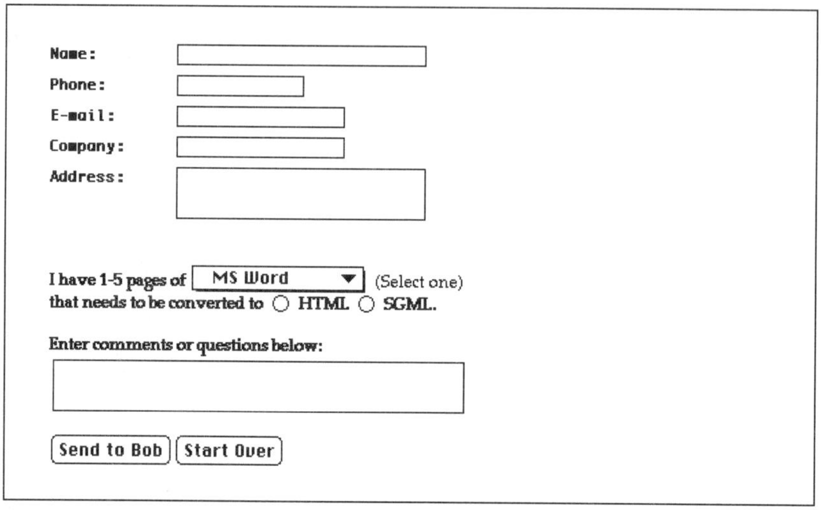

Name:

Phone:

E-mail:

Company:

Address:

I have 1-5 pages of [MS Word ▼] (Select one)
that needs to be converted to ○ HTML ○ SGML.

Enter comments or questions below:

[Send to Bob] [Start Over]

Figure 15-6:
The Web:
no money or
brains
required.

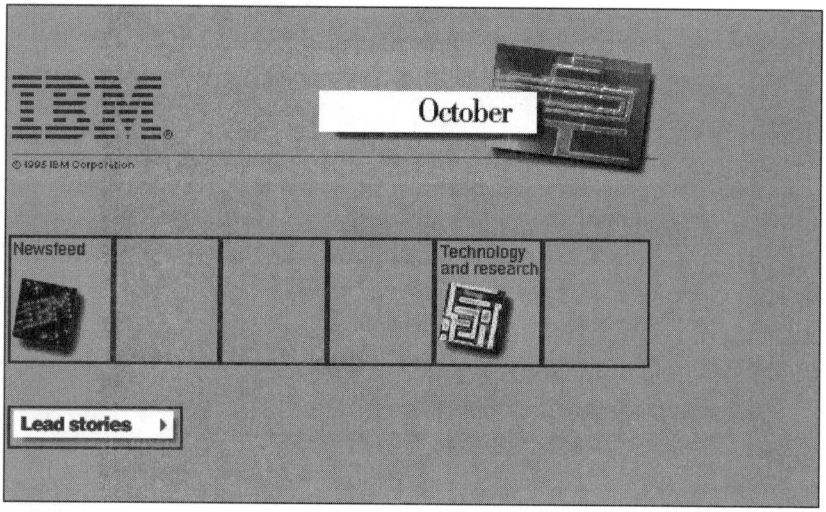

IBM®

© 1995 IBM Corporation

October

Newsfeed

Technology
and research

[Lead stories ▶]

Figure 15-7:
Even IBM
gets the
Web wake-
up call.

Stuff

AT&T is a natural Web resident, as are IBM, Apple, Compaq, MCI, Cisco, U.S. Robotics, or any company that does computers, modems, network hardware, or networking services. What's somewhat more remarkable is that businesses with non-computer products have flooded onto the Web in ways that may show how business will be organized in the near future. That's right, companies that actually make *real* stuff are here too! 3M, for example, (www.mmm.com), has put an agglomeration of material on the Web that amounts to a virtual version of the company, as shown in Figure 15-8. All the organization charts, all the press releases, all the regional offices, and all the *products* (and 3M has a huge product line) are up there on the Web site. One of my favorite substances in the world is epoxy resin for use in electronics, so I searched the product directory on "epoxy AND resin", and sure enough, there are 3M's top-notch offerings in this department, waiting for your order (see Figure 15-9).

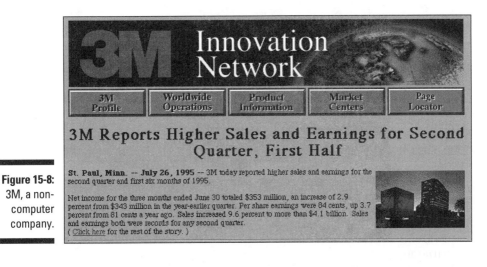

Figure 15-8:
3M, a non-
computer
company.

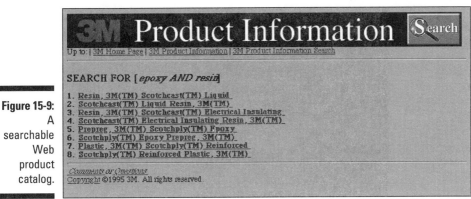

Figure 15-9:
A
searchable
Web
product
catalog.

If you are involved in product design, the idea of a single-source, computer-directed search over a whole range of products is tremendously exciting. The only possible cause for concern is that anyone, anywhere, from Bangkok to Bangor, now has the same access to design-critical information that you have.

Another American giant, Eli Lilly, has posted a Web site (http://www.lilly.com) that contains lots of press releases, product information, research data, elaborate legal disclaimers, and bits of medical advice (see Figure 15-10).

Because Lilly is a drug company, there's not much prospect of direct sales over the Web (all their big-money products are, naturally, prescription-only), but this site is interesting as a sort of online "second opinion" about pharmaceuticals. The Web sites of drug companies tend to have, probably for legal reasons, more information about side effects than you are likely to hear from a prescribing physician. The day is not far away when some Web site will offer computer-aided diagnosis of diseases based on entry of symptom keywords — systems that can do this already exist at medical schools, with diagnostic accuracy comparable to that of real clinicians.

Besides businesses that make stuff, there are businesses that move stuff around and businesses concerned with stuff that doesn't move at all. A good example of the former is shipping, and of course the main example of the latter is real estate.

At the UPS Web site (`http://www.ups.com`), you have as much information (see Figure 15-11) at your fingertips as a controller getting data from the famous fleet of brown trucks (have you ever noticed that you can't tell who makes the trucks?). Like FedEx, UPS lets you track parcels through the system if you have the parcel ID, or arrange for pickup, or set up a UPS service arrangement just from the Web site. Now that the information-handling capabilities of packages have been put on an equal footing, it will be interesting to see whether mergers naturally occur (maybe FedEx and UPS would be more efficient as a combo) or whether it's economically efficient to have smaller, regional companies with package-transfer agreements.

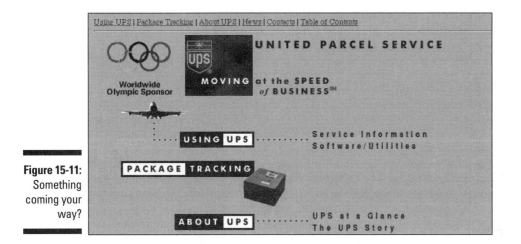

Using UPS | Package Tracking | About UPS | News | Contacts | Table of Contents

UNITED PARCEL SERVICE

Worldwide Olympic Sponsor

MOVING at the **SPEED** of **BUSINESS**SM

USING UPS · · · · · · · · · · Service Information
Software/Utilities

PACKAGE TRACKING

ABOUT UPS · · · · · · · · · UPS at a Glance
The UPS Story

Figure 15-11:
Something
coming your
way?

Real estate on the Web is an even larger business puzzle. For years, realtors' associations have cobbled together listings services, and multiple-listing services are the subject not only of technological transformation but of ferocious turf battles. With the advent of the Web, lots of previous decisions about who-gets-listed-where are simply washed away in the tide — the Web is immensely superior to any of the laboriously-constructed services strung together over the last few decades. Horror of horrors, some complete idiot can also post a color picture of his house with a description *all by himself*. It's not clear how the real estate profession will bring this phenomenon under control (trust me, they will), but since I wrote this chapter on a rainy Thursday afternoon in Northern California, I though I would give you a look (see Figure 15-12) at a timeshare in the Bahamas (`http://www.tiac.net/users/oline/ gazette/timesh.html`) as an example of this aspect of Web business. Hey, you can even check a Web weather map to see if the building is still there after hurricane season.

Money

Quick, how much money do you have right now? I mean, how much money in terms of paper currency and coins? Probably, unless you have some special reason (you trade unregistered guns out of a van in Calexico, for example), a tiny fraction of your net monetary worth is tangible. The rest is magnetic, in the form of bank records, merrily formed by electrons racing to and fro. And thus it is that investments are a rapidly growing area of business on the Web.

FOR SALE:

Nassau in the Bahamas:

Westwind II Timeshare *Red Week (Week 24, third week of June)*

All amenities, located on desirable **Cable Beach**. Short drive to downtown Nassau. Area boasts a variety of restaurants, night-life, including Carnival's Crystal Palace and Casino and numerous outdoor sports. On site, enjoy 2 outdoor pools, tennis court and poolside snack bar. **Market Value $13,000.00**. Will let it go for **$6500.00!**

Call 203-239-6581 after 6pm EST.

Figure 15-12:
Real estate
on the Web:
next door or
far away.

Surprisingly — well, it came as a surprise to the banks — online banking *per se* has been stubbornly resisted for more than a decade. Online banking faces several obstacles:

✔ The bank wants you to turn your computer into an ATM, and then charge you a hefty monthly fee for helping the bank with this convenience.

✔ Your disk drive slot cannot be readily modified to spit out $20 bills.

✔ The bankers of America somehow believe that you lie awake at night worrying about paying all your bills the day the bills arrive. For many people, this is simply not true. But somehow, it's a lesson that bank marketing VPs, whose $20,000 per month salaries are deposited automatically in overdraft-protected accounts, seem to have a hard time absorbing. Perhaps their world is not your world.

Paying bills may not be a screaming priority, but if you are a little bit ahead of the game, getting timely investment information might be. To this end, not only does every major brokerage house and mutual fund packager (for example, Fidelity at `http://www.fid-inv.com/index.html` — see Figure 15-13) have a Web site, but the raw data of the investment world, the info required by the Securities and Exchange Commission for listing stocks, is now automatically posted to a government-sponsored Web page at `http://www.sec.gov/edgarhp.htm` (see Figure 15-14). The smallest investor in the market now has instant access to the same public-access data as a fund manager, which is ultimately going to make insider trading more difficult to conceal.

Figure 15-13:
Fidelity on
the Web.

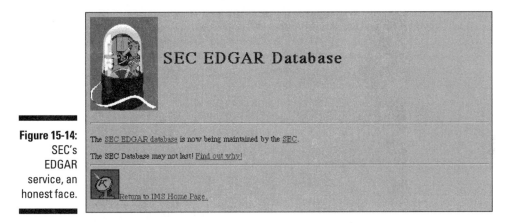

Figure 15-14:
SEC's
EDGAR
service, an
honest face.

The Web, Education, and Nonprofits

After all this talk about business, I'll tell you about the biggest single bright spot in the Internet's future: education. Ten years ago, I was involved in a noble effort to provide college-credit classes over a dial-up network. It was great fun and a worthwhile service — I ran a statistics class, sending out lessons, correcting homework, and designing an online final exam.

The system design had one problem, however. With the 300-bps modems of 1985, the service lost about a nickel in connect charges on every homework assignment. In the classic business joke, I guess we made it up on volume!

These days, when half the students at large universities skip the lectures and buy class notes from professional note-taking services anyway, the fundamental idea of remote classes looks better than ever. With a 28.8k-bps modem, you can even do so at a profit. Thus, I bring excellent news to everyone who took a job right after high school, every lab technician who's supposed to take classes every few years to stay certified, every real-estate agent who wants to become a mortgage broker, and every laid-off middle-aged engineer who now needs a quick skill-set overhaul. Help is on the way! The same universities that founded the Internet in the first place finally have found a convenient way to deliver their services to *you.* For anyone willing to crack the electronic books, great opportunities lie ahead. Get yourself an extension catalog from the college closest to you and see how much course work can now be delivered on the Web.

In fact, one of America's most progressive institutions, the New School for Social Research in New York (despite the name, it's a full function, general-purpose college), has started an Internet-based degree program using Web pages and e-mail as classrooms. Further validating the concept of university involvement in Web pitches, Harvard Business School (`http:www.hbs.harvard.edu/`) has set up a site (see Figure 15-15) that leads, through a classic vanity-graphic to a really valuable link-filled page of business information that points to many of the big-company sites reviewed earlier in this chapter (see Figure15-16).

Figure 15-15:
The Big
B-School
decides to B
there (rather
than be
square).

Welcome to the Harvard Business School

Harvard University
Graduate School of Business Administration
George F. Baker Foundation

This is the Home Page for the Harvard Business School. From here you can reach all other HBS WWW Pages. You may also search these pages.

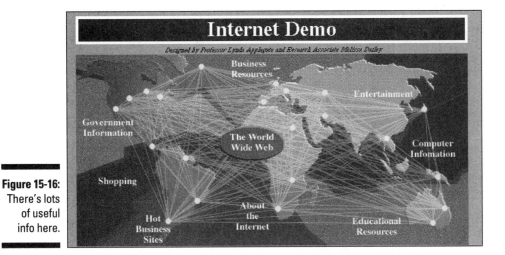

Figure 15-16:
There's lots
of useful
info here.

Nonprofit organizations have, potentially, a whole new way to reach people and to organize on the Web. Personally, I hope this opens up the Age of Aquarius, but for two reasons I have doubts about whether the larger and more famous nonprofs will lead this revolution. The first doubt is this: After working at a large and famous nonprofit for a year or so, I asked my supervisor how the accounting worked from one year to the next. He said, "Oh, it's simple. We look at the books at the end of the year and divide up any leftover money among the top management people. That's how we stay nonprofit."

The second doubt is based on statistical consulting for a direct-mail agency specializing in nonprofit organizations. A business will typically run a direct-mail campaign until the last round of the campaign loses money. A nonprofit will run a campaign until the whole campaign (sometimes on the tenth or twelfth mailing) is net negative. In other words, fund-raising for nonprofits usually proceeds until all the funds raised have been spent on fund-raising. As a prescription for generating vigorous social action, this method leaves something to be desired. Nonetheless, many nonprofit organizations are going to find that the Web's way of sending a zero-cost message to everyone with a computer is going to provide new power and a better-looking budget at the same time. I expect, for example, that Greenpeace at `http://www.greenpeace.org` (see Figure 15-17) managed to flood French e-mail channels with protests over nuclear testing.

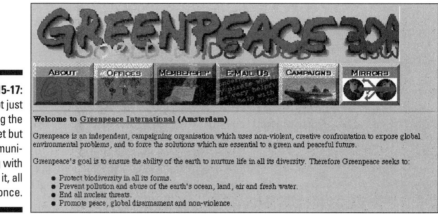

Figure 15-17:
Not just
saving the
planet but
communi-
cating with
it, all
at once.

Fringe Issues on the Web

Now that you've had a chance to look over some serious business applications of the World Wide Web, It's time for me to make a few remarks about some Internet issues that appear in the daily news. In a strange way, everything that happens fast seems to scare people. And beyond fears that arise in the general population, the agitation level among civil servants and others in charge of monitoring the communications industry borders on absolute hysteria.

As a little online exercise, check into the *Time* magazine area on America Online and do an article search on the keyword "internet". What you will find is that nearly 90 percent of the articles are about Internet dangers that are greatly exaggerated or just point-blank fictional. *Time's* notorious 1995 cover story on "CyberPorn," taken without further research from a fraudulent (and well-known as fraudulent) source, is not an isolated example, and other magazines have published material as useless and mistaken as *Time's*. I've been watching the Internet and the Web for years, but am still amazed at the fear print-media organizations and government information sources exhibit at the idea of an uncensored and unsupervised Internet. Thus, the newspapers serve up a daily diet of online Scary Monsters.

Web Scary Monster #1 has to do with security for credit card transactions. For some reason, people don't seem to have been bothered that their telephone-based credit card transactions are in some states handled by prison inmates, but they expect that wily online pirates are waiting to snag card numbers off the Web. Netscape Navigator 1.1 was supposedly secure for credit card transactions on the Web, but in fact had a flaw (based on its transaction time-stamping scheme) that took Netscape's programmers a day or so to fix. Rest assured that if Netscape's 2.0 edition has any security problems, they will be found by gleeful hackers in short order — and also fixed. To me, it's just amazing how much noise the *idea* of Web card fraud has generated, given that traditional non-computer credit card scams, a billion-dollar industry, are almost never mentioned. The 1995 movie *The Net* (look for a copy of this book next to Sandra Bullock's computer in the last few minutes of the film) brought up all sorts of Web financial and identity security issues, although, fortunately, the villain in the movie is a thinly-disguised version of Bill Gates.

Web Scary Monster #2 concerns pedophilia, perversion, and terror in general. Recent newspaper reports claim that police in large U.S. cities, and the FBI too, have taken to signing onto bulletin boards, chat groups, and e-mail lists in an attempt to decoy people who want to lure 12-year-olds into motel rooms. You may confidently expect to read plenty of lurid stories in the months ahead, as police departments react to the need to present themselves as high-tech. But you need to know an interesting fact. In the early 1980s, *The Los Angeles Times* did a retrospective study of every Halloween-candy tampering incident it had reported in the previous ten years. Every story, *every one,* was found to be unverifiable. Researchers in criminology report that no incident has ever been verified nationally, either.

Honest, they don't occur. It's been thoroughly documented. The most typical case is that some kid's older brother tampers with the candy and claims the kids got it from mean Mr. Johnson, the P.E. teacher. *The L.A. Times*, *The New York Times*, and the two standard college textbooks on criminology all agree about the Halloween stuff. And no one ever dried a poodle in a microwave either. I'm sad to report that crime statistics show that in-laws are still overwhelmingly a larger source of crimes against children than strangers on the Internet, too.

Similarly, everybody knows that terrorists are everywhere these days, just like bad Halloween candy, kept at bay only by expensive services that X-ray your underwear at every airport. The members of the Libyan hit squad who were said to be roaming the U.S. in the mid-1980s to assassinate President Reagan are now presumably using the newsgroup alt.kill.everyone to plan other fictitious capers. The historical record over the last three decades shows that various intelligence agencies do not hesitate to plant terror stories themselves. There are indeed some real terrorists in the world, but they won't be stopped by government security assaults on the Internet as long as there are still pay phones in New York.

REMEMBER

The conclusion of this little editorial is simple: You'll read lots of Web and Internet horror stories in the next few years, and a great many of them will be fabricated by people more interested in creating a need for their jobs than in protecting you and your family.

One Kind Of Future: The Web Takes Over Everything

In 1995, Sun Microsystems ("micro" is funny usage in this context, as Sun systems have been big-time UNIX workstations all along) released early versions of HotJava (see Figure 15-18 which is `http://java.sun.com`), a programming system that shows what the Web can be. In the Java language, an *application* can be dropped into a Web page just like a picture or sound. Sun is committed to doing versions of this language for Mac System 7.5, Windows 95 and beyond, and all popular UNIX variants.

Figure 15-18:
Java from
Sun: the
next big
thing.

Suppose you think of the HTML language of the Web as the basis of an operating system (well, actually, it's UNIX underlying the whole show) or at least a data-exchange scheme that works across *all computers currently used*. You may have your own local operating system on the box sitting on your desk, but the protocols of the Web amount to an operating system for all the computers in the world working together. And the Java initiative from Sun is a programming language for creating new applications specifically for the Web, small applications that can be written fairly quickly and ported among all the computers that make up the Web.

So what's the future? Is it bloated individual applications that take up 60MB on your hard drive? Proprietary groupware like Lotus Notes that never seems to get around to supporting the Mac properly? Or is it a Web-based scheme for exchanging information inside and between companies and organizations, with open, non-proprietary standards and a cool new language for developing small, fast, application? Personally, I'm betting that "better, faster, cheaper" has at least a fighting chance against the large, predatory vendors that seem to dominate the software business in the late 1990s short run.

Part IV
The Part of Tens

In this part...

The Part of Tens, a standard *Dummies* feature, is a concentrated dose of Internet trivia, serious matters, and convenience.

I provide some alternate ways to find information so that as you and I use the Net, we can avoid colliding at peak times.

Chapter 16

Ten Useful WWW Sites

In This Chapter

▶ A bunch of great WWW sites

*T*hese locations are good places to start roaming the World Wide Web. Actually, most WWW servers have some provision for jumping back out to one of the big sites, typically NCSA. Any Web browser (not just Mosaic) will have an Open URL command under the File menu. If you suddenly find yourself lost, bored, or irritable, just Open URL and type

```
http://www.yahoo.com/
```

This address will get you back to my favorite site, Yahoo. Alternatively, you can try

```
http://www.ncsa.uiuc.edu
```

and you arrive at the Mother of All Home Pages, the original Mosaic site.

Here are some of my favorites. Please note that the Web is growing so rapidly that providing this list is like naming a favorite bar in the Klondike during the Gold Rush. All these sites show links to the newer sites as well, so you can always just check the What's New section of the home page on your server.

1. galaxy.einet.net

I don't know what the hardware setup looks like down at MCC in Texas, but I know that this site is always up and running 24 hours each day, with apparently three zillion never-busy incoming lines. This is a very rich site, with content ranging from the businesslike to the bizarre.

2. info.cern.ch

The pioneer WWW site in Switzerland is still the source for lots of unique material of scientific interest and is a valuable reminder that, although America leads the world in Netheads per capita, the first W in WWW really does stand for World.

3. www.cyfer.net

This is a server devoted to nonprofit organizations. Instant international connectivity is dramatically amplifying the capabilities of organizations such as Amnesty International and ecology-monitoring groups. Electronic daylight is now penetrating some formerly murky geopolitical swamps.

4. www.commerce.net

CommerceNet is an aggressively expanding business society based in Silicon Valley. As it happens, Silicon Valley was just waiting for something like this — CommerceNet, after its first six months, was a bigger operation than the whole Web was in 1993.

5. http://rever.nmsu.edu/~elharo/faq/Macintosh.html

This site is the "Well Connected Mac" page, which leads out to all sorts of links to software connections for communications. This site is currently updated *weekly*, so it has the latest in Web browsers and HTML utilities.

6. www.yahoo.com

The current king of Web index sites, you can start here and find almost anything else. The Yahoos are supporting the service with advertising, but the ads are pretty small.

7. http://dutera.et.tudelft.nl/people/vdham/info-mac/

The Info-mac digests are a prime resource for all types of Mac information. Although you can find them in many places, this site always seems to be up, and Holland is sufficiently offset from the U.S. in world time that you can browse in the afternoon.

8. www.ncsa.uiuc

The last bit stands for University of Illinois, Urbana-Champaign. Although it's one of my favorite places (the town and, for that matter, the Web site), I'm convinced that this site's interest in supercomputing and Mosaic grew from the burning desire to produce something interesting from the flat, bare landscape of the cornfields.

9. hyperarchive.lcs.mit.edu/HyperArchive.html

This archive of Mac stuff has little descriptions of all the files and links to other sites. It's worth looking at the notes before you get stuck in a half-hour download.

10. www.well.sf.ca.us

Take a look at the future of private computer organizations on the Web. This famous bulletin board has constructed an admirably idiosyncratic WWW site, and as a nonmember of the WELL, you can look at most of it. It's not Mac-specific, but it's cool.

Chapter 17

Top Ten Mac Software Archives (FTP)

• •

In This Chapter

▶ mac.archive.umich.edu

▶ sumex-aim.stanford.edu

▶ ftp.apple.com

▶ ftp.ncsa.uiuc.edu

▶ ftp.funet.fi

▶ ftp.dartmouth.edu

▶ boombox.micro.umn.edu

▶ ftp.rrzn.uni-hannover.de (*)

▶ ftp.ucs.ubc.ca (*)

▶ shark.mel.dit.csiro.au (*)

• •

*M*ost of the sites listed in Table 17-1 are universities, so please try to tap in sometime after dinner or early in the morning. The directory given is where you can find the goodies.

In general, you should log in as **anonymous** and give your own Internet address as the password.

The Stanford site has practically everything worth having. But everyone knows this fact, so I marked three sites with an asterisk that are *mirrors,* or copies, of the Stanford collection. By the way, I included sites in different time zones, so you can access what you want without staying up round the clock. FTP may seem a bit old-fashioned compared to the Web, but if you are just trying to collect some software, it's more efficient than wading through graphics and such on your way to the files.

Table 17-1 Ten Mac Software Sites

Location	Number	Directory
mac.archive.umich.edu	141.211.32.2	/mac
sumex-aim.stanford.edu	36.44.0.6	/info-mac
ftp.apple.com	130.43.2.3	/dts
ftp.ncsa.uiuc.edu	141.142.20.50	/Mac (Mosaic)
ftp.funet.fi	128.214.6.100	/pub/mac
ftp.dartmouth.edu	129.170.16.54	/pub/mac (Dartmouth)
boombox.micro.umn.edu	128.101.95.95	/pub (gopher, more)
ftp.rrzn.uni-hannover.de (*)	130.75.2.2	/ftp1/mac [sumex]
ftp.ucs.ubc.ca (*)	137.82.27.62	/pub/mac/info-mac
shark.mel.dit.csiro.au (*)	144.110.16.11	/info-mac [sumex]

Chapter 18

Ten Communications Software Tips

Communications software is full of bugs. The fact that shareware programs still compete seriously with commercial applications indicates the unsettled state of things. If Apple had any sense of shame, it would have distributed a trouble-free Internet communications program as part of system software long ago.

Anyway, give thanks to the clever people who write shareware, or to the companies that now give Web browsers away. And be a good sport: Send in the modest registration fee if you use some shareware regularly.

Deflaking Your Modem

For a variety of reasons, communications software doesn't always reset your modem correctly when it starts up, and it doesn't always hang up properly at the end.

The solution: Keep your modem close enough to turn it off between sessions. Crude advice, I know, but sometimes it's the only way to get the darn thing to reset.

 Sometimes the modem doesn't hang up. *If you're still connected, you're paying for it!* Make sure that you turn it off when you're done. I have friends who thought they were logged off of America Online when they went a way for a weekend, but they weren't. Multiply 48 hours times a few bucks per hour and it's pretty miserable.

Deflaking Your Session Files, Part 1

Any good communications software (Microphone LT, for example) keeps a *session log*, which is a record of all the stuff you saw on-screen while you were connected. Mastering your software's session log can save you untold grief if you connect to bulletin board systems. For example, there's nothing like watching a 10K text file roll past you on-screen and then finding that your software only logged the last page.

If you look under the File menu in your program, there will usually be a choice like Save Archive As or Save Log File As. This choice lets you set the program to capture the entire session.

Deflaking Your Session Files, Part 2

As a Macintosh user, you are familiar with proportionally spaced fonts. Most of the BBS host computers running around the Internet, however, have never even heard of these lovely things. On UNIX computers, all the spacing considerations for laying out tables and lists assume that every character has the same width. When you capture a session file and open it with Geneva or Times as the font, all the tables and lists look ragged because the spacing has been changed by using a font in which *l* is narrower than *w*.

If you have a table of some sort in your session file, open the file in a word processor, select the table, and pick the Monaco font. Presto! All the text in the columns aligns properly.

Dealing with Weird Files

Stuff on the Internet and the Web comes in a baffling array of file formats. You may see .zip, .z, .tar, and all sorts of non-Mac creatures. You can collect a whole set of utilities for dealing with this situation (including HQXer, uuencode, and a half dozen others). Or, as soon as you have an account anywhere (AOL, eWorld, and others), you can download StuffIt Lite, which can turn the majority of these files into something you can recognize.

Upgrading Your Communications Software

StuffIt Lite can solve lots of BBS file decoding problems. I also recommend downloading ZTerm if you are using the communications module in an integrated (Works-type) program.

Experiment with Downloads

Most communications programs support several download protocols, among them XMODEM, YMODEM, and Kermit. There are considerable differences in the actual download speed from one online service to the next, depending on the protocol you use. It's worth doing several experiments with small files to compare speeds.

Serious Money

CompuServe, Delphi, and GEnie have special interface applications that let you design searches offline and set up e-mail message handling at high speed. My measurements with CompuServe Navigator, for example, show that the actual online time can be crunched down by a factor of ten!

These kinds of programs can type faster than you, and they don't sit there staring at the screen wondering what to do next: You can already have devised a plan, at no charge, offline. If you take advantage of these timesaving applications, you can typically get all your online work done inside the "free" time allotment.

Modem Speed Optimism

Don't you just hate it when you sign on with your brand-new 28.8K-bps modem, only to be told that the service is still running at 9600 bps? But don't despair: National online services and bulletin boards upgrade their hardware all the time, often without telling you. As a result, try a faster modem setting every week or so; it costs you only a few seconds of connect time and can save you gobs of time and money if it works.

If you set your communications software for 28.8K bps and the service is running at only 9600, either your modem drops down to the slower speed or you get some nonsense characters and are forced to turn the modem off to disconnect.

File Name Creativity

Most communications software gives you a generic name for session logs. If you do online Archie searches in a shell account or telnet to look through some directory, the software assigns every session the same name. The solution: For your sanity, come up with file names that clearly indicate the content of your session logs. And you should usually include the date in the file name, too.

Don't get lazy when you are naming your online files. After you cruise the Net for a month, you'll have so much stuff that you'll never find anything if you don't label your files clearly.

For Hotshots Only

If you're a hard-core Mac hotshot who bought this book just for a quick overview of Internet access, be sure to get the shareware program Modem Maker. You can use it to write modem scripts that can be used as small Internet telecommunications applications.

Chapter 19
Ten Internet Service Providers

In This Chapter

▶ PSINet

▶ CRL

▶ Pipeline NY

▶ US Cyber

▶ HookUp Communications Corporation

▶ IDT

▶ Millennium Online

▶ Netcom Online Communication Services

▶ NovaLink

▶ eWorld

*M*ost Internet service providers are scrambling to accommodate the dramatic increase in Internet demand. Meanwhile, conflicting factors affect access and cost. On the one hand, it's more efficient to run a service with a thousand subscribers than 50, especially if the providers aren't fussy about handing out busy signals. On the other hand, increased demand gives the providers incentive to keep the rates up as long as they can. (It's like running the only restaurant at the edge of a gold rush town: the owners want to charge $5 for an egg, but at some point the miners start raising their own chickens.)

Note that some online services provide 800 numbers so that you can avoid long-distance phone charges from the phone company. The catch is that the service charges you extra (beyond your standard per-hour charge) for using the 800 number. It used to be common to see 800-charges of $5 to $10 per hour, but increased competition is now bringing these charges down. Another consideration is that the big national online services are chasing the independent service providers as hard as they can. Whatever else may be true, the third edition of this book probably won't have two provider names in common with this list.

PSINet

This service has local numbers all over the U.S., and it has a nice bundle of Mac software. The simplest way to contact these people is to send an e-mail to info@psi.net or buy the set-up package Internet Valet, which automatically connects you to PSINet. Or call 800-774-0852.

CRL

This is one of the few organizations practiced enough to get you online as a Macintosh SLIP user. And you can access it cheaply across the country via more and more local numbers (CR Laboratories does shell accounts, too). Call 415-381-2800 and ask someone to fax their spiel. Internet address is crl.com.

Pipeline NY

Don't let the name throw you — it has access all over the U.S. and a pretty cheap flat-fee service. Call 212-267-3636 and get their easy-to-use Mac software.

US Cyber

These people have both free and pay (for businesses) service. The address is dconcepts.com, or call at 715-743-1700 for an explanation of their unique spectrum or services.

HookUp Communication Corporation

This Canadian service has shell or SLIP access with an 800 number and a reasonable price. Call 519-747-4110 or send a note to info@hookup.net for information.

IDT

This service gives you unlimited access for a flat fee per month and provides uncensored access to everything. When you sign up, they send you the current version of Netscape, and they're a Mac-oriented service. Call 800-743-4343.

Millennium Online

This is a shell service with a network of local numbers. Call 800-736-0122 or e-mail `mill.com`.

Netcom Online Communication Services

Netcom has local numbers in most big cities, shell and SLIP accounts, and customer support that knows something about Macintoshes. Call 800-501-8649 or e-mail `info@netcom.com`. Unfortunately, Netcom's cool NetCruiser package is Windows-only.

NovaLink

This Boston-based shell service, which uses Sprint for national access, has laudably modest access fees. Call 800-274-2814 or send e-mail to `info@novalink.com`. (Have you noticed a pattern in some of these e-mail addresses?)

eWorld

Most of the companies on this list are direct-connection specialists. With eWorld, you go through a separate Web browser now, but the service is changing rapidly and could emerge as a really hip alternative. And every time you have to call customer support, they know what your computer is. In a Mac-minority universe, this service feels pretty cozy. See the eWorld chapter (Chapter 10) for details.

Chapter 20

Ten Web Consulting Services for Business

● ●

In This Chapter

▶ 5 Circles Internet Consulting

▶ CyberNet

▶ Alteris Communications

▶ BBN Systems

▶ Cogwheel

▶ ETC Nextnet

▶ GetSet! Communications

▶ Internet Publication Services, Inc.

▶ Nexus Communications Corporation

▶ Virtual Communications

● ●

*W*hat a difference a year makes! In the first edition of this book, Chapter 20 was devoted to nonprofits and good causes. The hundreds and hundreds of response cards that readers sent me, however, all asked for business information. I guess the nonprofits will have to wait until people feel a little more prosperous.

This chapter contains an assortment of ten sites that I have reviewed. For the most up-to-date names in this explosively-growing area, you should try the index at Yahoo. Just go to the Yahoo home page, click Search, and use the keywords "Web" and "consulting". While this edition was prepared, this search went from 150 to 400 entries, and it's a cinch there will be more than a thousand as you read this. Also, the actual http addresses of many of these companies change in time, so rather than list URLs that are likely to go out of date in a few months, I recommend that you log onto Yahoo and do a search on the company name.

5 Circles Internet Consulting

These people, against the background of all sorts of blue-sky popular-media hype about the Web, offer realistic advice about what works and what doesn't.

CyberNet

I can't give up on altruism altogether. This organization specializes in Web services for nonprofits and has lots of experience in fundraising.

Alteris Communications

Attention, Canadian pals. This consulting service is equally proficient in French and English. I haven't given the matter much thought, but I would expect that if Canadian cereal boxes have to be bilingual, the Web sites should be also.

BBN Systems

This organization helped establish ARPANET, so they're not four guys in a room with HTML books open in their laps. If you make the Web decisions in a large organization, you probably should check here first.

Cogwheel

Cogwheel is based in Hong Kong. For lots of political reasons, Hong Kong will probably still be the gateway to China after 1997, and this organization has a serious group of Web workers.

ETC Nextnet

This well-regarded service will design Web pages for you and then take care of the details like hosting your site and getting you noticed.

GetSet! Communications

GetSet! provides more hand-holding than most other Web consulting services. If you think you are missing out on a hot business opportunity but don't know much about the Web, this organization would be a good first contact.

Internet Publication Services, Inc.

IPS does Web consulting down to the level of individuals. I included them in this list because some friends had a good experience here. Even in cyberspace, service makes a difference.

Nexus Communications Corporation

This organization specializes in services for the lambda communities of North America and beyond. If you don't know what this means, then you're not in a lambda community. If you do know, you'll like this service.

Virtual Communications

At last, a Mac-specific Web consultant. This exceptionally competent service can do it all for you in one gulp, and they won't ask you about Chameleon or Winsock or all sorts of other stuff they use on "other platforms."

Oh, you might also want to call Net.Solutions at 817-756-0390. They have a very low-cost Web page creation-plus-hosting service.

Chapter 21

Ten Absolutely Free Access Sites

*1*n this chapter, I provide tips on contacting no-charge Internet hosts. If you're lucky, you may live in a community where this free access service is already established. If you're not lucky, you may be soon because organizations that provide free access are making new sites spring up every month.

If you don't see a site you can access conveniently, call your local library. As libraries put their own catalogs online, they find that it's relatively simple to get online access to remote catalogs, and from there it's a short step to full Internet access. In addition, pick up a copy of *Computer Currents*, *MicroTimes*, or a similar tabloid at a newsstand and check the bulletin board directories, which are always located near the want ads (in the last few pages).

By the time you read this book, someone probably will have started an Internet access site in your area code, but it takes six months before the site turns up in national lists.

Some of the sites listed here don't offer every possible Internet feature. But they don't want $20 a month either, so they're a good place to begin learning about the Net. Most of them allow you to have a shell account, and you only need basic communications software like ZTerm or the communications module of a "Works" software package.

The people who provide these services are wonderful folks; their hospitality is not to be abused. If you sign onto one of these services and use it, for example, to send a chain letter to 20 million people, I will be obliged to track you down like a dog and smash your modem. Remember, IDG's henchmen are everywhere.

Our motto: Be nice.

Nyx

Nyx is a site in Denver, Colorado, maintained by the University of Denver. The dial-up number is 303-871-3324, and the Internet address is `nyx.cs.du.edu`. Its volunteer staff accepts donations if you are moved to offer them.

digitalNation

The easiest way to reach these people is at the Web page `www.csgi.com/`. If you want everything to be absolutely free, just take the free sign-up time offered by AOL and then check out this site.

US Cyber

US Cyber's "free.org" service is a free connection, for all Internet services, but it's an area code 715 number. Call them at 715-743-1700 and have them explain it to you.

m-net

A reliable contact operated by a nonprofit organization, m-net accepts donations. Its dial-up number is 313-996-4644; Internet address is `m-met.ann-arbor.mi.us`.

EasyAccess Information Systems

This is a free access site that supports itself by accepting advertising. Fair enough — that's how you used to get TV in the good old days. Find them at www.easyaccess.com.

Big Sky Telegraph

I don't know what's going on in Montana, but it certainly is an Internet hot spot. Probably for the same reason that Finland is Internet-happy — for lots of the year, it's easier to log on than to drive. Log in as "bbs" at the dial-up number 406-683-7680. For some reason, the Internet address is usually listed as 192.231.192.1.

O, Canada!

The National Capital free Internet site (freenet.carleton.ca) lets you log in as "guest" at the dial-up number 613-780-3733. Out on the West Coast, the Victoria free net (freenet.victoria.bc.ca) is at the dial-up number 604-595-2300.

I also should point out that Saskatoon is a major center of free Internet activity. I included these sites in an attempt to shame U.S. locations into catching up with the Canadians.

O, Hio!

Cleveland has one of the largest free nets in the country. Somehow, when talking about free access, everywhere else seems to be ahead of New York or Los Angeles — these other towns simply may not be as aggressive commercially. The dial-up number is 216-368-3888; the Internet address is freenet-in-a.cwru.edu.

Part V
Appendices

The 5th Wave — By Rich Tennant

"For further thoughts on that subject, I'm going to down-load Leviticus and go through the menu to Job, chapter 2, verse 6, file 'J', it reads..."

In this part...

Lots of information about the Internet is contained in Net documents and lists of various sorts. I even threw in a glossary for kicks. This part gives you the essentials you need to find interesting topics on the Net and a few other tips to help you become a fine, upstanding Internet citizen.

Appendix A

The Pedestrian's Guide
to Internet Addresses

• •

*I*nternet addressing can be confusing because it wasn't designed for you: it was designed for computers.

That explains everything.

I Want Oot, Find Me a Route!

After you get an account with an Internet service provider, you dial up the service, using your Mac and modem. At this point, you're connected to a network.

Now suppose that you want to use the telnet command to connect to another computer. For example, say that you want to visit the WELL in San Francisco as a guest. So you type

```
telnet well.sf.ca.us
```

to start the process.

Your network now calls another network — the main Internet high-speed network sponsored by the National Science Foundation.

Networks have relatively slow ports to the outside of modems (for your purposes, a *port* is just a phone number you can use) but faster connections inside the network. You may think that your 9600-bps modem is fast, but it's a poky little critter compared to real network-connection hardware. Networks call each other through a *router*, or a special hardware box that can connect networks that use the same plan for addresses and for message size. Technically, your messages are broken into little chunks called *packets*; the networks need to agree on the size of the packets.

You may think that you're calling up well.sf.ca.us. The machines involved, however, don't know a WELL from a bucket. The computer on the network won't tell you this, but inside the computer everything is a number. In the process of connecting to the WELL, both networks agree that the WELL is called

```
198.93.4.10
```

Strictly speaking, it's not even that user-friendly. The computers at either end of the transaction see a 32-digit *binary* number (0s and 1s).

The *real* Internet addresses, therefore, are numbers. But individuals can pick Internet addresses like

```
goofball@fishnet.org
```

and

```
starman@hollywood.ca.us
```

The routing system has translated the *domain names* (fishnet and hollywood) and the *top-level domain names* (org and us) into numbers. And it gets the numbers from a listing of Internet-assigned domain names, which are guaranteed to be unique.

When you issue a telnet command, the routing system gets the number of the site you're trying to reach; finding a file or a person at that site is up to you. When you send e-mail, the network at the other end calls up a table of *usernames* on that Net to determine that goofball is, in fact, Xenophon T. Biggles, cruelly nicknamed "goofball" in early childhood by playmates unable to pronounce the name of the great Athenian general.

What Domain Names Mean

You can usually count on the top-level domain name to be a type of group or a country name. Country names are usually easy to guess, but some are a bit harder, like those little oval stickers you sometimes see on cars. (*Hint:* the Germans don't call their country Germany, for example — it's Deutschland.)

Here are some common top-level domain names for groups:

.com	businesses
.edu	schools
.gov	government
.mil	military
.net	networks
.org	nonprofits

These are top-level domain names for countries you're likely to encounter:

.an	Australia
.au	Austria
.ca	Canada
.ch	Switzerland
.de	Germany
.fi	Finland
.it	Italy
.jp	Japan
.nz	New Zealand
.uk	United Kingdom
.us	United States

If you want to get the name for Brunei or other exotic climes (OK — you're dying of curiosity — Brunei is .bn), send a message to the Internet Society itself:

`isoc@isoc.org`

Appendix B
Your Internet Phone Book

● ●

1 wish I could tell you that this was going to be easy. Well, I could tell you, but you would find out anyway and send me nasty letters at *Macworld*.

You can make up a text file of Internet names and addresses and then just cut and paste them into the *To:* part of messages. You'll have your very own Internet phone book, and once you get the entries right in the first place, you won't make any typos (a truly dreaded Internet problem). This method works not only if you have a service with a cool interface like America Online, but even if you're just using primitive terminal software on a shell account on a UNIX network somewhere.

That's the good news. The bad news is that after years of explosive growth, it is very difficult to track down names and Internet addresses. In this appendix, I tell you some resources to use, but you're on your own after that. Good luck!

Just Say What?

If you're talking to someone whom you think you may want to reach someday by e-mail, ask that person for an Internet address on the spot. Maybe you won't need it for months, but months from now you probably won't be able to get it. Also, at least for the next few years, before Internet numbers are assigned at birth, asking for an e-mail address will make you look cool.

I know that this plan sounds simple, but it's the most reliable.

Da Phone, Boss, Da Phone!

Many organizations provide lists of e-mail addresses; simply ask the reception-ist at the other end of the phone. Take it from me, the boss's nephew who's answering the phone for the summer has more intelligence than the cleverest UNIX network utility. And if he doesn't know what you need to know, he can almost always find someone who does.

(In case you couldn't tell, I just delivered a searing indictment of the pitiful lack of organization in modern online communications. Welcome to the information supersidewalk.)

Secret Agent X.500

Many Internet sites have online directory services called X.500. If you know practically enough to guess the address anyway, try the command

```
person tim langly, apple, us
```

on your Internet host directories (lots of commercial shell service providers have X.500). If this method doesn't work, please notice that if you have the person's name and organization, you can track down the address with a phone call anyway.

Netfind: Just What the Name Implies

I have had pretty good luck with netfind. Telnet to

```
bruno.cs.colorado.edu
```

(Do this during off-peak hours, please.) Then log in as "netfind" — with no password. Follow the subsequent menu, in which you provide almost but not quite as much information as you need to search an X.500 directory.

The search procedure is quite easy to follow, and good old bruno delivers the goods more often than anything else I've tried.

Appendix C

Netiquette, or Playing Nicely Together

• •

As the Internet expanded, it gradually shed its role as an online gentlemen's club whose members were university researchers. Old hands felt obliged, however, to post some of the informal rules of conduct that they had developed over the years.

Back when there were only a few million people on the Net, these considerations were simply good manners, like not leaving chewing gum on a subway seat. Now that there are 60 million Net denizens, these "rules" take on new importance, like signs that make sure that you drive on the right side of the freeway.

In essence, this thing ain't gonna work any more unless we all behave like proper little ladies and gentlemen.

Here are four simple rules. Please take them seriously as friendly advice.

Watch Your) and (

Probably 90 percent of the content of face-to-face messages lies in expression and tone (this is even more true in Japan, which is why Internet e-mail is not so popular there). When you send e-mail, all these little clues to meaning we have developed over the centuries are absent. My advice is if you're saying anything that might be taken two ways, throw in a smile (see the list below). And look over your mail carefully before you send it.

The Keyboard Symbol	What It Says
:)	smile
;)	wink
: *	kiss
: (	things are not OK
: >	fiendish grin

Download FAQs First and Read Them Offline

Every newsgroup has a file of FAQs (*f*requently *a*sked *q*uestions). You will be amazed (and I cast no aspersions on your originality) how often the things you want to know about rhododendrons or seismology are the *same things everyone else* wants to know. Don't bother the poor newsgroup moderators with questions that they've answered a hundred times.

In addition, you should read at your leisure the guide to local customs, a file usually called `etiquette.txt`.

Don't Send E-Mail to Thousands of People at Once

After you use the Internet for a while, you will figure out how to post e-mail to platoons of potential victims automatically. I didn't tell you how to do so, though. And for a good reason. I don't want you to. Neither does anyone else.

Think about the Simplest Way to Get What You Want

All the national online services support telnet. You can telnet to Finland (and elsewhere around the globe) to fetch chess games (and whatnot). Or you can find the same stuff on your own service.

If you want to get DNA sequence data from the molecular biology archives at Indiana University, please do so. Just don't bother the Hoosiers for calculator DAs, OK?

Appendix D

alt.newsgroups

● ●

*T*he alt newsgroups arose as a way to distinguish popular topics from the original core topics (physics, math, computer science, and other serious matters) in the Usenet universe. They loom large in the mythology of the Internet because they're where the fun is, among other things.

This list is a severely edited version of a list posted regularly to a newsgroup called `news.lists`, which you can join from any Internet provider that offers Usenet newsgroups. The list is maintained by a volunteer named David C. Lawrence (Internet address `tale@uunet.uu.net`), who is the person to notify when groups are created or disappear. It's another example of the remarkable way the Internet operates — the list is a key piece of information about the Internet, and it's not under the control of an organization or business.

If you want the full version of the list, you should download it yourself; just look for it in the Internet-files library of any national online service. The complete list has topics and descriptions that are too X-rated for this little fun-for-the-whole-family book, and there's also an amazing amount of repetition — very similar topics often appear in three or four separate newsgroups. The groups identified as "moderated" here have someone who edits out the worst flames or the most inappropriate postings. The rest are just the absolute, raw, unedited transcript of all the messages contributed to the newsgroup.

Social Issues

This list is about one-fourth of the social-issue groups on Usenet. Different types of activist communities staked out their turf fairly early in Internet history.

`alt.abuse.recovery`	Helping victims of abuse to recover.
`alt.activism`	Activities for activists.
`alt.activism.d`	A place to discuss issues in `alt.activism`.
`alt.activism.death-penalty`	For people opposed to capital punishment.

`alt.adoption`	For those involved with or contemplating adoption.
`alt.child-support`	Raising children in a split family.
`alt.censorship`	Discussion about restricting speech/press.
`alt.current-events.bosnia`	The strife of Bosnia-Herzegovina.
`alt.current-events.clinton.whitewater`	The Clinton Whitewater scandal.
`alt.current-events.russia`	Current happenings in Russia.
`alt.current-events.usa`	What's new in the United States.
`alt.dads-rights`	Rights of fathers. (Moderated)
`alt.discrimination`	Quotas, affirmative action, bigotry, persecution.
`alt.education.disabled`	Education for people with physical/mental disabilities.
`alt.education.distance`	Learning from teachers who are far away.
`alt.feminism`	Like `soc.feminism`, only different.
`alt.fraternity.sorority`	Discussions of fraternity/sorority life and issues.
`alt.individualism`	Philosophies where individual rights are paramount.
`alt.missing-kids`	Locating missing children.
`alt.parents-teens`	Parent-teenager relationships.
`alt.politics.greens`	Green-party politics and activities worldwide.
`alt.politics.usa.constitution`	U.S. Constitutional politics.
`alt.recovery`	For people in recovery programs (for example, AA, ACA, GA).
`alt.recovery.codependency`	Mutually destructive relationships.
`alt.sexual.abuse.recovery`	Helping others deal with traumatic experiences.
`alt.support`	Dealing with emotional situations and experiences.
`alt.support.cancer`	Emotional aid for people with cancer.
`alt.support.depression`	Depression and mood disorders.

`alt.support.divorce`	Discussion of marital breakups.
`alt.support.step-parents`	Helping people with their step parents.
`alt.support.stuttering`	Support for people who stutter.
`alt.war`	Not just collateral damage.

At the Extremes

These groups contain plenty of interesting speculative material.

`alt.alien.visitors`	Space Aliens on Earth! Abduction! Gov't Cover-up!
`alt.conspiracy`	Be paranoid — they're out to get you.
`alt.out-of-body`	Out-of-body experiences.
`alt.paranet.skeptic`	"I don't believe they turned you into a newt."
`alt.paranet.ufo`	"Heck, I guess naming it 'UFO' identifies it."
`alt.paranormal`	Phenomena that are not scientifically explicable.
`alt.sci.physics.new-theories`	Scientific theories you won't find in journals.

Computer Stuff

Please note that these are discussion groups, rather than sources of software. You can, however, get plenty of advice if you want it.

`alt.bbs.internet`	BBSs that are hooked up to the Internet.
`alt.best.of.internet`	It was a time of sorrow, it was a time of joy.
`alt.gopher`	Discussion of the gopher information service.
`alt.irc.questions`	How-to questions for IRC (International Relay Chat).

`alt.lang.basic`	The language that would not die.
`alt.online-service`	Large commercial online services and the Internet.
`alt.online-service.america-online`	Discussions and questions about America Online.
`alt.online-service.compuserve`	Discussions and questions about CompuServe.
`alt.online-service.delphi`	Discussions and questions about Delphi.
`alt.online-service.freenet`	Public FreeNet systems.
`alt.online-service.prodigy`	The Prodigy system.
`alt.sources.mac`	Source file newsgroup for the Apple Macintosh computers.

Critters

I expect that as more dog and cat owners get on the Internet, there will be postings of upcoming shows and the like. It's pretty hard to believe there's a skunks group and not at least one for Persian cat fanciers.

`alt.animals.badgers`	Badgers (meles meles and others).
`alt.animals.dolphins`	Flipper, Darwin, and all their friends.
`alt.animals.foxes`	Everything you ever wanted to know about vulpines.
`alt.aquaria`	The aquarium and related as a hobby.
`alt.fan.lemurs`	Little critters with BIG eyes.
`alt.pets.rabbits`	Coneys abound.
`alt.skunks`	Enthusiasts of skunks and other mustelidae.
`alt.wolves`	Discussing wolves and wolf-mix dogs.

Games

There are more groups actually playing games on the Internet than discussing them.

alt.anagrams	Playing with words.
alt.games.mtrek	Multi-Trek, a multiuser Star Trek-like game.
alt.games.netrek.paradise	Discussion of the paradise version of netrek.
alt.games.video.classic	Video games from before the mid-1980s.
alt.sega.genesis	Another addiction.
alt.super.nes	Like rec.games.video.nintendo, only different.

Sports

I'm only listing a few of the groups for professional sports teams. Your favorite team is almost certainly listed, in the same format as these, as alt.sports.<sports>.<team-name>.

alt.archery	Robin Hood had the right idea.
alt.caving	Spelunking.
alt.fishing	Like rec.outdoors.fishing, only different.
alt.skate-board	Discussion of all aspects of skateboarding.
alt.sport.bowling	In the gutter again.
alt.sport.darts	Look what you've done to the wall!
alt.sport.falconry	The taking of live game by using a trained raptor.
alt.sport.jet-ski	Discussion of personal watercraft.
alt.sport.officiating	Problems related to officiating athletic contests.
alt.sport.pool	Knock your balls into your pockets for fun.
alt.sport.racquetball	All aspects of indoor racquetball and related sports.

`alt.sport.squash`	With the proper technique, vegetables can go very fast.
`alt.sports.baseball.chicago-cubs`	Chicago Cubs major league baseball.
`alt.sports.basketball.nba.la-lakers`	Los Angeles Lakers NBA basketball.
`alt.sports.college.ivy-league`	Ivy League athletics.
`alt.sports.football.mn-vikings`	Minnesota Vikings NFL football.
`alt.sports.football.pro.gb-packers`	Green Bay Packers NFL football.
`alt.sports.hockey.nhl.tor-mapleleafs`	Toronto Maple Leafs NHL hockey.
`alt.surfing`	Riding the ocean waves.

Fan Clubs

This listing represents roughly 8 percent of the fan-club material on the lists. These were selected for no other reason than personal eccentricity.

`alt.books.anne-rice`	The vampire stuff.
`alt.elvis.king`	You've heard of this guy.
`alt.fan.blues-brothers`	Jake and Elwood ride again!
`alt.fan.disney.afternoon`	Disney Afternoon characters and shows.
`alt.fan.hofstadter`	Douglas Hofstadter, Godel, Escher, Bach and others.
`alt.fan.howard-stern`	Fans of the abrasive radio and TV personality.
`alt.fan.jimmy-buffett`	A white sports coat and a pink crustacean.
`alt.fan.laurie.anderson`	Will it be a music concert or a lecture this time?
`alt.fan.letterman`	One of the top ten reasons to get the alt groups.
`alt.fan.noam-chomsky`	Noam Chomsky's writings and opinions.
`alt.fan.oingo-boingo`	Have you ever played Ping-Pong in Pago Pago?

`alt.fan.penn-n-teller`	The magicians Penn and Teller.
`alt.fan.rush-limbaugh`	Just what it says.
`alt.fan.u2`	The Irish rock band U2.
`alt.fan.wodehouse`	Discussion of the works of humor author P.G. Wodehouse.
`alt.fan.woody-allen`	The diminutive director.
`alt.music.peter-gabriel`	Discussion of the music of Peter Gabriel.
`alt.ql.creative`	The *Quantum Leap* TV show.
`alt.tv.barney`	He's everywhere. Now appearing in several alt groups.

The Arts, More or Less

This list uses a fairly elastic definition of art.

`alt.artcom`	Artistic community, arts and communication.
`alt.arts.ballet`	All aspects of ballet and modern dance as performing art.
`alt.binaries.pictures.cartoons`	Images from animated cartoons.
`alt.binaries.pictures.fine-art.d`	Discussion of the fine-art binaries. (Moderated)
`alt.binaries.pictures.fine-art.digitized`	Art from conventional media. (Moderated)
`alt.binaries.pictures.fine-art.graphics`	Art created on computers. (Moderated)
`alt.books.reviews`	"If you want to know how it turns out, read it!"
`alt.folklore.urban`	Urban legends, a la Jan Harold Brunvand.
`alt.guitar`	Strumming and picking.
`alt.magic`	For discussion about stage magic.
`alt.music.a-cappella`	Like `rec.music.a-cappella`, only different.
`alt.music.alternative`	For groups having two or less platinum-selling albums.
`alt.music.blues-traveler`	For "All fellow travelers."

`alt.music.progressive`	Yes, Marillion, Asia, King Crimson, and so on.
`alt.music.synthpop`	Depeche Mode, Erasure, Pet Shop Boys, and much more!
`alt.music.techno`	Bring on the bass!
`alt.music.world`	Discussion of music from around the world.
`alt.prose`	Postings of original writings, fictional and otherwise.
`alt.tv.mst3k`	The finest cultural newsgroup on earth (author's opinion)!
`alt.zines`	Small magazines, mostly noncommercial.

Religion

This area is full of many lively discussions. It's sometimes strange to think of comments on ancient manuscripts flying back and forth on high-speed, fiber-optic links.

`alt.christnet`	Gathering place for Christian ministers and users.
`alt.christnet.bible`	Bible discussion and research.
`alt.christnet.philosophy`	Philosophical implications of Christianity.
`alt.christnet.theology`	The distinctives of God of Christian theology.
`alt.hindu`	The Hindu religion. (Moderated)
`alt.messianic`	Messianic traditions.
`alt.philosophy.zen`	Zen for everyone.
`alt.religion.christian`	Unmoderated forum for discussing Christianity.
`alt.religion.gnostic`	History and philosophies of the gnostic sects.
`alt.religion.islam`	Discussion of Islamic faith and society.

Funny Business

Humor is a giant newsgroup topic. If you're the only person in Nonesuch, Wyoming who thinks Dave Barry is funny, you can find pals on the Net. In Usenet humor newsgroups like alt.humor.best-of-usenet, off-color jokes are typically encoded in a simple substitution cipher, so if you go to the trouble of decoding it, you don't have much business complaining about your sensibilities being assaulted.

alt.comedy.british	Discussion of British comedy in a variety of media.
alt.comedy.british. blackadder	The Black Adder programme.
alt.comedy.firesgn-thtre	Firesign Theatre — in all its flaming glory.
alt.comedy.standup	Discussion of stand-up comedy and comedians.
alt.fan.dave_barry	Electronic fan club for humorist Dave Barry.
alt.fan.monty-python	Electronic fan club for those wacky Brits.
alt.fan.mst3k	A forum of incisive cultural comment.
alt.humor.best-of-usenet	What the moderator thinks is funniest. (Moderated)

Appendix E
Glossary

These are terms you are likely to encounter while roaming the Net or planning your next adventure.

account

There are two main kinds of Internet access for civilians: shell accounts and SLIP accounts. In a shell account, you usually dial up a computer with your modem and then navigate with UNIX commands. With a SLIP account (see SLIP), you are a real Internet site yourself, so you can use special Mac software for graphical-interface access.

address

A person's Internet address is the line with the @, as in chseiter@aol.com. From the Internet's point of view, an address is a set of four numbers, such as 132.34.115.31. The numbers correspond to a name that you can remember, such as zapp.com or simple.net. Check Appendix A for more on addresses.

alt

The newsgroups with the highest entertainment value are all in the unofficial alternative newsgroup hierarchy, and their names start with alt. Look in Appendix D for examples.

Anarchie

Anarchie is a Macintosh shareware program (see Chapter 5) that performs Archie searches. It's very good, and every national online service has it in Mac software libraries.

anonymous FTP

Anonymous FTP (see Chapter 5) is a procedure for logging into computers that maintain file archives that are accessible to anyone. You use *anonymous* as your user name and your e-mail address as your password.

AppleLink

Apple's own online service, soon to be merged into eWorld.

AppleTalk

Apple's own set of hardware and software for managing local-area networks. It's a slow protocol, best for smaller networks.

Archie

Archie is the basic Internet system for finding files. An Archie server is a computer that has lists of available archived files all over the Internet.

archive

An archive is a collection of files. At a site that maintains archives, someone is responsible for updating files and checking the archive for viruses.

ARPA

The Advanced Research Projects Agency, the government agency that funded ARPANET, a precursor to the Internet.

ARPANET

The ARPANET was the basis for networking research in the 1970s. The ARPANET has esentially disappeared into the Internet.

ASCII

ASCII stands for *A*merican *S*tandard *C*ode for *I*nformation *I*nterchange, a definition that associates each character with a number from 0 to 255. An ASCII file is a text file of characters.

backbone

A high-speed set of network connections. On the Internet, this usually means the NSFNET, a government-funded set of links between large computer sites.

BBS

Shorthand for *b*ulletin *b*oard *s*ystem. A BBS can be an old Mac II in a garage or a gigantic system with 10,000 users.

Big Sky Telegraph

A public-access Internet service, located in Montana. One of the best of its kind.

binary file

A file of 0s and 1s, which can represent pictures and sound as well as text.

binhex

A file transmission fix-up. Most mail programs can only handle ASCII, so a binhex utility program converts binary programs to ASCII so that people can mail you a binary file. At the receiving end, you have to decode the file back to binary with the programs BinHex (4.0 or 5.0), HQXer, or uudecode.

BITNET

A large network that passes material back and forth to the Internet. See Chapter 2.

biz

A newsgroup where you find discussions that have to do with (gasp!) money. Generally, you're not supposed to use other newsgroups for commercial purposes.

bounce

When you send a piece of e-mail and it comes back as undeliverable, it is said to have "bounced," much like an uncashable check.

bridge

A bridge is a set of hardware and software that lets two different networks appear to be a single larger network to people connecting from outside the system.

bug

A software programming or design problem. Unfortunately, bugs are plentiful in communications software.

chat

If you send messages to an electronic mailbox, that's e-mail. If you're sending messages back and forth to someone in real time, that's chat. See *IRC*.

ClariNet

ClariNet is a special newsgroup system that provides first-rate, commercially important news and charges a fee. Some Internet service providers carry it; some don't.

ClarisWorks

ClarisWorks is an integrated software package with a communications module that's better than some but not particularly useful in a world where you can get older versions of ZTerm for free.

com

This is the top-level domain name that identifies businesses.

communications software

The software that controls your modem and dials out to other networks. Mac examples are ZTerm, Microphone, White Knight, and the communications modules of Microsoft Works and ClarisWorks.

comp

The term comp in the middle of a newsgroup name means that the discussions will be computer-oriented. I'm sorry to report that the majority of these groups are oriented towards UNIX or PCs, not Macintoshes.

Computer Currents

A tabloid-format computer magazine that turns up on newspaper racks in big cities. A good source of local bulletin board numbers.

country code

A top-level domain name that identifies a site by country: `well.sf.ca.us`, for example, has the country code `us` because San Francisco is physically, if not emotionally, part of the United States.

.cpt

The file extension .cpt at the end of a filename means that the file was compressed with Compact Pro. You can expand it either with that program or with one of the StuffIt series from Aladdin Software.

CR Laboratories

A shell and SLIP account provider in Larkspur, California, with local dial-up numbers all over the United States. They're *my* SLIP provider, and they know how to set up MacTCP and InterSLIP for you.

cyberspace

This somewhat overworked term first appeared in the science fiction novel *Neuromancer*, by William Gibson. It refers to the digital world represented by all computers and their interaction.

dial-up

A dial-up connection is one that works only while you're connected by phone. The other type of connection is direct, where you're wired to a network and are connected all the time.

Dial 'n' cerf

A national Internet access provider.

DIALOG

A huge information service, managed by Lockheed, with lots of technical databases.

DNS

The domain name system, used to convert Internet names to their corresponding Internet numbers.

domain

An Internet site address has two parts, the domain and the top-level domain name. For America Online — `aol.com` — `aol` is the domain name and `com` is the top-level part. The domain roughly corresponds to the name of a particular network.

DOS

The original operating system that Microsoft cooked up (actually, Microsoft bought it in a one-sided deal) for IBM PCs. Don't bother looking in DOS file collections.

dotted quad

Every now and then you'll hear an old-time Internet hipster refer to the four numbers of an Internet address as a "dotted quad."

Electronic Frontier Foundation (EFF)

This organization is something like the conscience of the Internet, as opposed to its administration. Go look for the EFF area on your Internet service provider.

elm

This is considered a "good" UNIX e-mail utility, meaning that as a Mac user, you've probably never seen anything as cryptic or difficult.

e-mail

Electronic mail. It's a message you compose on your computer to be received on someone else's computer, although some services let your message be delivered as a fax or (this sounds weird, but it's true) *an actual piece of paper!*

edu

Usually this is the Internet address identifier for a university. The universities of the United States are the reason the Internet is the vast wonderland it is today.

Ethernet

An Ethernet network is a very common, much faster alternative to Apple's original built-in networking stuff. Newer Macs for business now have Ethernet capability as part of the system.

Eudora

A Macintosh program for handling e-mail. The first versions were shareware, but now it's a commercial program from QualComm software.

FAQ

*F*requently *a*sked *q*uestion. Trust me, your questions will be just like anyone else's. When you sign up with an Internet service provider — and before you make any contributions to newsgroups— read the FAQ files that are prominently displayed in menus. This saves you embarrassment and saves everyone else from your three-millionth-time newbie questions.

Fetch

A truly wonderful Macintosh FTP program from Dartmouth, available from all Internet service providers.

file transfer protocol

See *FTP*.

finger

On UNIX-based Internet systems, finger is a utility that lets you get a profile of a user (including the user's real name).

firewall

You may wonder how other computers you can reach by telnet keep you out of private areas. Networks have *firewalls* in different places to block access to unauthorized users.

flame

A flame is the sort of extreme opinion that the sender probably wouldn't have the nerve to deliver in person. Although some Internet old-timers seem to generate four flames a day, I think that as a matter of decorum you should never flame (it's a verb or a noun) anyone ever, no matter what.

freenet

There are about 30 or 40 freenets around the United States. These are networks that don't charge you a monthly or per-hour fee. Cool, huh? Your local librarian is likely to have the phone numbers.

freeware

Freeware is software that is offered by its author for no charge. This is different from shareware (see *shareware*). There's some amazingly good freeware on the Net.

FTP

FTP stands for *file transfer protocol*. On the Internet, it usually refers to a UNIX-system utility program that lets you collect files from archives at other sites (see Chapter 5).

gateway

A gateway is hardware that lets messages be sent between two different kinds of networks. You need a gateway, for example, to communicate at network speeds between a Macintosh AppleTalk-based network and a UNIX-based network.

Graphic Interchange Format (GIF)

GIF stands for graphics interchange format — you see it as a file extension on picture files such as flower.gif. GIF files are very common on the Internet, and most sites offer a shareware program called GIFwatcher to read them. Adobe Photoshop and other large image-handling programs also can work with GIF files.

gnu

Every time you look in a big archive, you see gnu folders. The Free Software Foundation has developed gnu as a sort of UNIX-clone operating system, complete with C-language compiler and lots of utilities, that it distributes for free, as a matter of principle.

Gopher

A Gopher is a file search-and-retrieval system that's usually the right basic Internet tool for finding the file you want. For the Macintosh, there's TurboGopher.

Gopherspace

Gopherspace is a cutesy name for the total of all the Gophers in the world and the information in them.

gov

Gov is the top-level domain name, or zone, for any type of government organization.

host

Most kinds of Internet access using a modem will have you dialing a host computer, which is a big computer with its own Internet address.

.hqx

When you see this as a file extension, it means that the file is in binhex (see binhex) format. You have to decode it to get the original file, and the easiest way to decode it is with HQXer.

HQXer

As you can guess from the name, this shareware utility processes files into and out of .hqx format. It's available in the libraries of every Internet service provider.

hypertext

Hypertext is a set of text files in which individual words link one file to the next.

HyTelnet

This program can be used to manage telnet functions, but it can also be used offline as a comprehensive directory of telnet sites.

information superhighway

No one knows what this means, including me, so I thought I'd put it in the glossary. Internet fans think it means the Internet, cable TV companies think it's what will happen when cable fibers carry data, and phone companies think it's what will happen when they can force you to buy computers from them. The Internet fans are closest.

Internet protocol (IP)

A set of definitions that govern transmission of individual packets of information on the Internet.

Internet Society

A bunch of good people who discuss policies and make recommendations about Internet management.

InterNIC

The name stands for _Inter_net _N_etwork _I_nformation Center. The word _InterNIC_ turns up on the menus of many Internet service providers, and it's a good place to look for the history and future of the Net.

InterSLIP

A freeware program from Intercon that works with MacTCP to give your Mac a SLIP connection.

IRC

IRC stands for _I_nternet _R_elay _C_hat, an online forum of almost unimaginable liveliness that's offered by real Internet providers, such as Delphi.

jpeg

A compressed file format for images.

Jughead

Because there was a program called Archie and another called Veronica, someone decided that Jughead would be a good name for a Gopher searching tool.

Kermit

A slow but reliable file transfer protocol named, in fact, after the frog on *The Muppet Show*.

LISTSERV

LISTSERV programs manage mailing lists by sending messages automatically to everyone on a given list.

log in

Log in and *log on* are different terms for making contact with a remote computer. They're used interchangeably.

lurking

In Internet jargon you are said to be lurking if you join a discussion group and just read other people's messages. Oh, well, better a lurker than a flamer.

Mac Binary

A special format for storing Macintosh binary files on other computers.

MacTCP

Apple's program (a control panel, actually) that you need to use a SLIP account (see Chapter 13). MacTCP translates your files and messages into Internet-compatible chunks of information.

MacSLIP

An alternative to InterSLIP.

MacWAIS

An excellent shareware program for WAIS, the *wide area information server*.

mail server

A mail server is a program on a host computer that saves your mail for you until you make a dial-up connection and have a chance to download your mail and read it.

Matrix

Lots of early Net visionaries use the term Matrix to denote the total of all connected computers in the world. It used to be used as a cool name for the Internet plus everything else.

Metaverse

A graphical version, more or less, of the Internet, but with a better plot. This electronic structure is the basis of Neal Stephenson's science fiction masterpiece *Snow Crash*.

MicroTimes

A tabloid-format computer magazine that turns up on newspaper racks in big cities. A good source of local bulletin board numbers.

mil

The top-level domain name of military sites on the Internet. Just about all U.S. military sites are Internet sites.

MIME

This acronym stands for *M*ultipurpose *I*nternet *M*ail *E*xtension, an Internet standard that lets you add sound and images to e-mail. It's not widely implemented yet, but it will be.

mirror

A mirror site is an archive that keeps a copy of the files in another site.

misc

Newsgroups that don't fit under any other recognizable category get put into misc.

modem

The device that lets your computer make telephone calls to other computers.

moderated

A moderated newsgroup has someone who filters out the really pointless or offensive material, leaving only moderately pointless or offensive messages.

Mosaic

Mosaic is the original freeware program for access to the World Wide Web hypertext system. Commercial versions of Mosaic are now available.

MUD

*M*ulti-*U*ser *D*ungeons are online fantasy games that can have dozens of players.

Multi-User Simulated Environment (MUSE)

A *M*ulti-*U*ser *S*imulated *E*nvironments is a sort of highbrow MUD. A multiplayer version of the Mac game SimCity would be a MUSE.

NCSA

*N*ational *C*enter for *S*upercomputing *A*pplications, managed by the University of Illinois, is the home of Mosaic, along with lots of big computers.

Netcom

A large national Internet service provider and a big FTP server.

network

Any set of computers that can communicate directly with each other constitutes a network.

newbie

A faintly derogatory term for users in their first months on the Internet, employed freely by people who have been on the system one week longer.

newsgroup

A collection of people and messages on a particular topic of interest.

node

The term *node* in Internet context means a central computer that's part of an Internet-connected network. Sometimes used interchangeably with "site" or "host."

NovaLink

A big-time Internet service provider. Look in Chapter 19 for the phone number.

NSFNET

The *N*ational *S*cience *F*oundation *Net* is a principal Internet traffic carrier.

packet

A block of information, complete with addresses for destination and source, traveling over the Internet.

page

The basic unit of the World Wide Web information service is the page. Pages are linked by hypertext references to other pages.

password

OK, you know what a password is. Just try to think of a nonobvious password (usually, it shouldn't be a real word from a dictionary, much less your nickname) to save yourself potential grief.

PDIAL

The PDIAL list, available on every Internet service, is a regularly updated registry of public Internet access providers.

ping

An Internet program that is used to determine if a site is still active.

poker

OK, you may be wondering why I keep putting definitions next to their acronyms. Years ago at Caltech, I asked a French postdoc in my research group if he wanted to join the lunchtime graduate student poker game. He looked puzzled (he was just learning vernacular English, although he could write better than we could). I wrote the word "poker" on a blackboard, he looked at it, frowned, and looked it up in a bilingual dictionary, where the entry read (I'm not kidding)

> poker (n.) *poker*

The light bulb went off, he said, "Ah, poker!", sat down, and cleaned us out.

point of presence

A local phone number for high-speed access maintained by an Internet provider.

POP

*P*ost *O*ffice *P*rotocol is an e-mail protocol used for downloading mail from a mail server.

PPP

*P*oint to *P*oint *P*rotocol is an alternative to SLIP for dial-up full Internet access. You would use MacPPP instead of InterSLIP or MacSLIP for this kind of connection. Your Internet service provider's system administrator will tell you which to use.

protocol

A protocol is a definition that controls communication on a network.

rec

Newsgroups for recreational purposes are signaled with `rec`. There's plenty of overlap between `rec` and `alt`, in practice.

RFC/RFD

*R*equests *F*or *C*omment and *R*equests *F*or *D*iscussion are study-group documents with an important role in settling general Internet questions about design and use.

rlogin

An alternative to telnet, rlogin is a UNIX command for connecting to remote computers.

router

A router is a gateway (see gateway) between two networks that use Internet protocol.

sci

Serious research newsgroups in science and mathematics belong to this newsgroup hierarchy.

.sea

This file extension stands for *self-extracting archive*. If you double-click on a .sea file, it usually turns itself into a folder containing an application and some documentation files.

server

A computer that stores files as a central resource for other computers, called clients, that can connect to the server to get files for themselves.

shareware

Shareware is software you can download free to test. If you like it and use it, you are obliged as a matter of honor to send the requested payment to the author.

.sit

Files compressed with StuffIt from Aladdin Software show this file extension. You can expand them with UnStuffIt or Stuffit Expander, available from all the national online services and most bulletin boards.

SLIP

Serial Line Internet Protocol lets you become a dial-up Internet site. You also need MacTCP to make a SLIP connection with a Macintosh (see Chapter 13). SLIP is an alternative to PPP.

SMTP

The *S*imple *M*ail *T*ransport *P*rotocol is the e-mail protocol standard for the Internet.

soc

The soc newsgroups on social issues overlap many of the alt social issue newsgroups.

.tar

This file extension indicates files compressed with a special UNIX program. You can expand them with StuffIt Deluxe.

TCP/IP

The whole system, *T*ransport *C*ontrol *P*rotocol and *I*nternet *P*rotocol, makes up a standard guideline for network hardware and software design.

telnet

The core of all Internet services is the UNIX utility telnet, a program that lets users connected to one host dial up a different Internet host.

terminal

In the old days, a terminal could only receive and send characters to the real computer at the other end of the wires. A terminal program lets your sophisticated Macintosh mimic this primitive arrangement.

thread

A series of connected messages in a newsgroup.

TurboGopher

A brilliant Macintosh Gopher program for searching all the files of the Internet. As freeware, TurboGopher is available everywhere in the libraries of online services.

UNIX

The operating system that runs the Internet. Developed over many years, it's capable of meeting any networking challenge and is very thrifty with computing resources. The downside consequence of these virtues is that UNIX is hard for beginners to use.

Usenet

The network, linked at different points to the Internet, that supports all the newsgroups.

uuencode

Uuencode is a program that turns binary files into ASCII files so that you can send them through e-mail. Uudecode takes the files back to binary. Mac shareware utilities for this function are available in most online libraries.

Veronica

Veronica is a program that searches for files over all available Gopher servers, making it the program to use whenever it's available. Higher-level searches are preferable to direct use of Archie.

VT-100/102

These are two very common terminals and, hence, two very common terminal-software options. As a first guess, pick VT-100 as the terminal setting when you dial up almost any service using standard communications software.

WAIS

*W*ide *a*rea *i*nformation *s*ervers are text databases with a superior search method that looks inside the text rather than just looking at document titles.

WELL

A very popular Bay Area bulletin board with full Internet access. About half the computer journalists on earth seem to hang out on this service.

Windows

An attempt to stick a Macintosh-like face on the ugly reality of DOS.

WWW

*W*orld *W*ide *W*eb is an Internet service consisting of hypertext-linked documents. It's easy and fun, and it's taking over the Internet (see Chapter 6).

whois

A command available on some Internet services to find the real name of a user based on the user's screen name.

X, Y, and ZMODEM

XMODEM is a 15-year-old file transfer protocol; YMODEM is newer; and ZMODEM is the fastest and best.

.Z

Another type of UNIX-system compressed file extension, also expandable with UnStuffIt.

zip

The most common compressed-file format for PCs. Unless it's a text file, you probably won't be able to do anything with a .zip file on a Mac, even if you expand it, so don't bother unless there's a compelling reason to put yourself through the trouble.

ZTerm

The favorite communications software for many Mac users. It's reliable and fast for downloading large files from bulletin boards.

Index

• Q •

• R •

• S •

10/31/9[?]

Title	Author	ISBN	Price
The Internet For Macs® For Dummies® 2nd Edition	by Charles Seiter	ISBN: 1-56884-371-2	$19.99 USA/$26.99 Canada
The Internet For Macs® For Dummies® Starter Kit	by Charles Seiter	ISBN: 1-56884-244-9	$29.99 USA/$39.99 Canada
The Internet For Macs® For Dummies® Starter Kit Bestseller Edition	by Charles Seiter	ISBN: 1-56884-245-7	$39.99 USA/$54.99 Canada
The Internet For Windows® For Dummies® Starter Kit	by John R. Levine & Margaret Levine Young	ISBN: 1-56884-237-6	$34.99 USA/$44.99 Canada
The Internet For Windows® For Dummies® Starter Kit, Bestseller Edition	by John R. Levine & Margaret Levine Young	ISBN: 1-56884-246-5	$39.99 USA/$54.99 Canada

MACINTOSH

Mac® Programming For Dummies®	by Dan Parks Sydow	ISBN: 1-56884-173-6	$19.95 USA/$26.95 Canada
Macintosh® System 7.5 For Dummies®	by Bob LeVitus	ISBN: 1-56884-197-3	$19.95 USA/$26.95 Canada
MORE Macs® For Dummies®	by David Pogue	ISBN: 1-56884-087-X	$19.95 USA/$26.95 Canada
PageMaker 5 For Macs® For Dummies®	by Galen Gruman & Deke McClelland	ISBN: 1-56884-178-7	$19.95 USA/$26.95 Canada
QuarkXPress 3.3 For Dummies®	by Galen Gruman & Barbara Assadi	ISBN: 1-56884-217-1	$19.99 USA/$26.99 Canada
Upgrading and Fixing Macs® For Dummies®	by Kearney Rietmann & Frank Higgins	ISBN: 1-56884-189-2	$19.95 USA/$26.95 Canada

MULTIMEDIA

Multimedia & CD-ROMs For Dummies® 2nd Edition	by Andy Rathbone	ISBN: 1-56884-907-9	$19.99 USA/$26.99 Canada
Multimedia & CD-ROMs For Dummies® Interactive Multimedia Value Pack, 2nd Edition	by Andy Rathbone	ISBN: 1-56884-909-5	$29.99 USA/$39.99 Canada

OPERATING SYSTEMS:

DOS

MORE DOS For Dummies®	by Dan Gookin	ISBN: 1-56884-046-2	$19.95 USA/$26.95 Canada
OS/2® Warp For Dummies® 2nd Edition	by Andy Rathbone	ISBN: 1-56884-205-8	$19.99 USA/$26.99 Canada

UNIX

MORE UNIX® For Dummies®	by John R. Levine & Margaret Levine Young	ISBN: 1-56884-361-5	$19.99 USA/$26.99 Canada
UNIX® For Dummies®	by John R. Levine & Margaret Levine Young	ISBN: 1-878058-58-4	$19.95 USA/$26.95 Canada

WINDOWS

MORE Windows® For Dummies® 2nd Edition	by Andy Rathbone	ISBN: 1-56884-048-9	$19.95 USA/$26.95 Canada
Windows® 95 For Dummies®	by Andy Rathbone	ISBN: 1-56884-240-6	$19.99 USA/$26.99 Canada

PCS/HARDWARE

Illustrated Computer Dictionary For Dummies® 2nd Edition	by Dan Gookin & Wallace Wang	ISBN: 1-56884-218-X	$12.95 USA/$16.95 Canada
Upgrading and Fixing PCs For Dummies® 2nd Edition	by Andy Rathbone	ISBN: 1-56884-903-6	$19.99 USA/$26.99 Canada

PRESENTATION/AUTOCAD

AutoCAD For Dummies®	by Bud Smith	ISBN: 1-56884-191-4	$19.95 USA/$26.95 Canada
PowerPoint 4 For Windows® For Dummies®	by Doug Lowe	ISBN: 1-56884-161-2	$16.99 USA/$22.99 Canada

PROGRAMMING

Borland C++ For Dummies®	by Michael Hyman	ISBN: 1-56884-162-0	$19.95 USA/$26.95 Canada
C For Dummies® Volume 1	by Dan Gookin	ISBN: 1-878058-78-9	$19.95 USA/$26.95 Canada
C++ For Dummies®	by Stephen R. Davis	ISBN: 1-56884-163-9	$19.95 USA/$26.95 Canada
Delphi Programming For Dummies®	by Neil Rubenking	ISBN: 1-56884-200-7	$19.99 USA/$26.99 Canada
Mac® Programming For Dummies®	by Dan Parks Sydow	ISBN: 1-56884-173-6	$19.95 USA/$26.95 Canada
PowerBuilder 4 Programming For Dummies®	by Ted Coombs & Jason Coombs	ISBN: 1-56884-325-9	$19.99 USA/$26.99 Canada
QBasic Programming For Dummies®	by Douglas Hergert	ISBN: 1-56884-093-4	$19.95 USA/$26.95 Canada
Visual Basic 3 For Dummies®	by Wallace Wang	ISBN: 1-56884-076-4	$19.95 USA/$26.95 Canada
Visual Basic "X" For Dummies®	by Wallace Wang	ISBN: 1-56884-230-9	$19.99 USA/$26.99 Canada
Visual C++ 2 For Dummies®	by Michael Hyman & Bob Arnson	ISBN: 1-56884-328-3	$19.99 USA/$26.99 Canada
Windows® 95 Programming For Dummies®	by S. Randy Davis	ISBN: 1-56884-327-5	$19.99 USA/$26.99 Canada

SPREADSHEET

1-2-3 For Dummies®	by Greg Harvey	ISBN: 1-878058-60-6	$16.95 USA/$22.95 Canada
1-2-3 For Windows® 5 For Dummies® 2nd Edition	by John Walkenbach	ISBN: 1-56884-216-3	$16.95 USA/$22.95 Canada
Excel 5 For Macs® For Dummies®	by Greg Harvey	ISBN: 1-56884-186-8	$19.95 USA/$26.95 Canada
Excel For Dummies® 2nd Edition	by Greg Harvey	ISBN: 1-56884-050-0	$16.95 USA/$22.95 Canada
MORE 1-2-3 For DOS For Dummies®	by John Weingarten	ISBN: 1-56884-224-4	$19.99 USA/$26.99 Canada
MORE Excel 5 For Windows® For Dummies®	by Greg Harvey	ISBN: 1-56884-207-4	$19.95 USA/$26.95 Canada
Quattro Pro 6 For Windows® For Dummies®	by John Walkenbach	ISBN: 1-56884-174-4	$19.95 USA/$26.95 Canada
Quattro Pro For DOS For Dummies®	by John Walkenbach	ISBN: 1-56884-023-3	$16.95 USA/$22.95 Canada

UTILITIES

Title	Author	ISBN	Price
Norton Utilities 8 For Dummies®	by Beth Slick	ISBN: 1-56884-166-3	$19.95 USA/$26.95 Canada

VCRS/CAMCORDERS

Title	Author	ISBN	Price
VCRs & Camcorders For Dummies™	by Gordon McComb & Andy Rathbone	ISBN: 1-56884-229-5	$14.99 USA/$20.99 Canada

WORD PROCESSING

Ami Pro For Dummies®	by Jim Meade	ISBN: 1-56884-049-7	$19.95 USA/$26.95 Canada
MORE Word For Windows® 6 For Dummies®	by Doug Lowe	ISBN: 1-56884-165-5	$19.95 USA/$26.95 Canada
MORE WordPerfect® 6 For Windows® For Dummies®	by Margaret Levine Young & David C. Kay	ISBN: 1-56884-206-6	$19.95 USA/$26.95 Canada
MORE WordPerfect® 6 For DOS For Dummies®	by Wallace Wang, edited by Dan Gookin	ISBN: 1-56884-047-0	$19.95 USA/$26.95 Canada
Word 6 For Macs® For Dummies®	by Dan Gookin	ISBN: 1-56884-190-6	$19.95 USA/$26.95 Canada
Word For Windows® 6 For Dummies®	by Dan Gookin	ISBN: 1-56884-075-6	$16.95 USA/$22.95 Canada
Word For Windows® For Dummies®	by Dan Gookin & Ray Werner	ISBN: 1-878058-86-X	$16.95 USA/$22.95 Canada
WordPerfect® 6 For DOS For Dummies®	by Dan Gookin	ISBN: 1-878058-77-0	$16.95 USA/$22.95 Canada
WordPerfect® 6.1 For Windows® For Dummies® 2nd Edition	by Margaret Levine Young & David Kay	ISBN: 1-56884-243-0	$16.95 USA/$22.95 Canada
WordPerfect® For Dummies®	by Dan Gookin	ISBN: 1-878058-52-5	$16.95 USA/$22.95 Canada

Fun, Fast, & Cheap!™

10/31/95

NEW!

The Internet For Macs® For Dummies® Quick Reference
by Charles Seiter

ISBN:1-56884-967-2
$9.99 USA/$12.99 Canada

NEW!

Windows® 95 For Dummies® Quick Reference
by Greg Harvey

ISBN: 1-56884-964-8
$9.99 USA/$12.99 Canada

SUPER STAR

Photoshop 3 For Macs® For Dummies® Quick Reference
by Deke McClelland

ISBN: 1-56884-968-0
$9.99 USA/$12.99 Canada

SUPER STAR

WordPerfect® For DOS For Dummies® Quick Reference
by Greg Harvey

ISBN: 1-56884-009-8
$8.95 USA/$12.95 Canada

Title	Author	ISBN	Price
DATABASE			
Access 2 For Dummies® Quick Reference	by Stuart J. Stuple	ISBN: 1-56884-167-1	$8.95 USA/$11.95 Canada
dBASE 5 For DOS For Dummies® Quick Reference	by Barrie Sosinsky	ISBN: 1-56884-954-0	$9.99 USA/$12.99 Canada
dBASE 5 For Windows® For Dummies® Quick Reference	by Stuart J. Stuple	ISBN: 1-56884-953-2	$9.99 USA/$12.99 Canada
Paradox 5 For Windows® For Dummies® Quick Reference	by Scott Palmer	ISBN: 1-56884-960-5	$9.99 USA/$12.99 Canada
DESKTOP PUBLISHING/ILLUSTRATION/GRAPHICS			
CorelDRAW! 5 For Dummies® Quick Reference	by Raymond E. Werner	ISBN: 1-56884-952-4	$9.99 USA/$12.99 Canada
Harvard Graphics For Windows® For Dummies® Quick Reference	by Raymond E. Werner	ISBN: 1-56884-962-1	$9.99 USA/$12.99 Canada
Photoshop 3 For Macs® For Dummies® Quick Reference	by Deke McClelland	ISBN: 1-56884-968-0	$9.99 USA/$12.99 Canada
FINANCE/PERSONAL FINANCE			
Quicken 4 For Windows® For Dummies® Quick Reference	by Stephen L. Nelson	ISBN: 1-56884-950-8	$9.95 USA/$12.95 Canada
GROUPWARE/INTEGRATED			
Microsoft® Office 4 For Windows® For Dummies® Quick Reference	by Doug Lowe	ISBN: 1-56884-958-3	$9.99 USA/$12.99 Canada
Microsoft® Works 3 For Windows® For Dummies® Quick Reference	by Michael Partington	ISBN: 1-56884-959-1	$9.99 USA/$12.99 Canada
INTERNET/COMMUNICATIONS/NETWORKING			
The Internet For Dummies® Quick Reference	by John R. Levine & Margaret Levine Young	ISBN: 1-56884-168-X	$8.95 USA/$11.95 Canada
MACINTOSH			
Macintosh® System 7.5 For Dummies® Quick Reference	by Stuart J. Stuple	ISBN: 1-56884-956-7	$9.99 USA/$12.99 Canada
OPERATING SYSTEMS:			
DOS			
DOS For Dummies® Quick Reference	by Greg Harvey	ISBN: 1-56884-007-1	$8.95 USA/$11.95 Canada
UNIX			
UNIX® For Dummies® Quick Reference	by John R. Levine & Margaret Levine Young	ISBN: 1-56884-094-2	$8.95 USA/$11.95 Canada
WINDOWS			
Windows® 3.1 For Dummies® Quick Reference, 2nd Edition	by Greg Harvey	ISBN: 1-56884-951-6	$8.95 USA/$11.95 Canada
PCs/HARDWARE			
Memory Management For Dummies® Quick Reference	by Doug Lowe	ISBN: 1-56884-362-3	$9.99 USA/$12.99 Canada
PRESENTATION/AUTOCAD			
AutoCAD For Dummies® Quick Reference	by Ellen Finkelstein	ISBN: 1-56884-198-1	$9.95 USA/$12.95 Canada
SPREADSHEET			
1-2-3 For Dummies® Quick Reference	by John Walkenbach	ISBN: 1-56884-027-6	$8.95 USA/$11.95 Canada
1-2-3 For Windows® 5 For Dummies® Quick Reference	by John Walkenbach	ISBN: 1-56884-957-5	$9.95 USA/$12.95 Canada
Excel For Windows® For Dummies® Quick Reference, 2nd Edition	by John Walkenbach	ISBN: 1-56884-096-9	$8.95 USA/$11.95 Canada
Quattro Pro 6 For Windows® For Dummies® Quick Reference	by Stuart J. Stuple	ISBN: 1-56884-172-8	$9.95 USA/$12.95 Canada
WORD PROCESSING			
Word For Windows® 6 For Dummies® Quick Reference	by George Lynch	ISBN: 1-56884-095-0	$8.95 USA/$11.95 Canada
Word For Windows® For Dummies® Quick Reference	by George Lynch	ISBN: 1-56884-029-2	$8.95 USA/$11.95 Canada
WordPerfect® 6.1 For Windows® For Dummies® Quick Reference, 2nd Edition	by Greg Harvey	ISBN: 1-56884-966-4	$9.99 USA/$12.99/Canada

PC PRESS

10/31/95

"A lot easier to use than the book Excel gives you!"

Lisa Schmeckpeper, New Berlin, WI, on PC World Excel 5 For Windows Handbook

Official Hayes Modem Communications Companion
by Caroline M. Halliday

ISBN: 1-56884-072-1
$29.95 USA/$39.95 Canada
Includes software.

1,001 Komputer Answers from Kim Komando
by Kim Komando

ISBN: 1-56884-460-3
$29.99 USA/$39.99 Canada
Includes software.

PC World DOS 6 Handbook, 2nd Edition
by John Socha, Clint Hicks, & Devra Hall

ISBN: 1-878058-79-7
$34.95 USA/$44.95 Canada
Includes software.

PC World Word For Windows® 6 Handbook
by Brent Heslop & David Angell

ISBN: 1-56884-054-3
$34.95 USA/$44.95 Canada
Includes software.

PC World Microsoft® Access 2 Bible, 2nd Edition
by Cary N. Prague & Michael R. Irwin

ISBN: 1-56884-086-1
$39.95 USA/$52.95 Canada
Includes software.

PC World Excel 5 For Windows® Handbook, 2nd Edition
by John Walkenbach & Dave Maguiness

ISBN: 1-56884-056-X
$34.95 USA/$44.95 Canada
Includes software.

PC World WordPerfect® 6 Handbook
by Greg Harvey

ISBN: 1-878058-80-0
$34.95 USA/$44.95 Canada
Includes software.

QuarkXPress For Windows® Designer Handbook
by Barbara Assadi & Galen Gruman

ISBN: 1-878058-45-2
$29.95 USA/$39.95 Canada

Official XTree Companion, 3rd Edition
by Beth Slick

ISBN: 1-878058-57-6
$19.95 USA/$26.95 Canada

PC World DOS 6 Command Reference and Problem Solver
by John Socha & Devra Hall

ISBN: 1-56884-055-1
$24.95 USA/$32.95 Canada

Client/Server Strategies™: A Survival Guide for Corporate Reengineers
by David Vaskevitch

ISBN: 1-56884-064-0
$29.95 USA/$39.95 Canada

"PC World Word For Windows 6 Handbook is very easy to follow with lots of 'hands on' examples. The 'Task at a Glance' is very helpful!"

Jacqueline Martens, Tacoma, WA

"Thanks for publishing this book! It's the best money I've spent this year!"

Robert D. Templeton, Ft. Worth, TX, on MORE Windows 3.1 SECRETS

Microsoft and Windows are registered trademarks of Microsoft Corporation. WordPerfect is a registered trademark of Novell. ----STRATEGIES and the IDG Books Worldwide logos are trademarks under exclusive license to IDG Books Worldwide, Inc., from International Data Group, Inc.

scholastic requests & educational orders please Educational Sales, at 1. 800. 434. 2086

FOR MORE INFO OR TO ORDER, PLEASE CALL ▶ 800. 762. 2974

For volume discounts & special orders please call Tony Real, Special Sales, at 415. 655. 3048

10/31/99

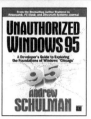

Unauthorized Windows® 95: A Developer's Guide to Exploring the Foundations of Windows "Chicago"
by Andrew Schulman

ISBN: 1-56884-169-8
$29.99 USA/$39.99 Canada

Unauthorized Windows® 95 Developer's Resource Kit
by Andrew Schulman

ISBN: 1-56884-305-4
$39.99 USA/$54.99 Canada

Best of the Net
by Seth Godin

ISBN: 1-56884-313-5
$22.99 USA/$32.99 Canada

Detour: The Truth About the Information Superhighway
by Michael Sullivan-Trainor

ISBN: 1-56884-307-0
$22.99 USA/$32.99 Canada

PowerPC Programming For Intel Programmers
by Kip McClanahan

ISBN: 1-56884-306-2
$49.99 USA/$64.99 Canada

Foundations™ of Visual C++ Programming For Windows® 95
by Paul Yao & Joseph Yao

ISBN: 1-56884-321-6
$39.99 USA/$54.99 Canada

Heavy Metal™ Visual C++ Programming
by Steve Holzner

ISBN: 1-56884-196-5
$39.95 USA/$54.95 Canada

Heavy Metal™ OLE 2.0 Programming
by Steve Holzner

ISBN: 1-56884-301-1
$39.95 USA/$54.95 Canada

Lotus Notes Application Development Handbook
by Erica Kerwien

ISBN: 1-56884-308-9
$39.99 USA/$54.99 Canada

The Internet Direct Connect Kit
by Peter John Harrison

ISBN: 1-56884-135-3
$29.95 USA/$39.95 Canada

Macworld® Ultimate Mac® Programming
by Dave Mark

ISBN: 1-56884-195-7
$39.95 USA/$54.95 Canada

The UNIX®-Haters Handbook
by Simson Garfinkel, Daniel Weise, & Steven Strassmann

ISBN: 1-56884-203-1
$16.95 USA/$22.95 Canada

Learn C++ Today!
by Martin Rinehart

ISBN: 1-56884-310-0
34.99 USA/$44.99 Canada

Type & Learn™ C
by Tom Swan

ISBN: 1-56884-073-X
34.95 USA/$44.95 Canada

Type & Learn™ Windows® Programming
by Tom Swan

ISBN: 1-56884-071-3
34.95 USA/$44.95 Canada

For scholastic requests & educational orders please call Educational Sales, at 1. 800. 434. 2086

FOR MORE INFO OR TO ORDER, PLEASE CALL ▶ 800 762 2974

For volume discounts & special orders please c Tony Real, Special Sales, at 415. 655. 3048

இப் புத்தகங்கள் மிகவும் நல்லவை

(way cool)

10/31/95

OS/2® Warp Internet Connection: Your Key to Cruising the Internet and the World Wide Web

by Deborah Morrison

OS/2 users can get warped on the Internet using the OS/2 Warp tips, techniques, and helpful directories found in *OS/2 Warp Internet Connection*. This reference covers OS/2 Warp Internet basics, such as e-mail use and how to access other computers, plus much more! The Internet gets more

complex every day, but for OS/2 Warp users it just got a whole lot easier! Your value-packed disk includes 10 of the best internet utilities to help you explore the Net and save money while you're on-line!

EXPERT AUTHOR PROFILE

Deborah Morrison (Raleigh, NC) is an award-winning IBM writer who specializes in TCP/IP and the Internet. She is currently the editor-in-chief of IBM's *TCP/IP Connection* quarterly magazine.

ISBN: 1-56884-465-4
$24.99 USA/$34.99 Canada
Includes one 3.5" disk

Available: Now

Official Guide to Using OS/2® Warp

by Karla Stagray & Linda S. Rogers

IDG Books and IBM have come together to produce the most comprehensive user's guide to OS/2 Warp available today. From installation to using OS/2 Warp's BonusPak programs, this book delivers valuable help to the reader who needs to get up and running fast. Loaded with working examples, easy tips, and operating system concepts, *Official Guide to Using OS/2 Warp* is the only official user's guide authorized by IBM.

EXPERT AUTHOR PROFILE

Karla Stagray and Linda Rogers (Boca Raton, FL) both have a unique understanding of computer software and hardware. As award-winning IBM writers, Stagray and Rogers have received Society of Technical Communicators awards for various endeavors.

ISBN: 1-56884-466-2
$29.99 USA/$39.99 Canada

Available: Now

OS/2® Warp Uncensored

by Peter G. Magid & Ira H. Schneider

Exploit the power of OS/2 Warp and learn the secrets of object technology for the Workplace Shell. This all new book/CD-ROM bundle, for power users and intermediate users alike, provides the real inside story—not just the "what," but the "how" and "why" — from the folks who designed and developed the Workplace Shell. Packed with tips and techniques for using IBM's REXX programming language, and the bonus CD includes new bitmaps, icons, mouse pointers, REXX scripts, and an Object Tool!

EXPERT AUTHOR PROFILE

Peter G. Magid (Boca Raton, FL) is the User Interface Design Lead for the Workplace Shell and has over 12 years of programming experience at IBM. He is a graduate of Tulane University, and holds a B.S. degree in Computer Science.

Ira H. Schneider (Boca Raton, FL) has focused on enhancements to the Workplace Shell and has over 25 years of experience with IBM. He has held numerous lead programming positions within IBM and graduated from Northeastern University with a B.S. degree in Electrical Engineering.

ISBN: 1-56884-474-3
$39.99 USA/$54.99 Canada
Includes one CD-ROM

Available: Now

OS/2® Warp FAQs™

by Mike Kaply & Timothy F. Sipples

At last, the ultimate answer book for every OS/2 Warp user. Direct from IBM's Service Hotline, *OS/2 Warp FAQs* is a comprehensive question-and-answer guide that helps you optimize your system and save time by putting the answers to all your questions right at your fingertips. CD includes FAQs from the book in an easy-to-search format, plus hard-to-find device drivers for connecting to peripherals, such as printers.

EXPERT AUTHOR PROFILE

Mike Kaply (Boca Raton, FL) is currently on the OS/2 Help Manager Development Team at IBM in Boca Raton, Florida. He holds a B.S. degree in Mathematics and Computer Science from Southern Methodist University.

Timothy F. Sipples (Chicago, IL) is an OS/2 Warp specialist from IBM. He has written for *OS/2 Magazine* and was named "Team OS/2er of the Year" by *OS/2 Professional*.

ISBN: 1-56884-472-7
$29.99 USA/$42.99 Canada
Includes one CD-ROM

Available: Now

OS/2® Warp and PowerPC: Operating in the New Frontier

by Ken Christopher, Scott Winters & Mary Pollack Wright

The software makers at IBM unwrap the IBM and OS/2 mystique to share insights and strategies that will take business computing into the 21st century. Readers get a long, hard look at the next generation of OS/2 Warp for PowerPC.

EXPERT AUTHOR PROFILE

Ken Christopher (Boca Raton, FL) is Program Director of Development for OS/2 for Power PC. He has been a key player in the development on OS/2 Warp.

Scott Winters (Boca Raton, FL) is lead architect of OS/2 for the PowerPC. He has been instrumental in the development on OS/2 Warp on the PowerPC platform.

Mary Pollack Wright (Boca Raton, FL) is currently the technical editor for the OS/2 Techinical Library. She has been part of the OS/2 team since 1985. Her technical articles on OS/2 have been published in the *OS/2 Developer* magazine and *OS/2 Notebooks*.

ISBN: 1-56884-458-1
$29.99 USA/$39.99 Canada

Available: Now

9/19/9

Order Center: **(800) 762-2974** *(8 a.m.–6 p.m., EST, weekdays)*

Quantity	ISBN	Title	Price	Total

Shipping & Handling Charges

	Description	First book	Each additional book	Total
Domestic	Normal	$4.50	$1.50	$
	Two Day Air	$8.50	$2.50	$
	Overnight	$18.00	$3.00	$
International	Surface	$8.00	$8.00	$
	Airmail	$16.00	$16.00	$
	DHL Air	$17.00	$17.00	$

*For large quantities call for shipping & handling charges.
**Prices are subject to change without notice.

Ship to:

Name _____

Company _____

Address _____

City/State/Zip _____

Daytime Phone _____

Payment: ☐ Check to IDG Books Worldwide (US Funds Only)

☐ VISA ☐ MasterCard ☐ American Express

Card # _____ Expires _____

Signature _____

Subtotal _____

CA residents add
applicable sales tax _____

IN, MA, and MD
residents add
5% sales tax _____

IL residents add
6.25% sales tax _____

RI residents add
7% sales tax _____

TX residents add
8.25% sales tax _____

Shipping _____

Total _____

Please send this order form to:
**IDG Books Worldwide, Inc.
7260 Shadeland Station, Suite 100
Indianapolis, IN 46256**

*Allow up to 3 weeks for delivery.
Thank you!*

IDG BOOKS WORLDWIDE REGISTRATION CARD

RETURN THIS REGISTRATION CARD FOR FREE CATALOG

Title of this book: The Internet For Macs For Dummies, 2E

My overall rating of this book: ❑ Very good [1]   ❑ Good [2]   ❑ Satisfactory [3]   ❑ Fair [4]   ❑ Poor [5]

How I first heard about this book:

❑ Found in bookstore; name: [6]

❑ Advertisement: [8]

❑ Word of mouth; heard about book from friend, co-worker, etc.: [10]

❑ Book review: [7]

❑ Catalog: [9]

❑ Other: [11]

What I liked most about this book:

What I would change, add, delete, etc., in future editions of this book:

Other comments:

Number of computer books I purchase in a year: ❑ 1 [12]   ❑ 2-5 [13]   ❑ 6-10 [14]   ❑ More than 10 [15]

I would characterize my computer skills as: ❑ Beginner [16] ❑ Intermediate [17] ❑ Advanced [18] ❑ Professional [19]

I use ❑ DOS [20] ❑ Windows [21] ❑ OS/2 [22] ❑ Unix [23] ❑ Macintosh [24] ❑ Other: [25]_____
(please specify)

I would be interested in new books on the following subjects:
(please check all that apply, and use the spaces provided to identify specific software)

❑ Word processing: [26]

❑ Data bases: [28]

❑ File Utilities: [30]

❑ Networking: [32]

❑ Other: [34]

❑ Spreadsheets: [27]

❑ Desktop publishing: [29]

❑ Money management: [31]

❑ Programming languages: [33]

I use a PC at (please check all that apply): ❑ home [35] ❑ work [36] ❑ school [37] ❑ other: [38] _____

The disks I prefer to use are ❑ 5.25 [39] ❑ 3.5 [40] ❑ other: [41]_____

I have a CD ROM: ❑ yes [42]   ❑ no [43]

I plan to buy or upgrade computer hardware this year: ❑ yes [44]   ❑ no [45]

I plan to buy or upgrade computer software this year: ❑ yes [46]   ❑ no [47]

Name: _____ Business title: [48] _____ Type of Business: [49] _____

Address (❑ home [50] ❑ work [51]/Company name: _____)

Street/Suite# _____

City [52]/State [53]/Zipcode [54]: _____ Country [55] _____

❑ **I liked this book!** You may quote me by name in future
IDG Books Worldwide promotional materials.

My daytime phone number is _____

IDG BOOKS

THE WORLD OF
COMPUTER
KNOWLEDGE

❏ YES!

Please keep me informed about IDG's World of Computer Knowledge.
Send me the latest IDG Books catalog.

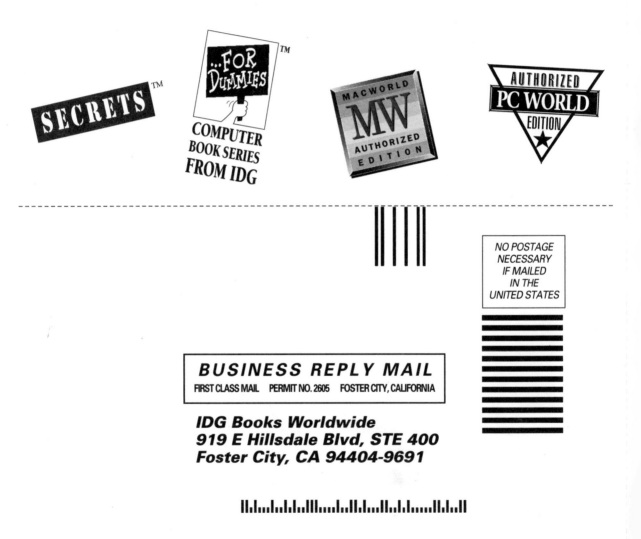